CLASSIC ELITE
Quick Knits

CLASSIC ELITE
Quick Knits

100 Fabulous Patterns
for Wraps, Socks, Hats, and More
from the studios of CLASSIC ELITE YARNS

The Taunton Press

ACKNOWLEDGMENTS

We thank the following people for their valuable contributions to this book: all the talented knitwear designers who contributed to this book; the technical editors at Classic Elite Yarns; Carol Kaplan, Sadie Dayton, Jared Flood, and Karen Lewis, photographers; Betsy Perry, owner of Classic Elite Yarns; Erica Sanders-Foege and Alex Giannini, editors at The Taunton Press.

The Taunton Press
Inspiration for hands-on living®

The Taunton Press, Inc., 63 South Main Street, PO Box 5506, Newtown, CT 06470-5506
e-mail: tp@taunton.com

Editor: Erica Sanders-Foege and Alex Giannini
Copy Editor: Candace B. Levy
Indexer: Lynne Lipkind
Front Cover Design: Teresa Fernandes
Interior Design & Layout: Susan Fazekas
Illustrations: Courtesy of Classic Elite Yarns
Photographers: Karen Lewis: pp. 8–9, 51–58, 60–61, 63, 74, 76, 78, 80, 82, 84, 86, 98, 159–161, 163–165, 167, 169, 171–172, 174–176, 178, 180–192, 201–202, 207–208; Carol Kaplan: pp. 10, 12–14, 16–23, 25–29, 31, 33, 49, 65, 73, 90–94, 96, 99, 100–101, 103–105, 110, 114–131, 133–135, 137, 139–140, 196–198, 203, 205, 209, 212; Sadie Dayton: pp. 35, 106, 141–144, 146–147; Classic Elite staff: pp. 37–38, 41, 67, 108–109, 148–150, 152; Jared Flood: pp. 39, 43–44, 46–47, 69–70, 153, 155

The following names/manufacturers appearing in *Classic Elite Quick Knits* are trademarks: Bernat®

Library of Congress Cataloging-in-Publication Data

Classic Elite quick knits : 100 fabulous patterns for wraps, socks, hats, and more / from the studios of Classic Elite Yarns.
   p. cm.
  Includes index.
  ISBN 978-1-60085-403-3
  1. Knitting--Patterns. 2. Knitwear. I. Classic Elite Yarns (Firm)
  TT825.C63237 2011
  746.43'2--dc23
            2011026744

Printed in the United States of America
10 9 8 7 6 5 4 3 2

contents

Introduction

CLASSIC ELITE YARNS has long been a well-loved and well-respected leader in the hand-knitting industry. We strive to provide quality yarns composed of some of the finest fibers. When choosing pattern designs, we look at current fashion while keeping in mind the elements that make for timeless garments. In this book, we have compiled some of the most interesting accessories published over the past few years. Because they are small, portable, and wearable, accessories lend themselves very well to all ranges of knitters, and, due to minimal sizing requirements, are great for gift-giving to friends and loved ones.

The 100 patterns included in this collection are sure to give knitters plenty of all levels to keep them busy and intrigued. For more information about yarns and patterns, please visit www.classiceliteyarns.com.

ABOUT CLASSIC ELITE YARNS

Classic Elite Yarns had its origin in the late 1940s when Ernest Chew, the company's founder, became a partner in Warley Worsted Mills, an old-line textile-manufacturing mill in Lowell, Massachusetts. Under Chew's direction, Warley Worsted became a specialty yarn mill, producing fine mohair yarns for fabric manufacturers and yarn companies like Bernat®.

In 1980, Classic Elite Yarns was created as a marketing division of the mill and catered to hand weavers and designers. In 1982, Classic Elite expanded its product line beyond mohairs to include cottons, silks, alpacas, wools, and natural fiber blends. The company then began presenting hand-knitting designs at national needlework shows and producing two annual collections—and the new company also began to make the pages of international fashion magazines.

Today, Classic Elite, no longer in the manufacturing business, is owned, managed, and staffed primarily by women. The company focuses on distributing beautiful hand-knitting yarns from international and domestic mills. In addition to providing exemplary customer service, Classic Elite's in-house staff manages all pattern writing, technical editing, desktop publishing, and much of the designing for its collections. Classic Elite still resides in an historic mill building on the banks of the Merrimack River in Lowell and prides itself on distributing fine hand-knitting yarns to the best yarn shops in America.

General Pattern Instructions

GAUGE

Obtaining the correct gauge is the single most important factor for a successful garment. Take time to save time; check your gauge. To check gauge: Knit a swatch at least 4" wide and long using the stitch pattern and needles recommended. Using the washing instructions on the yarn label, wash your swatch. This will tell you how your finished garment will behave after it has been washed. Measure the number of stitches over the 4" swatch. This should match the required gauge. If you have more stitches than the pattern specifies, increase your needle size; if you have fewer stitches, decrease your needle size.

BLOCKING

We recommend blocking all pieces to the measurements given before assembling.

SKILL LEVELS

EASY: Projects using basic stitches, repetitive stitch patterns, simple color changes, and simple shaping and finishing.

INTERMEDIATE: Projects with a variety of stitches, such as basic cables and lace and simple intarsia; use of double-pointed needles and knitting in the round techniques; mid-level shaping and finishing.

EXPERIENCED: Projects using advanced techniques and stitches, such as short rows, Fair Isle, more intricate intarsia, cables, lace patterns, and numerous color changes. Projects for crochet use intricate stitch patterns, techniques, and dimensions, such as nonrepeating patterns, fine threads, small hooks, detailed shaping, and refined finishing.

ABBREVIATIONS

1/3/1 Cross: sl 4 sts to cn, hold in back; k1; sl the last 3 sts from cn back to LH needle, bring rem st on cn to front bet needles; k3; k1 from cn

approx: approximately

BC: (baby cable) k2tog, leaving sts on LH needle; knit into the first st again, slip both sts off LH needle

beg: begin(ning)

beg-of-rnd (BOR): beginning of round

bet: between

BO: bind off

brk1: (brioche knit stitch) knit the next stitch (that was slipped in the previous row) together with the following yo

brp1: (brioche purl st) p the next st (that was slipped on the prev row) tog with the following yo

Btw: (back twist) wyib slip 1 st purlwise, drop next st off LH needle to front of work, slip the slipped st back to LH needle, pick up dropped st and knit it, p1

C1/3F: sl 1 st to cn, hold in front; k3; k1 from cn

C2B: sl 1 st to cn, hold to back; k1; k1 from cn

C2F: sl 1 st to cn, hold to front; k1; k1 from cn

C3/1B: sl 3 sts to cn, hold in back; k1; k3 from cn

C3F: sl 2 sts to cn, hold in front; k1; k2 from cn

C4B: sl 2 stitches to cn and hold in back; knit 2, knit 2 from cn

C4BP: sl 2 sts to cn, hold in back; k2; p2 from cn

C4F: sl 2 stitches to cn and hold in front; knit 2, knit 2 from cn

C4FP: sl 2 sts to cn, hold in front; p2; k2 from cn.

C5B: sl 4 sts to cn, hold in back; k1; k4 from cn

C5Bw2: sl 4 sts to cn, hold in back; k1; k3, kw2 from cn

C5F: Slip 1 st to cn, hold in front; k4; k1 from cn

C5Fw2: sl 1 st to cn, hold in front; kw2, k3; k1 from cn

C6B: sl 3 sts to cn, hold in back; k3, k3 sts from cn

C6F: sl 3 sts to cn, hold in front; k3, k3 sts from cn

C8B: sl 4 sts to cn, hold in back; k4; k4 from cn

C8F: st 4 sts to cn, hold in front; k4; k4 from cn

CC: contrast color

ch: chain stitch

cn: cable needle(s)

CO: cast on

cont: continue

dbld: doubled

dc: double crochet

dcd: (double centered decrease) sl 2 stitches together to right-hand needle knitwise, knit 1, pass both slip stitches together over knit stitch

dec: decrease

dpn: double-pointed needles

EOR: every other row

est: establish(ed)

foll: follows, following

Ftw: (front twist) drop next st off LH needle to front of work, p1, pick up dropped st and knit it

Gtr st: Garter stitch

inc: increase

k: knit

k1b: knit 1 stitch in row below

k1-f/b: knit into front and back of same stitch (1-stitch increase)

k2tog: knit 2 stitches together (1-stitch decrease)

k2tog-tbl: knit 2 stitches together through back loop (1-stitch decrease)

k3tog: knit 3 stitches together (2-stitch decrease)

kw2: knit 1 st wrapping yarn around needle 2 times

L1: lifted increase—increase 1 stitch by inserting tip of right-hand needle from top down into back of stitch on left-hand needle 1 row below; knit this stitch, then knit stitch on left-hand needle (1-stitch increase)

LH: left hand

LT: (left twist) sl 1 st and knit the next st tbl keeping both sts on needle, knit the skipped st, sl both sts from needle tog

LT-p: skip 1 st and purl the next st tbl, keeping both sts on needle, knit the skipped st, sl both sts from needle tog

m: meter(s)

m1: (m1k, m1l) make 1 stitch—insert left-hand needle, from front to back, under horizontal strand between st just worked and next stitch, knit through back loop (1-stitch increase)

m1p: make 1 stitch purlwise (1-stitch increase)

M1R: insert left-hand needle, from back to front, under horizontal strand between stitch just worked and next stitch, knit through front loop (1-stitch increase)

MB: (make Bobble) knit into the front, back, and then front again of the same st, turn—3 sts; p3, turn; k3, with LH needle, pull the 2nd and 3rd sts, 1 at a time, over th first st and off needle—1 st rem

MC: main color

meas: measure(s)

mm: millimeters

mos: months

mStar: K3, pass first st on RH needle over following 2sts (1 st decreased)

p: purl

P1-f/b: purl into the front loop, then the back loop of the next st (1 st inc)

p2tog: purl 2 stitches together (1-stitch decrease)

p2tog-tbl: purl 2 stitches together through back loop (1-stitch decrease)

p3tog: purl 3 stitches together (2-stitch decrease)

patt: pattern

pc: piece

pm(s): place marker(s)

psso: pass slipped stitch over

rem: remain(ing)

rep: repeat

rev: reverse, reversing

Rev St st: Reverse Stockinette stitch

RH: right hand

rnd(s): round(s)

RS: right side

RT: (right twist) sl 1 st and knit the next st, knit the skipped st, sl both sts from needle tog

RT-p: skip 1 st and knit the next st, purl the skipped st, sl both sts from needle tog

sc: single crochet

sep: separately

sk2p: slip 1 stitch knitwise, from left-hand needle to right-hand needle; knit 2 together, pass slipped stitch over knit stitch created by knitting 2 together (2-stitch decrease)

s2kp: sl 2 sts tog knitwise to the RH needle, k1, pass 2 slipped sts over knit st (2 sts decreased)

s2k3p: sl 2 sts tog knitwise (as if to k2tog), k3tog, pass the 2 slipped sts tog over the st made by the k3tog (4 sts dec)

skp: slip 1, knit 1, pass slipped stitched over

sl: slip

sl1k: slip 1 stitch knitwise

sl1p: slip 1 stitch purlwise

sl1yof: with working yarn in front, sl next st purlwise; bring yarn over the needle, back to the front and under the needle, ready to purl the foll st

srp: ssk, return st to LH needle, pass next st on LH needle over returned st and off needle; slip returned st back to RH needle (2 sts dec)

ssk: slip, slip, knit—slip 2 stitches, 1 at a time, knitwise to right-hand needle; return stitches, to left-hand needle in turned position and knit them together through back loop

ssp: slip, slip, purl—slip 2 stitches 1 at a time, knitwise to right-hand needle; return to left-hand needle in turned position and purl them together through back loop

st(s): stitch(es)

St st: Stockinette stitch

T2B: sl 1 st to cn, hold to back; k1; p1 from cn

T2F: sl 1 st to cn, hold to front; p1; k1 from cn

T3B: sl 1 st to cn, hold in back, k2, p1 from cn

T3F: sl 2 sts to cn, hold in front, p1, k2 from cn

T4B: sl 2 sts to cn, hold in back, k2, p2 from cn

T4F: sl 2 sts to cn, hold in front, p2, k2 from cn

T5F: sl 3 sts to cn, hold in front, k2 sl cn st from cn back to LH needles and purl it; K2 from cn

T6B: sl 4 sts to cn and hold in back, k2, replace last 2 sts on cn to LH and p2, k2 from cn

T6F: sl 4 sts to cn and hold in front; k2; replace last 2 sts on cn to LH and p2; k2 from cn

tbl: through back loop

tog: together

twisted skp: sl 1 st purlwise, from the LH needle to the RH needle; k1; psso (1 st dec)

tr: treble crochet

WS: wrong side

wyib: with yarn in back.

wyif: with yarn in front.

yb: yarn back

yd: yard(s)

yf: yarn forward

ytsl1yo: (yarn forward, sl 1 st purlwise, yo) bring working yarn under the needle to front of work, sl 1 st purlwise, bring the yarn over the needle (& over the st just slipped) to the back, ready to work the next st (the slipped st/yo unit is considered 1 st)

yo: yarn over

SUBSTITUTE YARNS

It is unfortunate when a yarn is discontinued, but Classic Elite has a wide variety of yarns that can be substituted for yarns that may no longer be found in the marketplace. Below is a list of yarns used in this book that are no longer offered (although they may still be found at some yarn shops) and suitable substitute yarns. As in all knitting, for best results knit a gauge swatch and check for accuracy before proceeding.

CLASSIC ELITE YARN	CLASSIC ELITE YARN SUBSTITUTE
Aspen	Ariosa, doubled
Bam Boo	Cotton Bam Boo, doubled
Charmed	Kumara
Commotion	Alpaca Sox and Giselle, held together
Duchess	Princess, doubled
Four Seasons	Solstice
Interlude	Solstice
Marley	Fresco
Moorland	Liberty Wool, Magnolia
Paintbox	Sprout; Waterlily doubled
Renaissance	Liberty Wool
Sinful	Ariosa
Star	Seedling
Summer Set	Solstice
Sundance	Solstice

STANDARD YARN WEIGHT SYSTEM

Yarn Weight Symbol and Category Name	Super Fine 1	Fine 2	Light 3	Medium 4	Bulky 5	Super Bulky 6
Types of yarn in category	Sock, fingering, baby	Sport, baby	DK, light worsted	Worsted, afghan, Aran	Chunky, craft, rug	Bulky, roving
Knit gauge range in St st in 4"*	27–32 sts	23–26 sts	21–24 sts	16–20 sts	12–15 sts	6–11 sts
Recommended metric needle size	2.25–3.25 mm	3.25–3.75 mm	3.75–4.5 mm	4.5–5.5 mm	5.5–8 mm	8 mm and larger
Recommended U.S. needle size	1–3	3–5	5–7	7–9	9–11	11 and larger
Crochet gauge range in sc in 4"*	21–31 sts	16–20 sts	12–17 sts	11–14 sts	8–11 sts	5–9 sts
Recommended metric hook size	2.25–3.5 mm	3.5–4.5 mm	4.5–5.5 mm	5.5–6.5 mm	6.5–9 mm	9 mm and larger
Recommended U.S. hook size	B/1–E/4	E/4–7	7–I/9	I/9–K/10.5	K/10.5–M/13	M/13 and larger

*The information in this table reflects the most commonly used gauges and needle or hook sizes for the specific yarn categories.

Hats, Mittens, Gloves

contents

Harriet Tam

SIZES
Small Child (Large Child, Small Adult, Large Adult)

FINISHED MEASUREMENTS
16 (16³/₄, 17¹/₂, 18¹/₂)" brim circumference unstretched

TO FIT MEASUREMENTS
18 (18³/₄, 19³/₄, 20³/₄)" head circumference

MATERIALS
Liberty Wool by Classic Elite
(100% washable wool; 50-gram ball = approx 122 yards)

2-Tone Striped (modeled in girls' size)
• 1 ball Color A—7895 Aubergine
• 1 ball Color B—7855 Raspberry

Self-Striping (modeled in adult size)
• 1 (1, 1, 2) balls—7898 Blue Twilight

Needles
• One 16" circular size U.S. 7 (4.5 mm)
• One set double-pointed needles size U.S. 7 (4.5 mm) **or size to obtain gauge**
• Tapestry needle
• Stitch marker

GAUGE
20 sts and 28 rows = 4" in Circular Stockinette stitch. *Take time to save time, check your gauge.*

PATTERN STITCHES

CIRCULAR 2 × 2 RIB (MULTIPLE OF 4 STS)
All rnds: *P1, k2, p1; rep from * around.

STRIPE SEQUENCE FOR 2-TONE STRIPED HAT
Rnd 1: Color A
Rnds 2 and 3: Color B.
Rnds 4 and 5: Color A.
Rep rnds 2–5 for Stripe Sequence.

NOTE
If you are interested in making the Isabella sweater on p. 9, please refer to Liberty Wool (9114) by Classic Elite.

HAT

With circular needle and Color A, CO 80 (84, 88, 92) sts. Join, being careful not to twist sts. Pm for beg of rnd. Begin 2 × 2 Rib and Stripe Sequence; work even until pc meas 1 (1, 1½, 1½)" from beg. **Inc Rnd:** *K2, m1; rep from * around—120 (126, 132, 138) sts. Change to St st; work even until pc meas 4 (4½, 5, 5)" from beg. **Shape Crown, Set-Up Rnd:** *Ssk, work 16 (17, 18, 19) sts, k2tog, pm; rep from * 5 more times—108 (114, 120, 126) sts rem. Work 1 rnd even. **Dec Rnd:** *Ssk, work to 2 sts before next marker, k2tog; rep from * around—12 sts dec'd. Rep dec rnd EOR 6 (7, 7, 8) more times, changing to dpns when necessary—24 (18, 24, 18) sts rem. **Next Rnd:** *K2tog; rep from * around—12 (9, 12, 9) sts rem.

FINISHING

For all sizes, break yarn, leaving a 6" tail. Thread tail onto tapestry needle and pull through all sts. Pull up tightly and fasten off.

Striped Hat

SKILL LEVEL: INTERMEDIATE

SIZES

Baby (Toddler, Child)

FINISHED MEASUREMENTS

16 (17$\frac{1}{2}$, 19)"

MATERIALS

Star by Classic Elite

(99% cotton, 1% lyrca; 50-gram hank = approx 112 yards)

- 1 hank Color A—5147 Aquarium
- 1 hank Color B—5102 Arizona Sun
- 1 hank Color C—5172 Lime Sherbert
- 1 hank Color D—5120 Purple Rain

Needles

- One 16" circular size U.S. 8 (5 mm)
- One set double-pointed needles size U.S. 8 (5 mm)
  or size to obtain gauge
- 1 stitch marker

GAUGE

22 sts and 40 rnds = 4" in Stockinette stitch, after washing. *Take time to save time, check your gauge.*

NOTES

1. Star is a lycra product. Our patterns allow for lycra to contract. When working with this yarn, machine wash/dry flat your gauge swatch, then adjust needle size if necessary. If you have difficulty finding the recommended yarn, you may consider using Classic Elite's Seedling as a substitute.

2. If you are interested in making the Star Color-Block Cardigan, please refer to Puddle Jumpers (9081) by Classic Elite. If you are interested in making the Child's Striped Socks, see p. 93.

PATTERN STITCHES

CIRCULAR STOCKINETTE STITCH (ST ST)

Knit every rnd.

CIRCULAR 1 × 1 RIB (MULTIPLE OF 2 STS)

Rnd 1: *K1, p1; rep from * around.

Rnd 2: Knit the knit sts and purl the purl sts as they face you.

Rep Rnd 2 for 1 × 1 rib.

STOCKINETTE AND GARTER STRIPE PATTERN

Rnds 1 and 3: With Color B, knit.

Rnds 2 and 4: With Color B, purl.

Rnds 5–8: With Color C, knit.

Rnds 9–12: With Color D, knit.

Rnds 13–16: Rep Rnds 5–8.

Rnds 17–20: With Color B, rep Rnds 1–4.

Rnds 21–24: With Color D, knit.

Rnds 25–28: With Color A, knit.

Rnds 29–32: Rep Rnds 21–24.

Rnds 33–36: With Color B, rep Rnds 1–4.

Rnds 37–40: With Color A, knit.

Rnds 41–44: With Color C, knit.

Rnds 45–48: Rep Rnds 37–40.

Rep Rnds 1–48 for Stripe patt.

HAT

Using circular needle and Color A, CO 88 (96, 104) sts; join, being careful not to twist sts, pm for beg of rnd. (RS) Begin St st; work even until piece meas 1" from beg. Change to 1 × 1 Rib; work even for 1". Change to Stockinette and Garter Stripes patt; work even until piece meas 31½ (4, 4½)" from end of Rib. **Shape Crown:** Cont in Stripe patt as est, change to dpn when necessary: Rnd 1: *K6, k2tog; rep from * around—77 (84, 91) sts rem. Rnd 2 and all even-numbered rnds: Knit. Rnd 3: *K5, k2tog; rep from * around—66 (72, 78) sts rem. Rnd 5: *K4, k2tog; rep from * around—55 (60, 65) sts rem. Rnd 7: *K3, k2tog; rep from * around—44 (48, 52) sts rem. Rnd 9: *K2, k2tog; rep from * around—33 (36, 39) sts rem. Rnd 11: *K1, k2tog; rep from * around 22 (24, 26) sts rem. Rnd 13: Knit, inc 2 (0, 2) sts—24 (24, 28) sts.

FINISHING

Noodles Embellishment: *Using dpn and Colors A, C or D, knit next 4 sts using color of choice; work even on these 4 sts for 33 rows. BO all sts. Rep from * 5 (5, 6) times— 6 (6, 7) noodles. Using Color B, wind yarn around base of noodles 20 times; fasten off securely. Weave end into wrap. Weave in all ends.

Garter Stitch Hat

SIZE

One size, 6–12 months

FINISHED MEASUREMENTS

18" circumference

MATERIALS

Summer Set by Classic Elite
(64% cotton, 19% alpaca, 12% polyester, 5% lyocel; 50-gram ball = approx 95 yards)
• 2 balls 2153 Convertible Red

Needles
• One pair each sizes U.S. 5 and 7 (3.75 and 4.5 mm)
  or size to obtain gauge
• Stitch markers
• Tapestry needle

GAUGE

20 sts and 36 rows = 4" in Garter stitch, using larger needles.
Take time to save time, check your gauge.

NOTE

If you have difficulty finding the recommended yarn, you may consider using Classic Elite's Solstice as a substitute.

PATTERN STITCH

GARTER STITCH (GTR ST)

Knit every row.

HAT

Using smaller needles, CO 90 sts. (RS) Begin Gtr st; work even until piece meas 3" from beg. Change to larger needles, work even until piece meas 7" from beg, end WS row, remembering that the brim of the hat will be turned up. *Dec Hat:* Row 1: (RS) *K8, k2tog, rep from * across—81 sts rem. Row 2 and all WS rows: Knit. Row 3: *K7, k2tog, rep from * across—72 sts rem. Row 5: *K6, k2tog, rep from * across—63 sts rem.

Row 7: *K5, k2tog, rep from * across—54 sts rem. Row 9: *K4, k2tog, rep from * across—45 sts rem. Row 11: *K3, k2tog, rep from * across—36 sts rem. Row 13: *K2, k2tog, rep from * across—27 sts rem. Row 15: *K1, k2tog, rep from * across—18 sts rem. Row 17: *K2tog, rep from * across—9 sts rem. Break yarn, leaving an 18" tail. Using a tapestry needle, run tail through sts on needle; pull tight and weave in. Sew seam on WS, remembering that the brim will be turned up.

Airy Hat

SKILL LEVEL: INTERMEDIATE

SIZE
One size

FINISHED MEASUREMENTS
20" circumference

MATERIALS
Aspen by Classic Elite
(50% alpaca, 50% wool; 100-gram hank = approx 51 yards)
• 2 hanks 1555 Ski Ticket
Needles
• One 16" circular size U.S. 17 (12.75 mm)
• One set double-pointed needles size U.S. 17 (12.75 mm)
  or size to obtain gauge

GAUGE
8 sts and 12 rows = 4" in Stockinette stitch. *Take time to save time, check your gauge.*

PATTERN STITCHES

CIRCULAR STOCKINETTE STITCH (ST ST)
Knit every rnd.

CIRCULAR HOLE PATTERN (MULTIPLE OF 6 STS, DEC'D TO MULTIPLE OF 5 STS)
Rnd 1: (RS) *K1, BO 5; rep from * around. [K1 equals the rem st on RH needle after the last BO; 1 st rem bet each set of BO's]

Rnd 2: *K1, CO 5; rep from * around. [First st of Rnd 2 has already been worked at the end of Rnd 1. See notes.]

Rnd 3: K1, BO 2, k1, *BO 5, k1; rep from * around to last 2 sts, BO 2.

Rnd 4: K1, CO 2, k1, *CO 4, k1; rep from * around, CO 1.

Work Rnds 1–4 for Hole patt.

NOTES
1. If you have difficulty finding the recommended yarn, you may consider using Classic Elite's Ariosa doubled as a substitute.
2. When working Hole patt, to work last BO of each rnd, remove marker and use first st of rnd to work last BO, sl st to LH needle, replace marker, sl st back to RH needle.
3. St count does not rem consistent. Count sts after Rnd 2 or 4 of Hole patt.

HAT

CO 48 st, join being careful not to twist sts; pm for beg of rnd. Begin Hole patt; work even for 4 rnds—40 sts rem. Knit 2 rnds. Purl 1 rnd. Knit 2 rnds. **Turning Rnd:** Bring yarn to front, sl 1 st, bring yarn to back and sl slipped st back to LH needle. Turn piece so you are looking at what was the WS. Begin St st; knit around to the last st. Knit last st, being sure to include the wrap in the st. Work even until piece meas 3½" from Turning Rnd. **Shape Crown:** Rnd 1: *K8, k2tog; rep from * around—36 sts rem. Rnd 2: Knit. Rnd 3: *K7, k2tog; rep from * around—32 sts rem. Rnd 4: *K6, k2tog; rep from * around—28 sts rem. Rnd 5: *K5, k2tog; rep from * around—24 sts rem. Rnd 6: *K4, k2tog; rep from * around—20 sts rem. Rnd 7: *K3, k2tog; rep from * around—16 sts rem. Rnd 8: *K2, k2tog; rep from * around—12 sts rem. Rnd 9: *K1, k2tog; rep from * around—8 sts rem. Rnd 10: *K2tog; rep from * around—4 sts rem. Pull yarn through 4 rem sts. Break yarn; fasten off.

Child's Fair Isle Hat

SKILL LEVEL: EXPERIENCED

SIZE

One size

FINISHED MEASUREMENTS

17³/₄" circumference

MATERIALS

Wool Bam Boo by Classic Elite

(50% wool, 50% bamboo; 50-gram ball = approx 118 yards)

- 2 balls Main Color—1650 Vanilla
- 1 ball Color A—1691 Bay Blue
- 1 ball Color B—1635 Key Lime
- 1 ball Color C—1660 Treasure

Needles

- One pair each size U.S. 4 and 6 (3.5 and 4 mm)
- Two double-pointed needles size U.S. 6 (4 mm) for I-cord
  or size to obtain gauge
- Stitch holders

GAUGE

21 sts and 29 rows = 4" in Stockinette stitch, using larger needles;
22 sts and 26 rows = 4" in Fair Isle patt, using larger needles.
Take time to save time, check your gauge.

PATTERN STITCHES

2 × 2 RIB (MULTIPLE OF 4 STS + 2)

Row 1: (WS) P2, *k2, p2; rep from * across.
Row 2: Knit the knit sts and purl the purl sts as they face you.
Rep Row 2 for 2 × 2 Rib.

STOCKINETTE STITCH (ST ST)

Knit on RS, purl on WS.

FAIR ISLE PATTERN (MULTIPLE OF 12 STS + 1)

See chart.

I-CORD

With 4 sts on dpn, *knit 1 row. Without turning the work, sl all sts to RH end of dpn. Pull yarn tightly from the end of the row. Rep from * until cord meas desired length.

NOTE

If you are interested in making the Fair Isle Yoke Cardigan, please refer to Puddle Jumpers (9081) by Classic Elite.

HAT

Using smaller needles and MC, CO 98 sts. ***Est 2 × 2 Rib:*** (WS) Work 1 st in St st (edge st, keep in St st throughout), 96 sts in 2 × 2 Rib, 1 st in St st (edge st, keep in St st, throughout). Work 6 rows even, end WS row. Change to larger needles and St st; (RS) work 2 rows even, end WS row. ***Est Fair Isle Patt:*** (RS) Maintaining edge sts, work 12-st rep across center 96 sts 8 times. Work Rows 1–21 of Fair Isle chart once, end RS row. (WS) Using MC only, purl 1 row. ***Shape Crown:*** (RS) Cont in St st, k1, *k10, k2tog; rep from * to last st, k1—90 sts. Work 1 row even. (RS) K1, *k9, k2tog; rep from * across to last st, k1—82 sts. Work 1 row even. Cont to dec in this manner, working 1 less st before each k2tog, EOR until 50 sts rem, end RS row. (WS) P1, *p2tog, p4; rep from * to last st, k1. Cont to dec in this manner every row, working 1 less st bet each p2tog or k2tog, until 10 sts rem, end WS row. (RS) K3tog twice, k2tog twice—4 sts rem. (WS) Purl 1 row. Sl rem sts to dpn and work I-cord for 2". BO all sts. Sew seam. Tie I-cord in overhand knot.

Color Chart
(multiple of 12 sts; 21 rows)

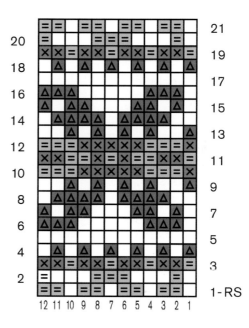

Work all sts in Fair Isle Stockinette stitch.

	MC
	Color A
	Color B
	Color C

Floppy Hat

SIZES

Small (Medium, Large)

FINISHED MEASUREMENTS

19¼ (20¾, 22½)"

MATERIALS

Inca Alpaca by Classic Elite

(100% alpaca; 50-gram hank = approx 109 yards)

• 3 hanks 1131 Blue Danube

Needles

• One 16" circular size U.S. 10½ (6.5 mm)

• One set double-pointed needles size U.S. 10½ (6.5 mm)
  or size to obtain gauge

• 6 stitch markers (1 a different color for beg of rnd)

GAUGE

15 sts and 24 rnds = 4" in Garter Ridge, using 2 strands of yarn held tog. *Take time to save time, check your gauge.*

PATTERN STITCHES

CIRCULAR GARTER RIDGE (GTR RIDGE)

Rnd 1: Purl.

Rnd 2: Knit.

Rnd 3: Knit.

Rep Rnds 1–3 for Gtr Ridge.

CIRCULAR STOCKINETTE STITCH (ST ST)

Knit every rnd.

HAT

Using 2 strands of yarn held tog and circular needle, CO 72 (78, 84) sts, pm for beg of rnd and join being careful not to twist sts. Beg Gtr Ridge; work even until piece meas 10½ (10½, 11)" from beg, end Rnd 2 of Gtr Ridge. *Change to St St and Shape Crown:* *K10 (11, 12), k2tog, pm; rep from * around—66 (72, 78) sts rem. *Dec Rnd:* *Work to 2 sts before next marker, k2tog, sl marker; rep from * around— 6 sts dec. Rep Dec Rnd 9 (10, 11) times, changing to dpn when necessary—6 sts rem. Remove markers on last rnd. K2tog 3 times—3 sts rem.

FINISHING

Break yarn leaving an 8" tail. Weave tail into rem 3 sts, pull tight to close top of hat.

Earflap Hat

SKILL LEVEL: INTERMEDIATE

SIZE
One size

FINISHED MEASUREMENTS
21³/4" circumference

MATERIALS
Inca Alpaca by Classic Elite
(100% alpaca; 50-gram hank = approx 109 yards)
• 2 hanks 1142 Cajamaica Maroon
Needles
• One pair size U.S. 7 (4.5 mm) **or size to obtain gauge**
• 6 stitch markers
• Stitch holder

GAUGE
18 sts and 30 rows = 4" in Hat Berry stitch. *Take time to save time, check your gauge.*

PATTERN STITCHES

HAT BERRY STITCH (MULTIPLE OF 4 STS + 2 AND 6 STS + 2)
Also see chart
Stitch count does not rem consistent; count sts after Rows 2 or 4.
Row 1: (RS) K1, *[k1, k1-tbl, k1] into next st, p3; rep from * to last st, k1—multiple of 6 sts + 2.
Row 2: K1, *p3tog, k3; rep from * to last st, k1—multiple of 4 sts + 2.
Row 3: K1, *p3, [k1, k1-tbl, k1] into next st; rep from * to last st, k1—multiple of 6 sts + 2.
Row 4: K1, *k3, p3tog; rep from * to last st, k1—multiple of 4 sts + 2.
Rep Rows 1–4 for Hat Berry st.

FLAP BERRY STITCH (MULTIPLE OF 6 STS + 5 AND 4 STS + 3)
Also see chart
Row 1: (RS) Slip 1 st knitwise wyib, p3, *[k1, k1-tbl, k1] into next st, p3; rep from * to last st, k1—multiple of 6 sts + 5.
Row 2: Slip 1 st knitwise wyib, p3tog, *k3, p3tog; rep from * to last st, k1—multiple of 4 sts + 3.
Row 3: Slip 1 st knitwise wyib, [k1, k1-tbl, k1] into next st, *p3, [k1, k1-tbl, k1] into next st; rep from * to last st, k1—multiple of 6 sts + 5.

Row 4: Slip 1 st knitwise wyib, k3, *p3tog, k3; rep from * to last st, k1—multiple of 4 sts + 5.
Rep Rows 1–4 for Flap Berry st.

NOTES

1. St count does not rem consistent. Count sts after Row 2 or 4 of Hat Berry st or after Row 2 of Flap Berry st.
2. If you are interested in making the Montera Lace Pullover, please refer to Autumn Book 1 (9092) by Classic Elite.

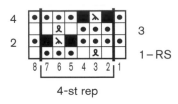

EARFLAP HAT

Hat Berry Chart
(multiple of 4 sts + 2; 4-row rep)

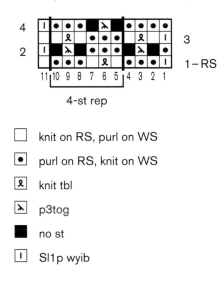

4-st rep

Flap Berry Chart
(multiple of 4 sts + 5; 4-row rep)

4-st rep

- ☐ knit on RS, purl on WS
- ⊡ purl on RS, knit on WS
- ⅃ knit tbl
- ⅄ p3tog
- ■ no st
- Ⅰ Sl1p wyib

HAT

CO 98 sts. (WS) Knit 1 row. **Beg Hat Berry St:** (RS) Work even until pc meas approx 4" from beg, end WS Row 4 of Hat Berry st. **Dec Row 1:** (RS) Work 13 sts as est, k1, p3tog, *work 12 sts as est, k1, p3tog; rep from * to last st, k1—122 sts. (WS) **K2tog, slip 1 st knitwise wyib, p3tog, psso, [k3, p3tog] 2 times, k2; rep from ** to last 2 sts, k2—74 sts rem. Beg Row 3 of Hat Berry st, work 10 rows even, end WS Row 4. **Second Dec Row:** (RS) Work 13 sts as est, k1, p3tog, pm, *work 8 sts as est, k1, p3tog, pm; rep from * 3 times, work to end—90 sts. (WS) Work to 1 st before marker as est, **remove marker, k2tog, slip 1 st knitwise wyib, p3tog, psso, k3, p3tog, k2; rep from ** 4 times, k1, p3tog, k4—54 sts rem. Beg Row 3 of Hat Berry st, work 6 rows even, end WS Row 4. **Third Dec Row:** (RS) Work 9 sts as est, k1, p3tog, pm, *work 8 sts as est, k1, p3tog, pm; rep from * 2 times, work to end—64 sts. (WS) Work to 1 st before marker as est, **remove marker, k2tog, slip 1 st knitwise wyib, p3tog, psso, k3, p3tog, k2; rep from ** 3 times, k2—38 sts rem. Beg Row 3 of Hat Berry st, work 6 rows even, end WS Row 4. **Final Dec Row:** (RS) Work 5 sts as est, k1, p3tog, pm, *work 8 sts as est, k1, p3tog, pm; rep from * 1 time, work to end—44 sts. (WS) K1, **p3tog, k2, remove marker, k2tog, slip 1 st

knitwise wyib, p3tog, psso, k3; rep from ** 2 times, k1—26 sts rem. Beg Row 3 of Hat Berry st, work 2 rows even. Fasten off.

FLAP (MAKE 2)

With RS facing, and pc held upside down, at CO edge pm 7 sts then 30 sts in from right edge for right flap; 8 sts, then 31 sts in from left edge for left flap. Pick up and knit 23 sts bet each set of flap markers. **Set-Up Row:** (WS) K1, *[k1, k1-tbl, k1] into next st, p3tog; rep from * to last 2 sts, [k1, k1-tbl, k1] into next st, k1—25 sts. **Beg Flap Berry St:** (RS) Work 6 rows, end WS Row 2. **Dec Row:** (RS) Skp, p3, *[k1, k1-tbl, k1] into next st, p3; rep from * to last 2 sts, k2tog—29 sts. (WS) Work Row 2 of Flap Berry st—19 sts rem. Rep last 2 rows 3 times—7 sts rem. Next Row: (RS) Skp, p3, k2tog—5 sts. Next Row: Slip 1 st knitwise wyib, p3tog, k1—3 sts rem. Next Row: (RS) S2kp. Fasten off.

FINISHING

Block lightly if desired. Sew seam.

Crochet Hat

SKILL LEVEL: INTERMEDIATE

SIZE
One size

FINISHED MEASUREMENTS
19¹/₂" circumference

MATERIALS
Lush by Classic Elite
(50% angora, 50% wool; 50-gram hank = approx 123 yards)
• 1 hank 4416 Natural
Crochet Hook
• One pair size U.S. H/8 (5 mm) **or size to obtain gauge**

GAUGE
15 sts and 9 rows = 4" in double crochet; 5 rnds = 5¹/₄" in pattern.
Take time to save time, check your gauge.

PATTERN STITCHES

CHAIN (CH)
Begin by making a slip knot on your hook. Wrap the yarn around the hook (yo) and draw it through the loop on the hook to form the first chain. Rep this step as many times as instructed. (The loop on the hook is never included when counting the number of chains).

HALF DOUBLE CROCHET (HDC)
Yo hook, insert hook into indicated st, yo and pull up a loop; yo and draw through all 3 loops on hook.

DOUBLE CROCHET (DC)
Yo hook, insert hook into indicated st, yo and pull up a loop; [yo and draw through 2 loops on hook] 2 times.

SINGLE CROCHET (SC)
Insert hook in indicated st, yo and pull up a loop; yo and draw through both loops on hook.

SLIP STITCH (SLIP ST)
Insert hook in the indicated st, yo and draw through both the st and the loop on the hook.

TREBLE CROCHET (TR)
Yo hook 2 times, insert hook in indicated st, yo and pull up a loop; [yo and draw through 2 loops] 3 times.

HAT

Beg at crown, ch 4, slip st to form ring.

Rnd 1: Ch 3 (counts as 1 dc), work 11 dc into ring, slip st into third ch of turning ch to join—12 dc. Rnd 2: Sc bet the turning ch and first dc, *ch 3, sc bet next 2 dc; rep from * around, ch 1, dc into beg sc to join—12 ch-3 loops. Rnd 3: Sc into space made by [ch-1, dc], tr into sc, * work 2 sc into next ch-3 space, tr into sc; rep from * around, sc into first [ch-1, dc space], slip st into beg sc to join. Rnd 4: *Sc into tr, ch 9; rep from * around, slip st into beg sc to join—12 ch-9 loops. Rnd 5: *Work [sc, hdc, 2 dc, 2 tr, ch 2] into next ch-9 space, work [2 tr, 2 dc, hdc, sc] in next ch-9 space, then slip st into

sc; rep from * around. Break yarn. Weave in end. Piece should measure 5¼" in diameter unstretched. Rnd 6: Attach yarn in any ch-2 space, ch 7, dc in slip st, ch 7, sc in next ch-2 space, *ch 3, sc in same ch-2 space, ch 7, dc in slip st, ch 7, sc in next ch-2 space; rep from * around, end ch 1, dc into joining st. Rnd 7: Sc into space made by [ch-1, dc], ch 2 (counts as dc), work 3 dc into same space, sc in ch-7 space, ch 6, sc in next ch-7 space, *work 7 dc in next ch-3 space, sc in ch-7 space, ch 6, sc in next ch-7 space; rep from * around, end work 3 dc in beg [ch-1, dc space], slip st in second ch of turning ch to join. Rnd 8: Sc into same st as slip st, ch 7, sc into ch-6 loop, ch 3, sc into same ch-6 loop, ch 7, *sc into fourth dc, ch 7, sc into ch-6 loop, ch 3, sc into same ch-6 loop, ch 7; rep from * around, slip st into beg sc to join. Rnd 9: [Slip st into ch-7 space, ch 1] 2 times, sc into same ch-7 space, work 7 dc into ch-3 space, sc in next ch-7 space, ch 7, *sc in next ch-7 space, work 7 dc into ch-3 space, sc in next ch-7 space, ch 7; rep from * around, slip st into first sc of rnd to join. Rnd 10: Slip st 3, sc in fourth dc, ch 7, sc in ch-7 space, ch 3, sc in same ch-7 space, ch 7, *sc in fourth dc, ch 7, sc into ch-7 space, ch 3, sc in same ch-7 space, ch 7; rep from * around, slip st into first sc of rnd to join. Rep Rnds 9 and 10 four times each. Rep Rnd 9 once more. Fasten off.

FINISHING

Block pc, if desired.

Stack Rib Hat

SKILL LEVEL: INTERMEDIATE

SIZES

Medium (Large)

FINISHED MEASUREMENTS

20 (22)" circumference

MATERIALS

Paintbox by Classic Elite

(100% merino wool; 100-gram ball = approx 110 yards)

• 1 (2) balls 6849 Pacific Island

Needles

• One set double-pointed needles size U.S. 11 (8 mm)

• One 16" circular size U.S. 11 (8 mm) **or size to obtain gauge**

• Stitch marker

GAUGE

11 sts and 26 rows = 4" in Stack Rib. *Take time to save time, check your gauge.*

NOTE

If you have difficulty finding the recommended yarn, you may consider using Classic Elite's Waterlily dbld as a substitute.

PATTERN STITCHES

CIRCULAR STOCKINETTE STITCH (ST ST)

Knit every rnd.

CIRCULAR STACK RIB

Rnds 1 and 2: Purl

Rnds 3 and 4: Knit

Rep Rnds 1–4 for Stack Rib.

CROWN

Using dpn, CO 12 sts, divide evenly on 3 needles, pm for beg of rnd and join being careful not to twist sts. *Beg St St and Inc:* Rnd 1 and all odd numbered rnds: Knit. Rnd 2: *K2, m1; rep from * around—18 sts. Rnd 4: *K3, m1; rep from * around—24 sts. Rnd 6: *K4, m1; rep from * around—30 sts. Rnd 8: *K5, m1; rep from * around—36 sts. Rnd 10: *K6, m1; rep from * around—42 sts. Rnd 12: *K7, m1; rep from * around—48 sts. Rnd 14: *K8, m1; rep from * around—54 sts.

Size L only: Rnd 16: *K9, m1; rep from * around—60 sts. *All Sizes:* Knit 1 rnd—54 (60 sts).

RISE

Change to circular needle and beg Stack Rib; work even for 34 rnds, end Rnd 2 of Stack Rib. Turn. (WS) BO all sts knitwise.

Lacy Hat

SIZES
Small (Medium, Large)

FINISHED MEASUREMENTS
21 (23, 25)" circumference, stretched

MATERIALS
Sundance by Classic Elite
(50% cotton, 50% microfiber; 50-gram ball = approx 83 yards)
• 1 (2, 2) balls 6201 Linen
Needles
• One 16" circular size U.Ss 6 (4 mm)
• One set double-pointed needles size U.S. 6 (4 mm) **or size to obtain gauge**

GAUGE
16 sts and 30 rnds = 4" in Circular Eyelet Rib, stretched. *Take time to save time, check your gauge.*

PATTERN STITCHES

CIRCULAR 2 × 2 RIB (MULTIPLE OF 4 STS)
Rnd 1: *K2, p2; rep from * around.
Rnd 2: Knit the knit sts and purl the purl sts as they face you.
Rep Rnd 2 for 2 × 2 Rib.

CIRCULAR EYELET RIB (MULTIPLE OF 4 STS)
Also see chart
Rnd 1: *P2, k2; rep from * around.
Rnds 2, 3, 4, and 5: Knit the knit sts and purl the purl sts as they face you.
Rnd 6: *P2, yo, ssk; rep from * around.
Rep Rnds 1–6 for Eyelet Rib.

CIRCULAR DECREASED EYELET RIB (MULTIPLE OF 3 STS)
Rnd 1: *P1, k2; rep from * around.
Rnd 2: *P1, yo, ssk; rep from * around.
Rnd 3: *P1, k2; rep from * around.
Rnds 4, 5, and 6: Knit the knit sts and purl the purl sts as they face you.
Rnd 7: *P1, k2; rep from * around.
Work Rnds 1–7 for Dec Eyelet Rib.

CIRCULAR STOCKINETTE STITCH (ST ST)
Knit every rnd.

NOTES

1. If you have difficulty finding the recommended yarn, you may consider using Classic Elite's Solstice as a substitute.
2. When measuring length, do not stretch the fabric.

HAT

CO 84 (92, 100) sts. Join, being careful not to twist sts; pm for beg of rnd. ***Beg Circular 2 × 2 Rib:*** Work 6 rnds. Change to Circular Eyelet Rib; work even until piece meas approx 4 (4¾, 5½)" from beg, end Rnd 3 of Circular Eyelet Rib. ***Dec Rnd 1:*** Change to double-pointed needles when necessary; Remove BOR marker, p1, replace marker, *p1, k1, k2tog; rep from * around—63 (69, 75) sts rcm. Change to Circular Dec Eyelet Rib; work 7 rnds. ***Dec Rnd 2:*** Remove BOR marker, p1, replace marker, *yo, sk2p; rep from * around—42 (46, 50) sts rem. Change to St st; work 6 rnds. ***Dec Rnd 3:*** Ssk around— 21 (23, 25) sts rem. Change to St st; work 3 rnds. ***Dec Rnd 4:*** *Ssk; rep from * to last st, k1—11 (12, 13) sts rem. Knit 1 rnd.

FINISHING

Break yarn with approx 6" tail. Draw tail through all live sts and pull tight.

Eyelet Rib Chart
(multiple of 4 sts; 6-rnd rep)

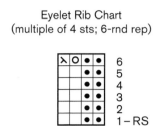

	knit
●	purl
O	yo
⅄	ssk

Lattice Rib Hat

SIZE
One size

FINISHED MEASUREMENTS
20" circumference

MATERIALS
Forbidden by Classic Elite
(100% cashmere; 50-gram hank = approx 65 yards)
• 2 hanks 10015 Natural
Needles
• One 16" circular size U.S. 10½ (6.5 mm)
• One set double-pointed needles size U.S. 10½ (6.5 mm) **or size to obtain gauge**
• Tapestry needle
• Cable needle

GAUGE
16 sts and 24 rows = 4" in Lattice patt; 18 sts and 22 rows = 4" in 2 × 2 Rib. *Take time to save time, check your gauge.*

PATTERN STITCHES

CIRCULAR 2 × 2 RIB (MULTIPLE OF 4 STS)
Rnd 1: * P2, k2; rep from * around.
Rnd 2: Knit the knit sts and purl the purl sts as they face you.
Rep Rnd 2 for 2 × 2 Rib.

CIRCULAR LATTICE PATTERN (MULTIPLE OF 4 STS)
Also see chart
Rnd 1: *C2B, p2; rep from * around.
Rnd 2 and all even numbered rnds: Knit the knit sts and purl the purl sts as they face you.
Rnd 3: K1, *T2F, T2B; rep from * around borrowing 1 st from beg of rnd to complete last T2B.
Rnd 5: *P2, C2F; rep from * around.
Rnd 7: P1, *T2B, T2F; rep from * around borrowing 1 st from beg of rnd to complete last T2F.
Rnd 8: Rep Rnd 2.
Rep Rnds 1–8 for Lattice patt.

NOTE
When ending a rnd, it will be necessary to "borrow" a st from the beg of that rnd to work the last 2-st cable.

HAT

Beg at lower edge, using circular needle, CO 80 sts. Join, being careful not to twist sts; pm for beg of rnd. *Est Rib:* *K2, p2; rep from * around. Change to Lattice patt; work even until piece meas approx 3½" from beg, end Rnd 5 of Lattice Patt. Change to 2 × 2 Rib; work even until piece meas 6" from beg. *Shape Crown, Change to Dpn When Necessary:* Rnd 1: *P2, k2, p2tog, k2; rep from * around—70 sts rem. Rnd 2 and all even numbered rnds: Knit the knit sts and purl the purl sts as they face you. Rnd 3: *P2tog, k2, p1, k2; rep from * around—60 sts rem. Rnd 5: *P1, k2tog, p1, k2; rep from * around—50 sts rem. Rnd 7: *P1, k1, p1, k2tog; rep from * around—40 sts rem. Rnd 9: *K2tog, p2tog; rep from * around—20 sts rem. Rnd 11: *K2tog, p2tog; rep from * around—10 sts rem. Break yarn, leaving an 8" tail; using tapestry needle threaded with tail, gather rem sts by running the tail 2 times through the rem sts, then pull tightly to close opening at top of hat; fasten off securely on WS of hat.

FINISHING

Block to measurements, being careful not to flatten texture.

LATTICE RIB HAT

Lattice Chart
(multiple of 4 sts; 8-rnd rep)

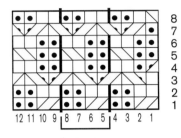

4-st rep

☐	knit	
⊡	purl	
▱	C2B	
◿	C2F	
◩	T2B	
◺	T2F	
◿	first part of T2B worked on 1st st of rnd	
◪	second part of T2B worked on 1st st of next rnd	
◸	first part of T2F worked on last st of rnd	
◹	second part of T2F worked on 1st st of next rnd	

Cabled Hat

SIZE
One size

FINISHED MEASUREMENTS
20" circumference

MATERIALS
Dutchess by Classic Elite

(40% merino, 28% viscose, 10% cashmere, 7% angora, 15% nylon; 50-gram ball = approx 75 yards)

• 2 balls 1058 Royal Red

Needles

• One 16" circular size U.S. 11 (8 mm)
• One set each size double-pointed needles U.S. 10 and 11 (6 and 8 mm) **or size to obtain gauge**
• Stitch marker
• Cable needle

GAUGE
16 sts and 19 rows = 4" in Cable Rib, slightly stretched using larger needles. *Take time to save time, check your gauge.*

NOTE
If you have difficulty finding the recommended yarn, you may consider using Classic Elite's Princess dbld as a substitute.

PATTERN STITCHES

CIRCULAR CABLE RIB (MULTIPLE OF 8 STS)
Also see chart

Rnd 1 and all odd-numbered rnds: *P2, k6; rep from * around.

Rnd 2: *P2, C6B; rep from * around.

Rnds 4 and 6: Rep Rnd 1.

Rep Rnds 1–6 for Cable Rib.

I-CORD
*Knit 1 row; without turning the work, slide the sts to RH end of needle, pull yarn tightly from the end of the row, (behind the sts); rep from * until cord meas desired length.

I-CORD EDGING
*Without turning the work, slip all sts to the RH end of needle. Pull yarn tightly from the end of the row, k2 sts, k2tog-tbl—3 sts rem. Pick up and knit 1 st along edge—4 sts; rep from * for length desired.

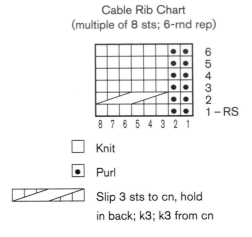

Cable Rib Chart
(multiple of 8 sts; 6-rnd rep)

☐ Knit

● Purl

Slip 3 sts to cn, hold
in back; k3; k3 from cn

HAT

Using larger dpn, CO 5 sts, pm for beg of rnd, join, being careful not to twist sts. Change to circular needle when enough sts are available. Rnd 1: Purl. Rnd 2: *P1, m1p; rep from * around—10 sts. Rnd 3: Rep Rnd 2—20 sts. Rnd 4: *P2, m1; rep from * around—30 sts. Rnds 5, 7, 9, 11 and 13: Work even as est, knit the knit sts and purl the purl sts as they face you. Rnd 6: *P2, k1, m1; rep from * around—40 sts. Rnd 8: *P2, k1, m1, k1; rep from * around—50 sts. Rnd 10: *P2, k2, m1, k1; rep from * around—60 sts. Rnd 12: *P2, k2, m1, k2; rep from * around—70 sts. Rnd 14: *P2, k3, m1, k2; rep from * around—80 sts. Change to Cable Rib; beg Rnd 1, work even until piece meas approx 3" from last inc rnd, end Rnd 3 of Cable Rib.

RIGHT EARFLAP

Cont in Cable Rib patt, beg working back and forth in rows, working sts on all WS rows as they face you, knit the knit sts and purl the purl sts; cont turning cable every 6 rows. Row 1: (RS) Work 4 sts, BO 2 sts, work across 31 more sts (32 sts from BO), turn. Row 2: (WS) BO 3 sts, work across to BO sts—29 sts rem. Row 3: BO 3 sts, work across to BO sts—26 sts rem. Row 4: BO 4 sts, work across to BO sts—22 sts rem. Row 5: BO 4 sts, turning cable as for Rnd 2, work across to BO sts—18 sts rem. Row 6: BO 4 sts, work across to BO sts—14 sts rem. Row 7: BO 3 sts, work across to BO sts—11 sts rem. Row 8: BO 4 sts, work across to BO sts—7 sts rem. Row 9: BO 3 sts, work across to BO sts—4 sts rem. Sl all sts to smaller dpn, cont on these 4 sts, work I-Cord until piece meas 13" from beg of I-Cord. BO all sts.

LEFT EARFLAP

With RS facing, attach yarn left of right earflap. (RS) BO 17 sts for the front of hat, work to end, turn—29 sts rem. Row 1: (WS) BO 3 sts, work to end—26 sts rem. Row 2: (RS) BO 4 sts, work to end—22 sts rem. Row 3: BO 4 sts, work to end—18 sts rem. Row 4: BO 4 sts, turning cable as for Rnd 2, work to end—14 sts rem. Row 5: BO 3 sts, work to end—11 sts rem. Row 6: BO 4 sts, work to end—7 sts rem. Row 7: BO 3 sts, work to end—4 sts rem. Work across 4 sts. Slip all sts to smaller dpn, cont on these 4 sts, work I-Cord until piece meas 13" from beg of I-Cord. BO all sts.

FINISHING

Back Edging: Using smaller dpn, CO 4 sts, work I-Cord until piece meas 13" from beg. With WS of hat facing, beg at back edge of right earflap I-Cord, Begin I-Cord Edging; work across back edge to Left Earflap I-Cord—4 sts. Change to I-Cord; work until piece meas 13" from beg. *Front Edging:* With WS of hat facing, work as for back edging, join at front edge of left earflap I-Cord. Braid the three I-Cords at each earflap. Tie a knot at the end.

Aspen Hat

SKILL LEVEL: INTERMEDIATE

SIZE
One size

FINISHED MEASUREMENTS
20" circumference, in relaxed ribbing; 24" circumference in Star Stitch; 9" tall

MATERIALS
Aspen by Classic Elite
(50% alpaca, 50% wool; 100-gram hank = approx 51 yards)
• 2 hanks 1595 Resort
Needles
• One 16" circular U.S. size 15 (10 mm) **or size to obtain gauge**
• Stitch marker

GAUGE
11 sts and 13 rnds = 4" in Star Stitch. *Take time to save time, check your gauge.*

NOTE
If you have difficulty finding the recommended yarn, you may consider using Classic Elite's Ariosa Dbld as a substitute.

STITCH PATTERNS

CIRCULAR 1 × 1 RIB: (MULTIPLE OF 2 STS)
Rnd 1: *K1, p1; rep from * around.
Rnd 2: Knit the knit sts and purl the purl sts as they face you.
Rep Rnd 1 for 1 × 1 Rib.

CIRCULAR STAR STITCH: (MULTIPLE OF 3 STS + 4)
Also see chart
Rnd 1: K1, *yo, make Star; rep from * around.
Rnd 2 and all even numbered rnds: Knit.
Rnd 3: *Yo, make Star; rep from * to last st, k1.
Rnd 5: K2, *yo, make Star; rep from * to last 2 sts, yo, make Star borrowing 1 st from beg of rnd; replace marker back 1 st; count borrowed st as the first knit st of Rnd 6.
Rnd 6: Rep Rnd 2.
Rep Rnds 1–6 for Star st.

Star Stitch Chart
(multiple of 3 sts + 4; 6 rnd rep)

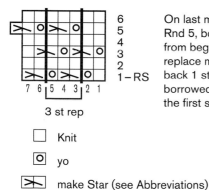

On last make Star of Rnd 5, borrow 1 st from beg of rnd; replace marker back 1 st; count borrowed st as the first st of Rnd 6.

3 st rep

- ☐ Knit
- ⊡ yo
- ⊠ make Star (see Abbreviations)

HAT
CO 44 sts, pm for beg of rnd, join, being careful not to twist sts. Begin 1 × 1 Rib; work 4 rnds, inc 5 sts evenly on last rnd—49 sts. Knit 1 rnd. Change to Star st; work even until pc meas 7" from beg, end on an odd numbered rnd. *Dec Rnd 1:* K3tog, *k2tog; rep from * around—24 sts rem. Knit 1 rnd. *Dec Rnd 2:* *K2tog; rep from * around—12 sts rem.

FINISHING
Break yarn, leaving 12" tail. Pull tail through all sts. Fasten off. Block lightly.

Montera Hat

SKILL LEVEL: INTERMEDIATE

SIZE

One size

FINISHED MEASUREMENTS

17" circumference, in relaxed ribbing; 22" circumference in Leaf Lace pattern; 10" tall

MATERIALS

Montera by Classic Elite

(50% llama, 50% wool; 100-gram hank = approx 127 yards)

• 2 hanks 3877 Smoke

Needles

• One 16" circular each size U.S. 7 and 10.5 (4.5 mm and 8 mm) Stitch markers

• One set double-pointed needles size U.S. 10.5 (8 mm) **or size to obtain gauge**

GAUGE

16 sts and 19 rows = 4" in Leaf Lace pattern with larger needles. *Take time to save time, check your gauge.*

PATTERN STITCHES

1 × 1 RIB (MULTIPLE OF 2 STS)

Rnd 1: *K1, p1; rep from * around.

Rnd 2: Knit the knit sts and purl the purl sts as they face you.

Rep Rnd 2 for 1 × 1 Rib.

CIRCULAR LEAF LACE PATTERN (MULTIPLE OF 12 STS)

Also see chart

Rnd 1: *K1, yo, ssk, k7, k2tog, yo; rep from * around.

Rnd 2: *K1, yo, k1, ssk, k5, k2tog, k1, yo; rep from * around.

Rnd 3: *K1, yo, k2, ssk, k3, k2tog, k2, yo; rep from * around.

Rnd 4: *K1, yo, k3, ssk, k1, k2tog, k3, yo; rep from * around.

Rnd 5: *K1, yo, k4, sk2p, k4, yo; rep from * around.

Rnd 6: *K4, k2tog, yo, k1, yo, ssk, k3; rep from * around.

Rnd 7: *K3, k2tog, k1, yo, k1, yo, k1, ssk, k2; rep from * around.

Rnd 8: *K2, k2tog, k2, yo, k1, yo, k2, ssk, k1; rep from around.

Rnd 9: *K1, k2tog, k3, yo, k1, yo, k3, ssk; rep from * around.

Rnd 10: K1, *k4, yo, k1, yo, k4, sk2p; rep from * around borrowing 1 st from beg of rnd for final sk2p; rep marker before sk2p, thus counting sk2p as the first st of Rnd 1.

Rep Rows 1–10 for Leaf Lace patt.

CIRCULAR DECREASE PATTERN (MULTIPLE OF 12 STS DEC'D TO 2)

Change to double-pointed needles when necessary.

Also see chart

Rnd 1: *K4, k2tog, k1, ssk, k3; rep from * around—80 sts rem.

Rnd 2: *K3, k2tog, k1, ssk, k2; rep from * around—64 sts rem.

Rnd 3: *K2, k2tog, k1, ssk, k1; rep from * around—48 sts rem.

Rnd 4: *K1, k2tog, k1, ssk; rep from * around—32 sts rem.

Rnd 5: *Sk2p, k1; rep from * around—16 sts rem.

Work Rnds 1–5 for Dec patt.

HAT

With smaller needle, CO 92 sts. Join to work in-the-rnd, being careful not to twist sts. Begin 1 × 1 Rib; work until pc meas 1" from beg, inc 4 sts evenly spaced on last rnd—96 sts. Change to larger needle and Leaf Lace Patt; work even for 35 rnds, end Rnd 5 of Leaf Lace Patt. Change to Dec patt; work 5 rnds— 16 sts rem. Break yarn, leaving 12" tail. Draw tail through rem sts 2 times. Fasten off.

FINISHING

Block lightly.

Leaf Lace Chart
(multiple of 12 sts; 10-rnd rep)

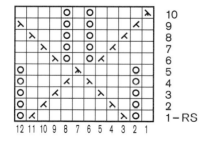

Decrease Chart
(multiple of 12 sts dec'd to 2; 5 rnds)

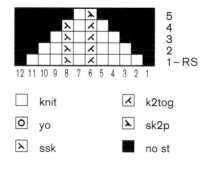

☐ knit	⊼ k2tog
⊙ yo	⅄ sk2p
⅄ ssk	■ no st

Starfish Hat

SIZE
One size

FINISHED MEASUREMENTS
16" circumference unstretched

MATERIALS
Dutchess by Classic Elite
(40% merino, 28% viscose, 10% cashmere, 15% nylon, 7% angora; 50-gram ball = approx 75 yards)
• 2 balls 1058 Royal Red

Needles
• One 16" circular each size U.S. 7 and 10 (4.5 and 6 mm)
• One set double-pointed needles size U.S. 9 (5.5 mm) **or size to obtain gauge**
• Stitch marker

GAUGE
14 sts and 20 rows = 4" in Reverse Stockinette stitch with largest needles. *Take time to save time, check your gauge.*

NOTE
If you have difficulty finding the recommended yarn, you may consider using Classic Elite's Princess dbld as a substitute.

PATTERN STITCHES

CIRCULAR 1 × 1 RIB (MULTIPLE OF 2 STS)
Rnd 1: *K1, p1; rep from * around.
Rnd 2: Knit the knit sts and purl the purl sts as they face you.
Rep Rnd 2 for 1 × 1 Rib.

CIRCULAR GARTER STITCH (GTR ST)
Rnd 1: Knit.
Rnd 2: Purl.
Rep Rnd 1 and 2 for Gtr st.

VINE PATTERN (MULTIPLE OF 13 STS)
Also see chart
Rnd 1: *P6, k2tog, [yo] 2 times, p5; rep from * around.
Rnd 2: *P6, k2, dropping the 2nd yo from previous rnd, p5; rep from * around.
Rnd 3: *P5, k2tog, [yo] 2 times, k1, p5; rep from * around.
Rnd 4: *P5, k1, p1, dropping the 2nd yo from previous rnd, k1, p5; rep from * around.
Rnd 5: *P4, k2tog, [yo] 2 times, p1, k1, p5; rep from * around.
Rnd 6: *P4, k1, p1, dropping the 2nd yo from previous rnd, p1, k1, p5; rep from * around.
Rnd 7: *P3, k2tog, [yo] 2 times, p2, k1, p5; rep from * around.
Rnd 8: *P3, k1, p1, dropping the 2nd yo from previous rnd, p2, k1, p5; rep from * around.
Rnd 9: *P2, k2tog, [yo] 2 times, p3, k1, p5; rep from * around.
Rnd 10: *P2, k1, p1, dropping the 2nd yo from previous rnd, p3, k1, p5; rep from * around.
Rnd 11: *P7, [yo] 2 times, ssk, p4; rep from * around.
Rnd 12: *P7, k1, dropping the 2nd yo from previous rnd, k1, p4; rep from * around.
Rnd 13: *P7, k1, [yo] 2 times, ssk, p3; rep from * around.
Rnd 14: *P7, k1, p1, dropping the 2nd yo from previous rnd, k1, p3; rep from * around.
Rnd 15: *P7, k1, p1, [yo] 2 times, ssk, p2; rep from * around.
Rnd 16: *P7, k1, p2, dropping the 2nd yo from previous rnd, k1, p2; rep from * around.
Rnd 17: *P7, k1, p2, [yo] 2 times, ssk, p1; rep from * around.
Rnd 18: *P7, k1, p3, dropping the 2nd yo from previous rnd, k1, p1; rep from * around.
Rnd 19: *P7, k1, p3, [yo] 2 times, ssk; rep from * around.
Rnd 20: *P7, k1, p4, dropping the 2nd yo from previous rnd, k1; rep from * around.
Rep Rnds 1–20 for Vine Patt.

Vine Chart
(multiple of 13 sts)

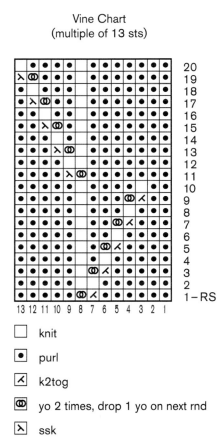

	knit
•	purl
⅄	k2tog
◍	yo 2 times, drop 1 yo on next rnd
⅃	ssk

HAT

With smaller circular needle, CO 72 sts; pm for beg of rnd. Join being careful not to twist sts. Begin Circular 1 × 1 Rib; work even until pc meas 2" from beg. *Inc Rnd:* Inc 6 sts evenly around—78 sts. Change to larger circular needle and Vine Patt; work 26 rnds, end Rnd 6 of Vine Patt. Change to dpn and Circular Gtr st; work 2 rnds. *Dec Rnd 1:* *K4, k2tog; rep from * around—65 sts rem. Purl 1 rnd. *Dec Rnd 2:* *K3, k2tog; rep from * around—52 sts rem. Purl 1 rnd. *Dec Rnd 3:* *K2, k2tog; rep from * around—39 sts rem. Purl 1 rnd. Dec Rnd 4: *K1, k2tog; rep from * around—26 sts rem. Purl 1 rnd. *Dec Rnd 5:* K2tog around—13 sts rem. Purl 1 rnd.

FINISHING

Pull yarn through rem sts. Block if desired.

Lace Beret

SKILL LEVEL: INTERMEDIATE

SIZE
One size

FINISHED MEASUREMENTS
20¼" circumference

MATERIALS
Classic Silk by Classic Elite
(50% cotton; 30% silk, 20% nylon; 50-gram ball = approx 135 yards)
• 1 ball 6916 Natural
Needles
• One 16" circular each size U.S. 5 and 6 (3.75 mm and 4 mm)
• One 24" circular size US 6 (4 mm)
• One set double-pointed needles size U.S. 6 (4 mm) **or size to obtain gauge**
• Stitch marker

GAUGE
19 sts and 24 rnds = 4" in Lace Patt with larger needles. *Take time to save time, check your gauge.*

PATTERN STITCHES

1 × 1 RIB (MULTIPLE OF 2 STS)
Rnd 1: *K1, p1; rep from * around.
Rnd 2: Knit the knit sts and purl the purl sts as they face you.
Rep Rnd 2 for 1 × 1 Rib.

LACE INCREASE PATTERN (MULTIPLE OF 6 STS INC'D TO 10 STS)
Also see chart
Rnds 1 and 3: Knit.
Rnd 2: *K1, yo, k5, yo; rep from * around—multiple of 8 sts.
Rnd 4: *P1, k1, yo, k1, sk2p, k1, yo, k1; rep from * around.
Rnd 5: *P1, k7; rep from * around.
Rnd 6: *P1, k2, yo, k3, yo, k2; rep from * around—multiple of 10 sts.
Rnd 7: *P1, k9; rep from * around.
Rnd 8: *P1, k3, yo, sk2p, yo, k3; rep from * around.
Work Rnds 1–8 for Lace Inc patt.

LACE PATTERN: (MULTIPLE OF 10 STS)
Also see chart
Rnds 1 and 3: Knit.
Rnd 2: *K1, yo, k3, sk2p, k3, yo; rep from * around.
Rnd 4: *P1, k1, yo, k2, sk2p, k2, yo, k1; rep from * around.
Rnds 5 and 7: *P1, k9; rep from * around.
Rnd 6: *P1, k2, yo, k1, sk2p, k1, yo, k2; rep from * around.
Rnd 8: *P1, k3, yo, sk2p, yo, k3; rep from * around.
Work Rnds 1–8 for Lace patt.

LACE DECREASE PATTERN (MULTIPLE OF 10 STS DEC'D TO 2 STS)
Also see chart
Rnds 1 and 3: Knit.
Rnd 2: *K1, yo, k3, sk2p, k3, yo; rep from * around.
Rnd 4: *P1, k1, yo, k2, sk2p, k2, yo, k1; rep from * around.
Rnd 5: *P1, k9; rep from * around.
Rnd 6: *P1, k2, yo, s2k3p, yo, k2; rep from * around—multiple of 8 sts.
Rnds 7 and 9: Knit.
Rnd 8: *K1, yo, k2, sk2p, k2, yo; rep from * around.
Rnd 10: *P1, k1, yo, k1, sk2p, k1, yo, k1; rep from * around.
Rnd 11: *P1, k7; rep from * around.
Rnd 12: *P1, k2, yo, sk2p, yo, k2; rep from * around.
Rnds 13, 15, 17, 19, 21, 23, and 25: Knit.
Rnd 14: Rep Rnd 8.
Rnd 16: *P1, k1, yo, s2k3p, yo, k1; rep from * around—multiple of 6 sts.
Rnd 18: *K1, yo, k1, sk2p, k1, yo; rep from * around.
Rnd 20: *P1, k1, yo, sk2p, yo, k1; rep from * around.
Rnd 22: *K1, yo, s2k3p, yo; rep from * around—multiple of 4 sts.
Rnd 24: *K1, yo, sk2p, yo; rep from * around.
Rnd 26: *K1, sk2p; rep from * around—multiple of 2 sts.
Rnd 27: Knit.
Work Rnds 1–27 for Lace Dec patt.

BERET

With smaller circular needle, CO 96 sts. Join, being careful not to twist sts; pm for beg of rnd. Begin 1 × 1 Rib; work even until pc meas ¾" from beg. Change to larger 16" needle and Lace Inc patt; work for 6 rnds, end after Rnd 6—160 sts. Change to longer circular needle; work 2 more rnds in Lace Inc patt, end after Rnd 8. Change to Lace patt; work 8 rnds, end after Rnd 8. Change to Lace Dec patt; work 27 rnds, change to shorter circular needle then dpn as necessary, end after Rnd 27 of Lace Dec patt—32 sts rem. **Dec Rnd 1:** K1,

*ssk; rep from * to last st, slip last st, rem marker, sl slipped st back to LH needle, replace marker, ssk—16 sts rem. Knit 1 rnd. **Dec Rnd 2:** *Ssk; rep from * to last st, sl last st, remove marker, sl slipped st back to LH needle, replace marker, ssk—8 sts rem.

FINISHING

Break yarn leaving approx 8" tail. Thread tail through rem 8 sts 2 times and pull tight with tail on WS of beret.

LACE BERET

Lace Chart
(multiple of 10 sts; 8 rnds)

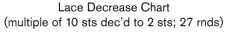

Lace Increase Chart
(multiple of 6 sts inc'd to 10 sts; 8 rnds)

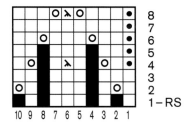

Lace Decrease Chart
(multiple of 10 sts dec'd to 2 sts; 27 rnds)

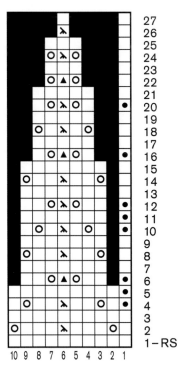

- ☐ knit
- ⊡ purl
- ⊙ yo
- ⅄ sk2p
- ▲ s2k3p
- ■ no st

Princess Hat and Neck Scrunchy

Because Nancy Marchant's instructions for brioche stitch are the clearest and most comprehensive we've come across, we've used her abbreviations and descriptive moves in this pattern. For lots more information on brioche stitch, visit www.briochestitch.com.

SIZE
One size

FINISHED MEASUREMENTS
21" circumference; 14" tall

MATERIALS
Princess by Classic Elite
(40% merino, 28% viscose, 10% cashmere, 7% angora, 15% nylon; 50-gram hank = approx 150 yards)
• 1 hank Color A   3446 Regal Teal
• 1 hank Color B—3409 Proud Peacock

Needles
• One 16" circular each size U.S. 6 and 7 (4 and 4.5 mm)
• Two double-pointed needles size U.S. 5 (3.75 mm) **or size to obtain gauge**

GAUGE
14 sts and 24 rows = 4" on larger needles in Circular Brioche stitch, unstretched. *Take time to save time, check your gauge.*

PATTERN STITCHES

CIRCULAR BRIOCHE STITCH (MULTIPLE OF 2 STS)
Rnd 1: With Color A, * brk1, yfsl1yo; rep from * around.
Rnd 2: With Color B, wyif, *sl1yof, brp1; rep from * around.
Rep Rnds 1 and 2 for Brioche st

I-CORD
Using 2 dpns, CO 2 sts onto 1 dpn. *Knit 1 row; without turning the work, slide the sts to RH end of needle, pull yarn tightly from the end of the row (behind the sts); rep from * until cord meas desired length.

NOTES

1. Make tie and pom-poms first to ensure that there is enough yarn for them.
2. On RS, knit columns are in Color A, purl columns are in Color B. Each rnd is worked with only 1 color, either A or B. On A rnds, B sts are slipped and on B rnds, A sts are slipped. 2 rnds make 1 complete rnd.
3. On every row, the yo and slipped sts are counted and worked as 1 st.

PRINCESS HAT AND NECK SCRUNCHY

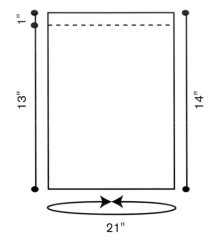

BODY

With Color A and larger circular needle, CO 74 sts. Do not join or turn work—RS is facing. Slide sts to opposite end of needle. ***Preparation Rnd:*** With Color B, wyif, *sl1yof, p1; rep from * to end. Pm and join to work in-the-round, being careful not to twist sts. Begin Circular Brioche st; work even in patt until pc meas 13" from beg, end after Rnd 2 of Brioche st. ***Change to smaller needles and Color A, Eyelet Rnd:*** *Yo, ssk (the first st in each ssk is the yo/st pair); rep from * around. Next rnd: *P1, k1; rep from * around. Next rnd: Knit the knit sts and purl the purl sts as they face you. BO all sts loosely in patt.

TIE

With Color A, work I-Cord until pc meas 24". Break yarn leaving a 6" tail and pull through 2 sts on needle. With Color A and Color B, make 2 pom-poms 2½" to 3" in diameter.

FINISHING

Block piece to required measurements. Thread tie through eyelets at top of hat, skipping 1 eyelet. Attach 1 pom-pom to each end of tie.

Quincy Hat

SIZE
One size

FINISHED MEASUREMENTS
20½" completely unstretched; approx 6½" tall. Fits head sizes 21"–23".

MATERIALS
Ariosa by Classic Elite
(90% merino, 10% cashmere; 50-gram ball = approx 87 yards)
• 2 balls 7827 Sangria
Needles:
• One size U.S. 10½ (6.5 mm)
• One set of double-pointed needles size U.S. 10 (6 mm) **or size to obtain gauge**
• Removable stitch markers

GAUGE
15 sts and 28 rows = 4" in Garter stitch with larger needles. *Take time to save time, check your gauge.*

NOTE
The main portion of the hat is a flat strip of Garter stitch, knit back and forth with built-in I-Cord on both sides. When this piece reaches sufficient length, you'll give the fabric a half twist and graft the live stitches together with the cast-on stitches (see illustration on p. 40). You will now have a möbius strip from which you will pick up crown stitches and close up the top as you would a traditional knitted cap.

HAT

With larger needle, use provisional method to CO 26 sts. Knit until 3 sts rem on needle, bring yarn to front, slip last 3 sts purlwise.

Rep the previous row establishing Gtr st with built-in I-Cord edging 143 more times [72 Gtr ridges].

Lay knitting flat. Keeping 1 end flat against table, take the other and flip it, putting half twist into fabric (see illustration). Fold to join edges, keeping half twist in fabric; join live sts tog with provisionally CO sts using the Kitchener st.

With grafted edge centered directly across from twist in fabric, count 20 ridges in each direction away from the grafted seam and pm on I-Cord trim at these points (marking 20th I-Cord st to the left of graft line, and 20th I-Cord st to the right of graft line); pm at graft line for beg of rnd (BOR marker).

CROWN

You now have 3 markers dividing your ring of fabric into three sections. With RS facing, roll the I-Cord edge toward you to pick up sts from WS into 1 st on backside of I-Cord edging as follows: With dpns, beg at graft line, pick-up and knit 20 sts to first marker, with second dpn, pick up and knit 10 sts to twist, 10 sts to second marker, then with third dpn, pick up and knit 20 sts to BOR marker—60 sts. Remove all markers and join to work in rnd, pm on needle to indicate beg of rnd.

Before proceeding, pm after every 10th st of rnd—6 markers on needles, including 1 for beg of rnd. Rnd 1: *Purl to 1 st rem before marker, slip 1 st purlwise wyib; rep from * around. Rnd 2: *Knit to 2 sts rem before marker, k2tog. Rep from * around—6 sts dec'd. Rep Rnds 1 and 2 6 more times—18 sts rem. Next Rnd: *P1, k2tog; rep from * around—12 sts rem. Next Rnd: *K2tog; rep from * around—6 sts rem. Break yarn leaving 6" tail. With blunt tapestry needle, thread rem live sts with yarn tail and pull tightly to snug top. Weave in ends.

QUINCY HAT ILLUSTRATION

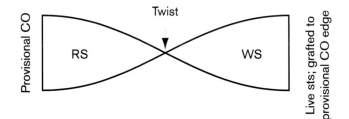

Princess Headwarmer

SIZE

One size

FINISHED MEASUREMENTS

3" wide and 18¼" long, excluding I-Cord ties

MATERIALS

Princess by Classic Elite

(40% merino, 28% viscose, 10% cashmere, 7% angora, 15% nylon; 50-gram hank = approx 150 yards)

• 1 hank Color A—3493 Choice Cobalt
• 1 hank Color B—3409 Proud Peacock
• 1 hank Color C—3485 Milord's Madder
• 1 hank Color D—3455 Patrician Port

Needles

• One pair each size U.S. 2 and 4 (2.75 and 3.5 mm) **or size to obtain gauge**
• One set of double-pointed needles size U.S. 2 (2.75 mm)

GAUGE

25 sts and 30 rows = 4" in Color pattern with larger needles. *Take time to save time, check your gauge.*

PATTERN STITCHES

STOCKINETTE STITCH (ST ST)

Knit on RS, purl on WS.

GARTER STITCH (GTR ST)

Knit all rows.

REVERSE GARTER ST (REV GTR ST)

Purl all rows.

COLOR PATTERN (MULTIPLE OF 24 STS + 9)

See chart on p. 42.

I-CORD

Using 2 dpns, slip 3 sts on one needle. *Knit 1 row; without turning the work, slide the sts to RH end of needle, pull yarn tightly from the end of the row (behind the sts); rep from * until cord meas desired length.

HEADWARMER

With smaller needles and Color A, CO 89 sts. ***Begin Gtr St Edging*** (RS): With Color A work 2 rows, join Color B and work 2 rows, with Color A work 2 rows. ***Change to Larger Needles and Beg Color Patt:*** (RS) With Color C, k4 (edge sts, keep in St st and Color C throughout), work 81 sts in Row 1 of Color patt, joining Color D as indicated by chart, k4 (edge sts, keep in St st and Color C throughout). Work Rows 2–13 of chart. ***Change to Smaller Needles, Rev Gtr St and Color A:*** (WS) Work 2 rows in Color A, work 2 rows in Color B, work 2 rows with Color A. With Color A, BO all sts.

FINISHING

Ties: With smaller needles and Color A, pick up and knit 16 sts along side edge of headwarmer. Begin Gtr st, work 3 rows even. ***Dec Row:*** (RS) K1, ssk, k to last 3 sts, k2tog, k1—14 sts rem. Rep dec row, EOR until 4 sts rem. Next Row: (RS) K1, ssk, k1—3 sts rem. ***Change to Dpn and I-Cord:*** Work for 11". With tail threaded through a tapestry needle, draw yarn through sts, pull tight, and weave in end. Work second tie on other side of headwarmer. ***Pom-poms:*** With Color B make two 2" pom-poms. Sew one pom-pom to end of each I-Cord tie. Block pc to measurements.

PRINCESS HEADWARMER

Color Chart
(multiple of 24 sts + 9; 13 rows)

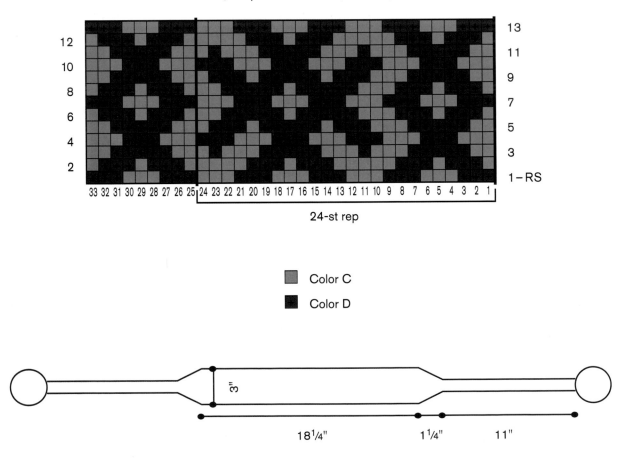

24-st rep

■ Color C

■ Color D

3"

18¼"   1¼"   11"

Fresco Beaumont

SIZE

Average adult 2-Color Tam version (average adult 4-Color Beanie)

FINISHED MEASUREMENTS

22³/₄ (21¹/₂)" circumference, stretched; 8¹/₂ (7¹/₄)" tall

MATERIALS

Fresco by Classic Elite

(60% wool, 30% alpaca, 10% angora; 50-gram hank = approx. 164 yards)

2-Color Tam

• 1 hank Main Color—5301 Parchment

• 1 hank Contrast Color—5355 Rumba Red

4-Color Beanie

• 1 hank Shade 1—5377 Charcoal Black

• 1 hank Shade 2—5375 Greystone

• 1 hank Shade 3—5303 Cinder

• 1 hank Shade 4—5301 Parchment

Needles

2-Color Tam

• One 16" circular each sizes U.S. 4 and 7 (3.5 and 4.5 mm)

• One set double-pointed needles size U.S. 7 (4.5 mm) **or size to obtain gauge**

4-Color Beanie

• One 16" circular each in sizes U.S. 3 and 5 (3.25 and 3.75 mm)

• One set double-pointed needles size U.S. 5 (3.75 mm) **or size to obtain gauge**

• Stitch marker

• Tapestry needle

GAUGE

2-Color Tam: 28 sts and 28 rows = 4" in Tam Colorwork patterns with larger needle (size U.S. 7)

4-Color Beanie: 31 sts and 32 rows = 4" in Beanie Colorwork patterns with larger needle (size U.S. 7)

Take time to save time, check your gauge.

PATTERN STITCHES

CIRCULAR 2 × 2 RIB (MULTIPLE OF 4 STS)

All rnds: *K2, p2; rep from * around.

NOTE

Instructions outside the parentheses are for the Tam version—those inside are for the Beanie version.

TAM (BEANIE)

With smaller needle (as indicated for each version) and CC (Shade 1), CO 108 sts; pm and join, being careful not to twist sts. Work 2 × 2 Rib until pc meas 1 (¾)" from beg. *Inc Rnd:* *K2, m1; rep from * to last 4 sts, k4—160 sts. Change to larger needle; with MC (Shade 1), knit 2 rnds. *Work Rows 1–3 of Chart A (as indicated for each version).* After completion of Chart A, cont as foll: *Inc Rnd:* With MC (Shade 1), k1, m1, k80, m1, k to end—162 sts. *Work Rows 1–25 of Chart B (as indicated for each version).* After completion of Chart B, cont as foll: *Dec Rnd:* With MC (Shade 1), *k2tog, k79; rep from * once more—160 sts. *Work Rnds 1–21 of Chart C (as indicated for each version).* Change to dpn when necessary. Marker placement will change at the end of rnd 20. Rnd 20: Work in patt to end of rnd, remove marker, wyib sl1p from LH to RH needle, replace marker. This indicates new beg of rnd—16 sts. After completion of Chart C, cont as foll: With CC (Shade 4), k 1 rnd. *Dec Rnd:* With CC (Shade 4), *K2tog; rep from * around—8 sts. Break yarn leaving 6" tail. With tapestry needle, thread tail through rem 8 sts, pull snugly to close top of hat. Weave in all ends.

Tam: Block over dinner plate or cardboard circle with approx. 10" diameter making sure not to stretch ribbing while blocking.

FRESCO BEAUMONT

TAM Chart A
(multiple of 8 sts; 3 rnds)

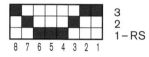

TAM Chart B
(multiple of 9 sts; 25 rnds)

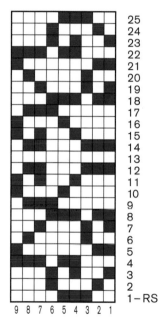

BEANIE Chart A
(multiple of 8 sts; 3 rnds)

BEANIE Chart B
(multiple of 9 sts; 25 rnds)

TAM Chart C
(multiple of 20 sts dec'd to 2 sts; 21 rnds)

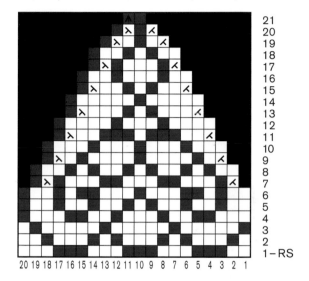

BEANIE Chart C
(multiple of 20 sts dec'd to 2 sts; 21 rnds)

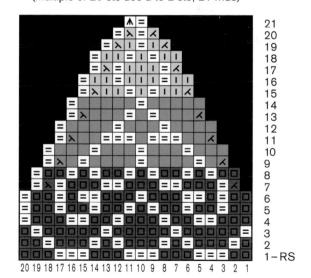

Work in Circular Fair Isle Stockinette stitch.

☐ MC

■ CC

▣ Shade 1

▨ Shade 2

Ⅰ Shade 3

= Shade 4

⟋ k2tog

⟍ ssk

⅄ s2kp

■ no st

Laurel Hat

SKILL LEVEL: INTERMEDIATE

SIZE
One size

FINISHED MEASUREMENTS
21" circumference

MATERIALS
Princess by Classic Elite
(40% merino, 28% viscose, 15% nylon, 10% cashmere, 7% angora;
50-gram ball = approx. 150 yards)
• 2 balls 3427 Côtes du Rhône
Needles
• One 16" circular each size U.S. 3 and 7 (3.25 and 4.5 mm)
• One set of double-pointed needles size U.S. 7 (4.5 mm) **or size to obtain gauge**
Notions
• Stitch marker
• Tapestry needle
• Cable needle

GAUGE
20 sts and 30 rows = 4" in Stockinette stitch with larger needle; 26 sts and 34 rows = 4" in Laurel Chart blocked, unstretched with larger needle. *Take time to save time, check your gauge.*

PATTERN STITCH

BOBBLE

[k1, p1, k1, p1] into 1 stitch. Turn work. P 4, turn work. ssk, k2tog, pass 2nd st on RH needle over 1st as if to BO.

BERET

With smaller circular needle, CO 120 sts; Pm and join, being careful not to twist sts; Rnd 1: *K2, p2 rep from * to end. Rep previous rnd, until pc meas 1" from beg. *Inc Rnd:* *[K2, p2] 3 times, k2, m1, p2, k2, p2; rep from * around—126 sts. *Change to Larger Needle and Work Rnds 1–53 of Laurel Chart as follows.*

NOTE

Laurel Chart begins as a 21-st motif that reps itself 6 times on every rnd. The st count changes throughout the pattern. Marker placement will change on Rnds 15, 17, 32, 34, 46 and 52; follow specific instructions listed below for each of these rnds: Rnds 15 and 32: Work in patt to end of rnd, remove marker, sl 2 sts purlwise wyib from LH to RH needle, replace marker. This indicates new beg of rnd. Rnds 14 and 34: Work

in patt until 1 st rems before marker, sl 1 st purlwise wyib, from LH to RH needle, remove marker, replace slipped st back onto LH needle, replace marker. This indicates new BOR.
Rnd 46: Work in patt until 2 sts before marker, sl 2 sts from LH to RH needle, remove marker, replace 2 slipped sts back onto LH needle. Replace marker. This indicates new beg of rnd.
Rnd 52: Work in patt to end of rnd. Rnd 53: Remove marker, sl 1 st from LH to RH needle, replace marker. *k2tog; rep from * around. After Rnd 53 has been completed, 12 sts rem on needle. Break yarn, leaving a 6" tail. Using a blunt tapestry needle, thread yarn tail through rem 12 sts and pull snugly to close top. Weave in all ends.

FINISHING

For tam shape, as shown in photograph, block finished hat over flat circular form approx 10" in diameter (dinner plate, cardboard circle, etc) making sure to not stretch ribbing at base of hat.

LAUREL HAT

Laurel Chart
(multiple of 21 sts dec'd to 2 sts; 53 rnds)

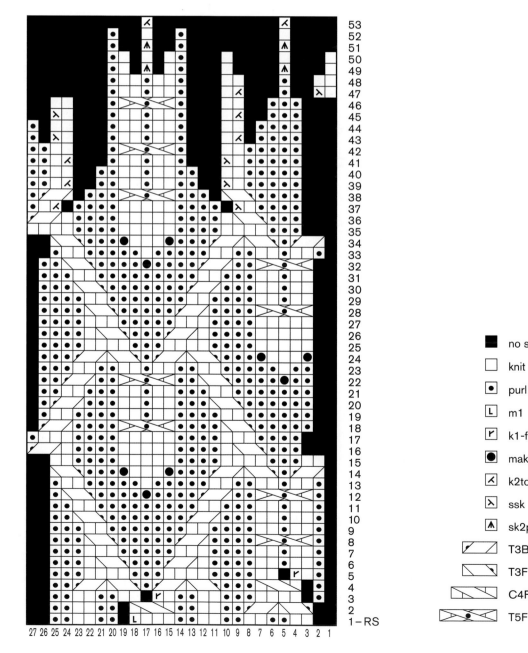

■	no st
□	knit
•	purl
L	m1
r	k1-f/b
●	make bobble
⊼	k2tog
⊻	ssk
Λ	sk2p
⟋	T3B
⟍	T3F
⟋	C4F
⟋•⟍	T5F

Child's Pillbox Hat

SKILL LEVEL: EXPERIENCED

SIZES

9 (18) months

FINISHED MEASUREMENTS

6 (7)" deep × 20" circumference

MATERIALS

Four Seasons by Classic Elite

(70% cotton, 30% wool; 50-gram hank = approx 103 yards)

• 1 hank Color A—7647 Pond

• 1 hank Color B—7697 Spring Green

• 1 hank Color C—7653 Very Berry

• 1 hank Color D—7619 Petal

• 1 hank Color E—7616 Natural

Needles

• One 16" circular size U.S. 6 (4 mm)

• One set double-pointed needles size U.S. 6 (4 mm)
  or size to obtain gauge

• 6 stitch markers (1 a different color for beg of rnd)

GAUGE

20 sts and 24 rows = 4" in Fair Isle Stockinette stitch. *Take time to save time, check your gauge.*

NOTE

If you have difficulty finding the recommended yarn, you may consider using Classic Elite's Solstice as a substitute.

PATTERN STITCHES

CIRCULAR GARTER STITCH (GTR ST)

Rnd 1: Knit.

Rnd 2: Purl.

Rep Rnds 1 and 2 for Gtr st.

CIRCULAR STOCKINETTE STITCH (ST ST)

Knit every rnd.

HAT

Using circular needle and Color E (A), CO 92 sts. Join, being careful not to twist sts; pm for beg of rnd. Begin Gtr st; work even for 5 rnds, end with knit rnd. Purl 1 rnd, inc 10 sts evenly across—102 sts. *Larger Size Only:* Change to St st and begin Chart A; changing colors as indicated, work even for 6 rnds. Change to Gtr st and Color E; beg with a knit rnd, work even for 6 rnds. *Both Sizes:* Change to St st and begin Chart B as indicated for your size; changing colors as indicated, work

rnd 1 (5) of Chart B, pm every 17 sts (between each rep). Cont as est, working Gtr st ridge (rnds 17 and 18) as indicated. *Shape Crown:* Work dcd as indicated on Chart B, changing to dpn when necessary—18 sts rem. Break tail of two ending colors, each 12" long. Using yarn needle, thread tails through rem sts and pull tightly to close top of hat. Bring rem tails to WS of hat; fasten off securely. Steam block, if desired.

CHILD'S PILLBOX HAT

Chart B
(17-st rep; 34 (38) rnds)

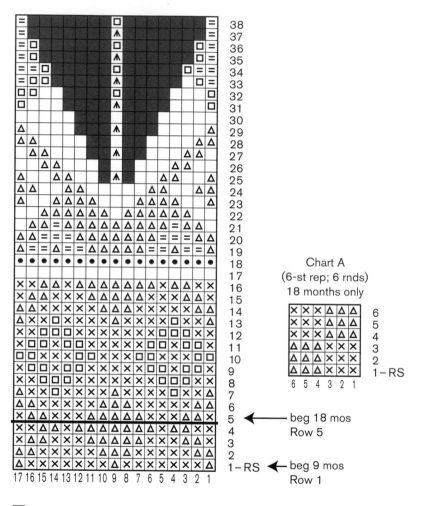

Chart A
(6-st rep; 6 rnds)
18 months only

← beg 18 mos
Row 5

← beg 9 mos
Row 1

△ Color A

□ Color B

☐ Color C

● Color C

⋀ Use same color as used in center st of
row before

✕ Color D

= Color E

■ No stitch

Wildwood Hat

SIZE

One size

FINISHED MEASUREMENTS

20" circumference in relaxed ribbing

MATERIALS

Woodland by Classic Elite, Verde Collection

(65% wool, 35% nettles; 50-gram ball = approx 131 yards)

• 2 balls 3103 Silver

Needles

• One 16" circular size U.S. 6 (4 mm)
• One set double-pointed needles size U.S. 6 (4 mm) **or size to obtain gauge**
• Cable needle
• Stitch marker

GAUGE

21 sts and 28 rows = 4" in Reverse Stockinette stitch. *Take time to save time, check your gauge.*

PATTERN STITCHES

CIRCULAR 2 × 2 RIB (MULTIPLE OF 4 STS)

All rnds: *K2, p2; rep from * around.

CROWN DECREASE PATTERN (MULTIPLE OF 32 STS DEC'D TO 12 STS)

Also see chart

Rnd 1: *P2tog, p1, k2, p10, k2, p2, k2, p10, k2; rep from * around— 160 sts.

Rnd 2: *P2, k2, p10, k2, p2, k2, p10, k2; rep from * around.

Rnd 3: *P2, C4F, p7, k2tog, k1, p2, k1, ssk, p7, C4B; rep from * around— 150 sts.

Rnd 4: *P2, k4, p7, k2, p2, k2, p7, k4; rep from * around.

Rnd 5: *P2, k2, T4F, p2tog, p3, k2, p2, k2, p3, p2tog, T4B, k2; rep from * around — 140 sts.

Rnd 6: *[P2, k2] 2 times, p4, k2, p2, k2, p4, k2, p2, k2; rep from * around.

Rnd 7: *P2, k2, p2, T3F, p2, k2tog, k1, p2, k1, ssk, p2, T3B, p2, k2; rep from * around— 130 sts.

Rnd 8: *P2, k2, p3, [k2, p2] 3 times, k2, p3, k2; rep from * around.

Rnd 9: *P2, k2, p3, k1, ssk, p1, k2, p2, k2, p1, k2tog, k1, p3, k2; rep from * around— 120 sts.

Rnd 10: *P2, k2, p3, k2, p1, k2, p2, k2, p1, k2, p3, k2; rep from * around.

Rnd 11: *P2, k2, p3, k1, ssk, k2, p2, k2, k2tog, k1, p3, k2; rep from * around— 110 sts.

Rnd 12: *P2, k2, p3, k4, p2, k4, p3, k2; rep from * around.

Rnd 13: *P2, k2, p3, k1, k2tog, k1, p2, k1, ssk, k1, p3, k2; rep from * around— 100 sts.

Rnd 14: *P2, k2, p3, k3, p2, k3, p3, k2; rep from * around.

Rnd 15: P2, k2, p3, k2tog, k1, p2, k1, ssk, p3, k2; rep from * around— 90 sts.

Rnd 16: *P2, k2, p3, k2, p2, k2, p3, k2; rep from * around.

Rnd 17: *p2, k2, p2, k2tog, k1, p2, k1, ssk, p2, k2; rep from * around— 80 sts.

Rnd 18: *P2, k2; rep from * around.

Rnd 19: *P2, k2, p1, k2tog, k1, p2, k1, ssk, p1, k2; rep from * around— 70 sts.

Rnd 20: *P2, k2, p1, k2, p2, k2, p1, k2; rep from * around.

Rnd 21: *P2, k2, k2tog, k1, p2, k1, ssk, k2; rep from * around— 60 sts.

Rnd 22: *P2, k4; rep from * around.

Rnd 23: *P2, C4F, p2, C4B; rep from * around.

Work Rnds 1–23 for Crown Dec patt.

WILDWOOD HAT

Crown Decrease Chart
(multiple of 32 sts; 23 rnds)

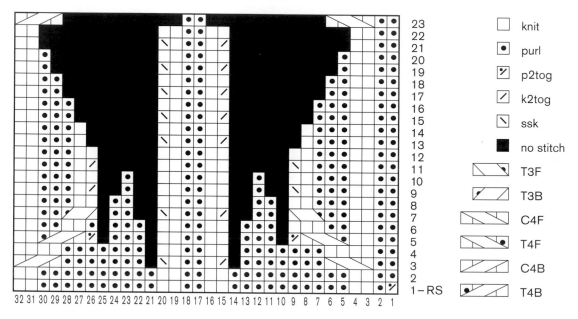

☐	knit
⊡	purl
⟋	p2tog
⟋	k2tog
⟍	ssk
■	no stitch
⟋	T3F
⟋	T3B
⟋	C4F
⟋	T4F
⟋	C4B
⟋	T4B

TAM

With circular needle, CO 100 sts; pm for beg of rnd. Join to work-in-the-rnd, being careful not to twist sts. Begin 2 × 2 Rib; work even for 8 rnds. *Inc Rnd:* *[P1, yo] 7 times, p1, k2, p2, k2, [p1, yo] 6 times; rep from * 4 more times—165 sts. *Est Patt:* *P15, k2, p2, k2, p12; rep from * 4 more times. Rep this rnd until pc meas 4½ " from beg. Change to Crown Dec patt; work 23 rnds, changing to dpns when necessary— 60 sts rem. Next Rnd: P1, *k2tog, k2, ssk; rep from *; the last ssk is worked with the last st this rnd tog with the first st from the next rnd—40 sts rem. Next Rnd: *K2tog; rep from *—20 sts rem. Next Rnd: *K2tog; rep from *—10 sts rem.

FINISHING

Break yarn, leaving 8" tail, thread through rem 10 sts and pull tight to close top of tam. Wet or steam block pc to measurements.

Trellis Hat

SKILL LEVEL: INTERMEDIATE

SIZE
One size

FINISHED MEASUREMENTS
19¼" circumference

MATERIALS
Ariosa by Classic Elite
(90% extrafine merino, 10% cashmere; 50-gram ball = approx 87 yards)
• 2 balls 4836 Tannin
Needles
• One 16" circular size U.S. 10 (6 mm)
• One set double-pointed needles size U.S. 10 (6 mm)
• One crochet hook size U.S. F/5 (3.75 mm) **or size to obtain gauge**
• Stitch marker
• Tapestry needle

GAUGE
15 sts and 20 rows = 4" in Trellis pattern. *Take time to save time, check your gauge.*

PATTERN STITCHES

CIRCULAR TRELLIS PATTERN (MULTIPLE OF 8 STS)
Also see chart
Rnd 1: *P3, k2, p3; rep from * around.
Rnd 2 and even-numbered rnds: Purl the purl sts and sl all knit sts purlwise wyib.
Rnd 3: *P2, Btw, Ftw, p2; rep from * around.
Rnd 5: *P1, Btw, p2, Ftw, p1; rep from * around.
Rnd 7: *Btw, p4, Ftw; rep from * around.
Rnd 9: *K1, p6, k1; rep from * around.
Rnd 11: *Ftw, p4, Btw; rep from * around.
Rnd 13: *P1, Ftw, p2, Btw, p1; rep from * around.
Rnd 15: *P2, Ftw, Btw, p2; rep from * around.
Rnd 16: Rep rnd 2.
Rep rnds 1–16 for Trellis patt.

CIRCULAR CROWN PATTERN (MULTIPLE OF 8 STS DEC'D TO 1 ST)
Also see chart
Rnd 1: *P2tog, p1, k2, p1, p2tog; rep from * around.
Rnd 2 and all even-numbered rnds: Purl the purl sts and slip all knit sts purlwise wyib.
Rnd 3: *P1, Btw, Ftw, p1; rep from * around.
Rnd 5: *Btw, p2tog, Ftw; rep from * around.
Rnd 7: *K1, p3tog, k1; rep from * around.
Rnd 9: K1, *p1, k2tog; rep from * to last st, k2tog using last st of this rnd and first st of next rnd. Rep marker before the final k2tog.
Rnd 11: *K2tog; rep from * around.
Work Rnds 1–11 for Crown patt.

HAT

With circular needle, CO 72 sts, pm for beg of rnd and join. Begin Trellis patt; work even for 32 rnds; end after Rnd 16. Change to Crown patt; work Rnds 1–11, changing to dpns when necessary—9 sts rem. Break yarn, leaving 8" tail, thread into tapestry needle and pull through rem sts tightly.

CORD LOOPS (MAKE 6)

With crochet hook, ch 5. Fasten off. Attach loops at different, random heights around the hat into Rnds 1 and 9 of Trellis patt.

CORD

With crochet hook, ch until pc meas 60". Fasten off.

FINISHING

Weave the cord through the 6 loops around the hat 2 times, crossing the cord at different places. Tie into a bow.

TRELLIS HAT

Trellis Chart
(multiple of 8 sts; 16-rnd rep)

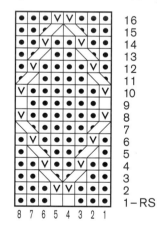

Crown Chart
(multiple of 8 sts, dec'd to 1 st; 11 rnds)

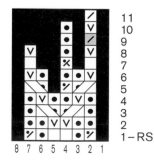

☐	knit
●	purl
V	sl1p wyib
╱	Btw
╲	Ftw
⊻	p2tog
⊠	p3tog
╱	knit 1st st of rnd; all other reps k2tog; on last rep borrow 1st st of next rnd to complete k2tog

Dawn Hat

SKILL LEVEL: INTERMEDIATE

SIZE

One size; to fit an average adult head

FINISHED MEASUREMENTS

17¼" circumference, unstretched

MATERIALS

Chesapeake by Classic Elite, Verde Collection

(50% organic cotton, 50% merino; 50-gram ball = approx 103 yards)

• 2 balls Main Color (MC)—5903 Mephisto
• 1 ball Color A—5912 Meyer Lemon
• 1 ball Color B—5981 Tendril Green
• 1 ball Color C—5957 True Blue
• 1 ball Color D—5955 Shanghai Red
• 1 ball Color E—5904 Scuba Blue

Needles

• One circular size U.S. 6 (4 mm)
• One set double-pointed needles size U.S. 6 (4 mm) **or size to obtain gauge**
• Stitch markers

GAUGE

21 sts and 30 rows = 4" in Stockinette stitch. *Take time to save time, check your gauge.*

PATTERN STITCHES

CIRCULAR 1 × 1 RIB (MULTIPLE OF 2 STS)

All rnds: *K1, p1; rep from * around.

STRIPE PATTERN (ANY NUMBER OF STS)

Rnds 1 and 2: With color A, purl.

Rnds 3 and 4: With color B, purl.

Rnds 5 and 6: With color C, purl.

Rnds 7 and 8: With color D, purl.

Rnds 9 and 10: With color E, purl.

Rep Rnds 1–10 for Stripe patt.

BRIM

With MC and circular needle, CO 100 sts; pm for beg of rnd and join, being careful not to twist sts. Beg 1 × 1 Rib; work even for 2". **Turning Rnd:** Knit all sts.

RISE

Dec Rnd: *P8, p2tog; rep from * around—90 sts rem. Change to Rev St st; work even until pc meas 1" from turning rnd. Change to Stripe Patt; work 20 rows. Change to MC and St st; work even until pc meas 8" from turning rnd.

CROWN

Shape Crown: Dec Rnd 1: *K7, k2tog, pm; rep from * around (beg-of-rnd marker counts as last marker)— 80 sts rem. Work 1 rnd even. **Dec Rnd 2:** *Knit to 2 sts before marker, k2tog, slip marker, rep from * around—10 sts dec'd. Rep Dec Rnd 2 EOR 5 more times, changing to dpns when necessary—20 sts rem; 2 sts bet markers. Work 1 rnd even. **Dec Rnd 3:** *K2tog; rep from * around, removing markers—10 sts rem. Break yarn, leaving approx 6" tail. Thread tail onto tapestry needle, and pull through rem sts. Pull tight to close top of hat.

FINISHING

Turn up brim at turning rnd and block lightly.

Canape Hat

SKILL LEVEL: EASY

SIZES

One size

FINISHED MEASUREMENTS

20½" circumference

MATERIALS

Kumara by Classic Elite

(85% extrafine merino, 15% baby camel; 50-gram ball = approx 128 yards)

• 2 balls 5709 Wild Duck

Needles

• One 16" circular each size U.S. 5 and 8 (3.75 and 5 mm)

• One set double-pointed needles size U.S. 8 (5 mm) **or size to obtain gauge**

• Stitch marker

• 2" pom-pom maker

• Tapestry needle

GAUGE

18 sts and 36 rows = 4" in Garter stitch with larger needles. *Take time to save time, check your gauge.*

PATTERN STITCHES

CIRCULAR 2 × 2 RIB (MULTIPLE OF 4 STS)

All rnds: *K2, p2; rep from * around.

CIRCULAR GARTER STITCH (GTR ST)

Rnd 1: Purl.

Rnd 2: Knit.

Rep Rnds 1 and 2 for Gtr st.

POM-POM

Follow instructions on pom-pom maker or make your own pom-pom maker following the tutorial on the Classic Elite website: www.classiceliteyarns.com/WebLetter/Stitches/PomPom/PomPom.php

HAT

With smaller needles, CO 92 sts, pm and join, being careful not to twist sts. Begin 2 × 2 Rib; work even until pc meas 2" from beg. *Inc Rnd 1:* *K9, m1; rep from * to last 2 sts, k2—102 sts. Change to larger needles; purl 1 rnd. *Inc Rnd 2:* [M1, k51] 2 times—104 sts. Change to Circular Gtr st; beg with a purl rnd, work even until pc meas 6¼" from beg, end after a purl rnd. *Shape Crown: Dec Rnd 1:* *K3, k2tog; rep from * to last 4 sts, k4—84 sts rem. Work 7 rnds even, ending after a purl rnd. *Dec Rnd 2:* *K2, k2tog; rep from * around—63 sts rem. Work 7 rnds even, ending after a purl rnd. *Dec Rnd 3:* *K2, k2tog; rep from * to last 3 sts, k3—48 sts rem. Work 5 rnds even, ending after a purl rnd. *Dec Rnd 4:* *K1, k2tog; rep

from * around—32 sts rem. Work 3 rnds even, ending after a purl rnd. *Dec Rnd 5:* *K2tog; rep from * around—16 sts rem. Purl 1 rnd. Rep dec rnd 5—8 sts rem. Break yarn leaving an 8" tail. With tail threaded on tapestry needle, thread through rcm sts and pull tightly. Do not cut tail, it will be used to attach pom-pom.

FINISHING

Block to measurements. Make a 2" pom-pom. Sew pom-pom to top center of hat.

Madeleine Beret

SKILL LEVEL: INTERMEDIATE

SIZE

One size

FINISHED MEASUREMENTS

18" brim, unstretched

MATERIALS

Princess by Classic Elite

(40% merino, 28% viscose, 15% nylon, 10% cashmere, 7% angora; 50-gram ball = approx 150 yards)

• I ball 3420 Brahman Blue

Needles

• One 16" circular each size U.S. 4 and 5 (3.5 and 3.75 mm)

• One set of double-pointed needles size U.S. 5 (3.75 mm) **or size to obtain gauge**

• Stitch markers

• Tapestry needle

GAUGE

20 sts and 28 rows = 4" in Reverse Stockinette stitch with larger needle. *Take time to save time, check your gauge.*

PATTERN STITCHES

CIRCULAR 1 × 1 RIB (MULTIPLE OF 2 STS)

All rnds.

BERRY BRANCH PANEL (PANEL OF 14 STS)

Also see chart

Rnd 1: P6, k1, LT, p5.

Rnd 2: P6, k3, p5.

Rnd 3: P6, k2, LT-p, p4.

Rnd 4: P6, k2, p1, k1, p4.

Rnd 5: P6, k2, p1, LT-p, MB, p2.

Rnd 6: P6, k2, p2, k1, p3.

Rnd 7: P6, k2, p1, MB, LT-p, p2.

Rnd 8: P6, k2, p3, k1, p2.

Rnd 9: P5, RT, k1, p3, LT-p, MB.

Rnd 10: P5, k3, p4, k1, p1.

Rnd 11: P4, RT-p, k2, p3, MB, LT-p.

Rnd 12: P4, k1, p1, k2, p5, k1.

Rnd 13: P2, MB, RT-p, p1, k2, p5, MB.

Rnd 14: P3, k1, p2, k2, p6.

Rnd 15: P2, RT-p, MB, p1, k2, p6.

Rnd 16: P2, k1, p3, k2, p6.

Rnd 17: MB, RT-p, p3, k1, LT, p5.

Rnd 18: P1, k1, p4, k3, p5.

Rnd 19: RT-p, MB, p3, k2, LT-p, p4.

Rnd 20: K1, p5, k2, p1, k1, p4.

Rnd 21: MB, p5, k2, p1, LT-p, MB, p2.

Rnds 22–24: Rep Rnds 6–8

Rnd 25: P6, k2, p3, LT-p, MB.

Rnd 26: P6, k2, p4, k1, p1.

Rnd 27: P6, k2, p3, MB, LT-p.

Rnd 28: P6, k2, p5, k1.

Rnd 29: P6, k2, p5, MB.

Work Rnds 1–29 for Berry Branch Panel.

BRIM

With smaller circular needles, CO 90 sts; pm for beg of rnd, join, being careful not to twist sts. Beg 1 × 1 Rib; work even until pc meas ¾" from beg. *Inc Rnd:* *K3, m1; rep from * to end—120 sts.

RISE

Change to larger circular needles. ***Est. Berry Branch Panel:*** *Work 6 sts in Rev St st, pm, work 14 sts in Berry Branch Panel, pm, work 4 sts in Rev St st; rep from * around. Cont as est for 28 more rnds, end after Rnd 29 of Berry Branch Panel. Rem all markers except beg-of-rnd marker. Est Patt: *P12, pm, k2, pm, p10; rep from * around.

CROWN

Shape Crown: Dec Rnd: *Purl to 2 sts before marker, p2tog, sl marker, k2, sl marker, ssp; rep from * 4 more times, purl to end—10 sts dec'd. Rep Crown Dec Rnd 9 more times, changing to dpns when necessary—20 sts rem. *Next Rnd:* *K2tog; rep from * around—10 sts rem. Break yarn, leaving approx 6" tail of yarn. Thread tail onto tapestry needle and thread through rem sts twice. Pull tight to close top of hat.

FINISHING

Wet block over 10" dinner plate, taking care not to stretch rib.

Berry Branch Chart
(panel of 14 sts; 29 rnds)

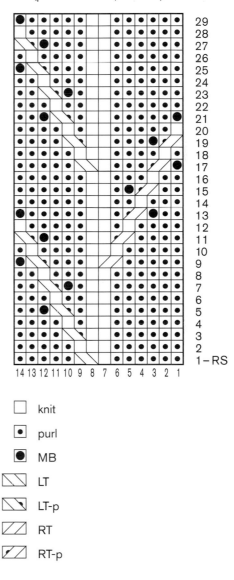

☐ knit

⊡ purl

⬤ MB

◢ LT

◥ LT-p

◣ RT

◤ RT-p

Bateau Mittens & Hat

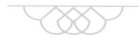

SKILL LEVEL: INTERMEDIATE

SIZE
One size

FINISHED MEASUREMENTS
Hat: 19½" circumference

Mittens: 8½" hand circumference; 6" finger length

MATERIALS
Inca Alpaca by Classic Elite

(100% baby alpaca, 50-gram hank = approx 109 yards)

• 2 hanks 1107 Camacho Periwinkle for hat

• 3 hanks 1107 Camacho Periwinkle for mittens

Needles

• One pair size U.S. 9 (5.5 mm) for hat and mittens

• One set double-pointed needles size U.S. 9 (5.5 mm) for mittens **or size to obtain gauge**

• Cable needle

• Stitch markers

• Stitch holder or waste yarn

GAUGE
16 sts and 21 rows = 4" in Stockinette stitch with 2 strands of yarn held together; 12 sts in Hourglass Cable = 2¼" wide with 2 strands of yarn held together. *Take time to save time, check your gauge.*

NOTE
A double-stranded hat and mitten set. Both the hat and mittens are worked flat and seamed; double-pointed needles are used only for the thumb.

PATTERN STITCHES

BABY CABLE RIB (MULTIPLE OF 4 STS + 2)
Also see chart

Row 1: (RS) P2, *k2, p2; rep from * to end.

Row 2: K2, *p2, k2; rep from * to end.

Row 3: P2, *BC, p2; rep from * to end.

Row 4: Rep Row 2.

Rep Rows 1–4 for Baby Cable Rib.

HOURGLASS CABLE (HC) (PANEL OF 12 STS)
Also see chart

Rows 1 and 5: (RS) P2, k8, p2.

Rows 2, 4, and 6: K2, p8, k2.

Row 3: P2, C4B, C4F, p2.

Row 7: P2, C4F, C4B, p2.

Row 8: Rep Row 2.

Rep Rows 1–8 for HC Panel.

HAT

With 2 strands of yarn held tog, CO 78 sts. (WS) Beg St st; work 1 row. Change to Baby Cable Rib; (RS) work 11 rows, end after RS Row 3 of Baby Cable Rib. *Inc Row:* (WS) Inc 8 sts evenly across as follows: k1, m1, k1, [p2, k2] twice, [p1, m1p, p1, k2] twice, *[p2, k2] 3 times, p1, m1p, p1, k2; rep from * twice more, p1, m1p, p1, [k2, p2] twice, k1, m1, k1—86 sts. *Est Patt:* Work 9 sts in St st, work 12 sts in HC Panel, *work 16 sts in St st, work 12 sts in HC Panel; rep from * once more, work to end in St st. Work 15 more rows as est, end after WS Row 8 of HC Panel. *Shape Crown: Dec Row:* (RS) Work to 2 sts before HC Panel, k2tog, work 12 st in HC Panel, ssk, *work to 2 sts before next HC Panel, k2tog, work 12 sts in HC Panel, ssk; rep from * once more, work to end—6 sts dec'd. Rep Crown Dec Row EOR 6 more times—44 sts rem. (WS) Work 2 rows even, end after RS row 7 of HC Panel. Break yarn, leaving a 12" tail. Thread tail onto tapestry needle and draw through live sts.

HAT FINISHING

Block to measurements if desired. Pull yarn tail to draw top of hat tightly together. Sew seam.

LEFT MITTEN

Cuff: Using 2 strands of yarn held tog, CO 34 sts. (WS) Beg St st; work 1 row. Change to Baby Cable Rib; work 23 rows, end after RS Row 3 of Baby Cable Rib. *Inc Row:* (WS) K2, p2, k2, [p1, m1p, p1, k] twice, p2, pm, k1, m1, k1, pm, [p2, k2] 4 times—37 sts. *Est Patt:* (RS) Work to first marker in St st, sl marker, work to next marker in Rev St st, sl marker, work 2 sts in St st, work 12 sts in HC Panel, work to end in St st. (WS) Work 1 row as est. *Shape Thumb Gusset: Inc Row:* (RS) Work to first marker, sl marker, p1, m1p, work in Rev St st to 1 st before next marker, m1p, p1, sl marker, work to end as est—2 sts inc'd bet markers. Rep thumb gusset inc row EOR 5 more times—49 sts; 15 sts bet markers. (WS) Work 1 row even as est. *Divide for Fingers:* (RS) Work to first marker as est, remove marker, sl next 15 unworked sts to st holder or waste yarn for thumb, remove marker, turn work so WS is

BATEAU MITTENS & HAT

Hourglass Cable Chart
(panel of 12 sts; 8-row rep)

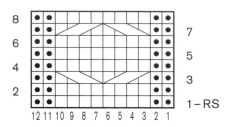

Baby Cable Chart
(multiple of 4 sts + 2; 4-row rep)

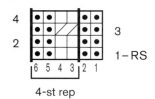

4-st rep

☐	knit on RS, purl on WS
⊡	purl on RS, knit on WS
⧅	BC
⧄	C4B
⧅	C4F

facing, use the Cable Method to CO 3 sts, turn work so RS is facing, work to end as est—37 sts. (WS) Work 25 more rows even as est, working CO sts in St st, end after WS row 8 of HC Panel. **Shape Fingers: Dec Row 1:** (RS) K1, [ssk, k2] 5 times, p2, k8, p2, k1, k2tog, k1—31 sts rem. (WS) Work 1 row even. **Dec Row 2:** K1, [ssk, k1] 5 times, p2, [k2tog] 4 times, p2, ssk, k1—21 sts rem. (WS) Work 1 row even. **Dec Row 3:** K1, [ssk] 5 times, p2, k4, p2, ssk—15 sts rem. **Dec Row 4:** (WS) P1, [p2tog] 7 times—8 sts rem. Break yarn, leaving a 12" tail. Thread tail onto tapestry needle and draw through live sts.

THUMB

Slip 15 sts from holder evenly onto dpns and join yarn preparing to work a RS row. (RS) Beg Rev St st; work 1 row, pick up and knit 3 sts in the CO sts for the hand. Pm for beg of rnd, and join, being careful not to twist sts—18 sts. Work even until pc meas 2" from pick-up rnd, or ½" less than desired length. **Dec Rnd 1:** *P1, p2tog; rep from * around—12 sts rem. Work 1 rnd even. **Dec Rnd 2:** *P2tog; rep from * around—6 sts rem. Break yarn, leaving a 6" tail. With tapestry needle, draw tail through rem sts and pull tight to close.

MITTEN FINISHING

Block to measurements if desired. Pull yarn tail to draw top of mittens tightly together. Sew side seam.

RIGHT MITTEN

Work as for left mitten to Inc Row. **Inc Row:** (WS) [K2, p2] 4 times, pm, k1, m1, k1, pm, p2, k2, [p1, m1p, p1, k2] twice, p2, k2—37 sts. **Est Patt:** (RS) Work 4 sts in St st, 12 sts in HC Panel, work to marker in St st, sl marker, work to next marker in Rev St st, sl marker, work to end in St st. (WS) Work 1 row as est. **Shape Thumb Gusset:** (RS) Cont as for left mitten to finger shaping. **Shape Fingers: Dec Row 1:** (RS) K1, ssk, k1, p2, k8, p2, [k2, k2tog] 5 times, k1—31 sts rem. (WS) Work 1 row even. **Dec Row 2:** (RS) K1, ssk, p2, [k2tog] 4 times, p2, [k1, k2tog] 5 times, k1—21 sts rem. (WS) Work 1 row even. **Dec Row 3:** K2tog, p2, k4, p2, [k2tog] 5 times, k1—15 sts rem. **Dec Row 4:** (WS) [P1, p2tog] 7 times—8 sts rem. Cont as for left mitten. Work thumb and mitten finishing as for left mitten.

Thistle Hat

SKILL LEVEL: INTERMEDIATE

SIZE

One size

FINISHED MEASUREMENTS

20" circumference, unstretched

MATERIALS

Portland Tweed by Classic Elite

(50% virgin wool, 25% alpaca, 25% viscose; 50-gram ball = approx 120 yards)

• 2 balls 5004 Tidal Foam

Needles

• One 16" circular size U.S. 7 (4.5 mm)

• One set double-pointed needles size U.S. 7 (4.5 mm) **or size to obtain gauge**

• Cable needle

• Stitch marker

GAUGE

27 sts and 31 rows = 4" in Cable pattern; 20 sts and 28 rows = 4" in Stockinette stitch. *Take time to save time, check your gauge.*

PATTERN STITCH

CIRCULAR CABLE PATTERN (MULTIPLE OF 11 STS)

Also see chart

Rnd 1: *P2, k5, p2, k2; rep from * around.

Cable Chart
(multiple of 11 sts; 6-rnd rep)

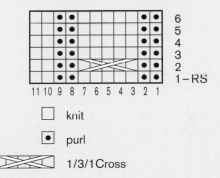

☐ knit

⊡ purl

⧓ 1/3/1 Cross

Rnd 2: *P2, 1/3/1Cross, p2, k2; rep from * around.

Rnds 3–6: *P2, k5, p2, k2; rep from * around.

Rep Rnds 1–6 for Cable patt.

HAT

CO 132 sts, pm for beg of rnd; join, being careful not to twist sts. Begin Cable Patt; work even until pc meas approx 2¾" from beg, ending after rnd 6 of patt. Purl 1 rnd. Change to St st; work even until pc meas 5½" from beg. *Shape Crown: Set-Up Rnd:* *K2tog, k10, pm; rep from * around—121 sts rem. Work 1 rnd even. *Dec Rnd:* *K2tog, knit to marker, sl marker; rep from * around—11 sts dec'd. Rep Crown Dec Rnd EOR 8 more times, changing to dpns when necessary—22 sts rem. Rem all markers except beg-of-rnd marker. Work 1 rnd even. *Dec Rnd 2:* *K2tog; rep from * around—11 sts rem. *Dec Rnd 3:* K1, *k2tog; rep from * around—6 sts rem. Break yarn leaving a 6" tail. Thread tail through rem sts, pull tightly to secure.

FINISHING

Block to measurements.

Fresco Mitts

SKILL LEVEL: INTERMEDIATE

SIZE
One size

FINISHED MEASUREMENTS
3" circumference, 9½" long

MATERIALS

Fresco by Classic Elite
(60% wool, 30% baby alpaca, 10% angora;
50-gram hank = approx 164 yards)
• 1 hank 5379 Purple Haze

Needles
• One set of 5 double-pointed needles
  size U.S. 4 (3.5 mm) **or size to obtain gauge**
• Stitch marker
• Waste yarn same weight as main yarn

GAUGE
32 sts and 40 rows = 4" in Eyelet Rib, relaxed. *Take time to save time, check your gauge.*

PATTERN STITCHES

CIRCULAR 1 × 1 RIB (MULTIPLE OF 2 STS)
Rnd 1: *K1, p1; rep from * around.
Rnd 2: Knit the knit sts and purl the purl sts as they face you.
Rep Rnd 2 for 1 x 1 Rib.

CIRCULAR EYELET RIB (MULTIPLE OF 7 STS)
Also see chart
Rnd 1: *P2, k2tog, yo, k1, yo, ssk; rep from * around.
Rnds 2, 3, and 4: *P2, k5; rep from * around.
Rep Rnds 1–4 for Eyelet Rib.

CIRCULAR STOCKINETTE STITCH (ST ST)
Knit every rnd.

RIGHT MITT

CO 48 sts. Divide sts evenly over 4 dpn. Join, being careful not to twist sts, pm for beg of rnd. Beg 1 × 1 Rib; work 4 rnds. *Inc Rnd:* K1-f/b in first st, work around in 1 × 1 Rib as est—49 sts. Change to Eyelet Rib; work even until pc meas approx 7" from beg, end Rnd 2 of Eyelet Rib. *Shape Thumb Opening:* With waste yarn, k8; sl 8 sts just worked back to LH needle and work them with main yarn in Eyelet Rib as est, work to end of rnd. Cont in patt until pc meas approx 9" from beg, end Rnd 1 of Eyelet Rib. *Change to 1 × 1 Rib and Dec Rnd:* K2tog, p1, work in 1 × 1 Rib around—48 sts rem. Work 4 rnds. BO all sts loosely in rib.

LEFT MITT

Work as for Right Mitt until pc meas approx 7" from beg, end Rnd 2 of Eyelet Rib. *Shape Thumb Opening:* Work 15 sts as est, end p1. With waste yarn, k8; sl 8 sts just worked back to LH needle and work them with main yarn in Eyelet Rib as est. Cont as for Right Mitt.

THUMB

Carefully pick out waste yarn 1 st at a time and slide 8 lower sts onto 1 dpn and 9 upper sts onto a second dpn—17 sts. Beg St st; beg at lower right corner, join yarn and work around, dividing sts over 3 dpn, pm for beg of rnd. Join, being careful not to twist sts, and work until thumb meas 1¼" from pick-up row. *Change to 1 × 1 Rib and Dec Rnd:* K2tog, p1, work in 1 × 1 Rib around—16 sts. Work 2 rnds. BO all sts loosely in rib.

Eyelet Rib Chart
(multiple of 7 sts; 4-rnd rep)

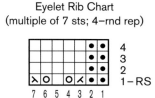

□ knit ⋉ ssk

● purl ○ yo

⋌ k2tog

Fluffy Mittens

SKILL LEVEL: INTERMEDIATE

SIZE

One size

FINISHED MEASUREMENTS

12½" long, 8½" circumference

MATERIALS

Fresco by Classic Elite

(60% wool, 30% baby alpaca, 10% angora; 50-gram hank = approx 164 yards)

• 1 hank Color A—5336 Oatmeal
• 1 hank Color B—5320 Ashley Blue
• 1 hank Color C—5335 Peacock Green
• 1 hank Color D—5385 Tandori Spice
• 1 hank Color E—5327 Wake Up Red

Needles:

• One set double-pointed needles size U.S. 5 (3.75 mm) **or size to obtain gauge**
• Stitch markers
• Waste yarn same weight as main yarn
• Tapestry needle

GAUGE

26 sts and 30 rows = 4" in Fair Isle pattern worked in circular Stockinette stitch. *Take time to save time, check your gauge.*

PATTERN STITCHES

CIRCULAR RIB PATTERN (MULTIPLE OF 4 STS)

Rnd 1: *K3, p1, rep from * around.

Rnd 2: Knit the knit sts and purl the purl sts as they face you.

Rep Rnd 2 for Circular Rib patt.

COLOR STRIPE PATTERN

Rnds 1–2: Color B.

Rnds 3–8: Color A.

Rnds 9–10: Color C.

Rnds 11–12: Color A.

Rnd 13: Color B.

Rnds 14–15: Color A.

Work Rnds 1–15 for Color Stripe patt.

CIRCULAR STOCKINETTE STITCH (ST ST)

Knit every rnd.

FAIR ISLE PATTERN

See chart; work in circular St st.

NOTES

The cuffs are extra long to keep your wrists warm, and the thumb is worked without a gusset—very simple indeed. The yarn, Fresco, is a blend of wool (for elasticity), alpaca (for warmth), and angora (just a touch—for softness), and it comes in many colors.

RIGHT MITTEN

With Color A, CO 56 sts, divide onto 4 dpns (14 sts on each needle). Join to work in-the-rnd being careful not to twist sts; pm for beg of rnd. *Begin Circular Rib Patt:* Work for 10 rnds. Cont working Circular Rib patt, begin Color Stripe patt, work 15 rnds. Change to Color A and St st; work 2 rnds. *Work Fair Isle Patt as Foll:* Work Rnds 1–6 of Fair Isle Patt, dec'ing 2 sts evenly on Rnd 6—54 sts. Work Rnds 7–15, inc'ing 2 sts evenly on Rnd 15—56 sts. Work Fair Isle Patt through Rnd 37. *Thumb Waste Yarn Placement:* Rnd 38, with Color A, k1, work 10 sts in waste yarn, slide 10 sts just worked back to LH needle, work 10 sts again and cont Rnd 38 of Fair Isle Patt. Work Fair Isle Patt through Rnd 66. Working in St st and Color A; work 4 rnds. *Shape Top:* *K2, k2tog; rep from * around—42 sts. Work 2 rnds even. *K1, k2tog; rep from * around— 28 sts. Work 1 rnd. *K2tog, rep from * around—14 sts rem. Break yarn, leaving 10" tail. With tapestry needle, draw yarn through 14 rem sts twice. Pull yarn to gather sts and close top of mitten. Fasten off yarn.

Fluffy
Mittens

2½"

12½"

8½"

THUMB

Carefully remove waste yarn and as you remove it, slip live sts to 2 dpns—10 sts from lower edge, 9 sts from upper edge. Working in circular St st with dpns, attach yarn to right end of lower needle. Using a third dpn, k6 sts; with fourth needle, k4 sts, pick up 1 st at corner; with another dpn, k5 sts from upper edge, then k last 4 sts from upper edge and pick up 1 st at right corner—21 sts on needles. Join, being careful not to twist sts; pm for beg of rnd. Work until thumb meas 2¼".
Shape Thumb: Next rnd; *K1, k2tog, rep from * to end—14 sts. Knit 1 rnd. *K2tog, rep from * around—7 sts. Break yarn and draw end through rem 7 sts twice. Pull yarn to close top of thumb. Fasten off.

LEFT MITTEN

Work as for right mitten through Rnd 37. *Thumb Waste Yarn Placement:* Work Rnd 38 in Fair Isle Patt for 45 sts. With Color A, k1, work 10 sts in waste yarn, slide 10 sts just worked back to LH needle and cont Rnd 38 of chart.

FINISHING

Block to required measurements.

FLUFFY MITTENS

Fair Isle Chart
(panel of 56 sts; 66 rnds)

 Color A

Color B

Color C

Color D

Color E

k2tog

no st

Using Color B, m1

Grove Mittens

SKILL LEVEL: INTERMEDIATE

SIZE
One size

FINISHED MEASUREMENTS
7" circumference at palm

MATERIALS
Princess by Classic Elite

(40% merino, 28% viscose, 15% nylon, 10% cashmere, 7% angora; 50-gram ball = approx 150 yards)

• 2 balls 3425 Tawny Chestnut

Needles

• One set double-pointed needles size U.S. 6 (4 mm) **or size needed to obtain gauge**

• Cable needle

• Stitch marker

• Tapestry needle

• Two short lengths waste yarn in same weight as main yarn

GAUGE
25 sts and 18 rows = 3" following sts 1–25 of Mitten Charts, blocked, unstretched. *Take time to save time, check your gauge.*

NOTES
These mittens have an intricate, twisted stitch motif that creates a beautiful relief pattern—inspired by twisting vines and tree roots. Knitted stitches are all worked through the back loop to create the sculptural texture characteristic of twisted stitch motifs. Shaping of the vine-like motifs on the hand is done with the use of yarn overs and decreasing—except for the cuff, no cabling occurs in the main portion of the mitten. The cuff motif, a spiraling 1 × 1 rib is mirrored on each hand, and involves moving the marker as you work, to keep the spiral pattern unbroken.

LEFT MITTEN

CO 42 sts; divide sts evenly over 3 or 4 dpns; pm for beg of rnd. Join, being careful not to twist sts. Purl 1 rnd to marker, remove marker, slip 1 st purlwise wyib, replace marker. Knit 1 rnd. Rep previous 2 rnds once more, establishing Circular Gtr st—2 Gtr ridges. Work Set-Up Rnd and Rnd 1 from Left Cuff Chart. Marker placement will change on Rnd 2; work as foll.

Rnd 2: Work in patt until 1 st rem before marker. Sl 1 st from LH to RH needle, remove marker, return slipped st to LH needle, replace marker. This indicates new beg of rnd. Rep Rnds 1 and 2, until pc meas just under 2" from beg. After completion of Left Cuff Chart, cont as foll. Purl 1 rnd to marker, remove marker, slip 1 st purlwise wyib, replace marker. Knit 1 rnd. Purl 1 rnd to marker, remove marker,

Left Cuff Chart
(multiple of 2; 2-rnd rep)

Right Cuff Chart
(multiple of 2; 2-rnd rep)

Thumb Chart
(panel of 20 sts dec'd to 8 sts; 16 rnds)

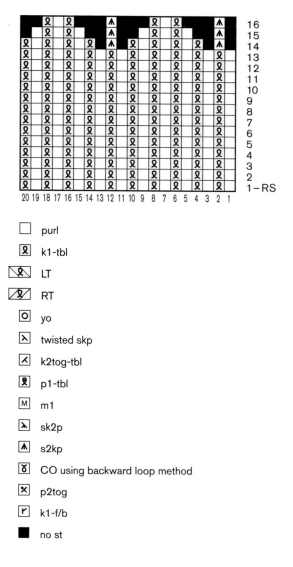

☐	purl
☒	k1-tbl
⬚	LT
⬚	RT
☐	yo
☒	twisted skp
☒	k2tog-tbl
☒	p1-tbl
Ⓜ	m1
☒	sk2p
⚠	s2kp
☒	CO using backward loop method
☒	p2tog
☒	k1-f/b
■	no st

slip 1 st purlwise wyib, replace marker. *Inc Rnd:* K1, m1, knit to end—43 sts. Work Rnds 1–16 of Left Mitten Chart. After completion of Rnd 16 of Left Mitten Chart, cont as foll. ***Divide for Thumb:*** Work Rnd 17 of Left Mitten Chart until 1 st rem in Rnd, sl 11 sts just worked (thumb sts) onto waste yarn (these sts are indicated by red bold line in chart); work to end of rnd—43 sts. On Rnd 18, when you reach held sts, use backward loop method to CO 9 sts, as indicated in chart; cont to end of Rnd—52 sts. Work Rnds 19–50 of Left Mitten Chart—20 sts. After completion of Left Mitten Chart, cont as foll: Slip first half of rnd onto 1 dpn and second half onto another dpn, so 10 sts are on either side, mirroring each other. Turn mitten inside out and work a three-needle BO from WS. *Note:* Left Cuff Chart is a multiple of 2 sts that reps itself 21 times on every Rnd. Marker placement will change on Rnd 2.

LEFT THUMB

With RS facing, beg at right edge of held sts, slip the 11 held sts from waste yarn onto 2 dpns, join yarn and with a third dpn, pick up 9 sts along CO edge of thumb hole—20 sts. Pm for beg of rnd; join, being careful not to twist sts. Work Rnds 1–16 of Thumb Chart. Marker placement will change on Rnds 15 and 16; work as foll. Rnds 15 and 16: Work in patt until 1 st rem in rnd; sl 1 st from LH to RH needle, rem marker, return slipped st back to LH needle, replace marker. This indicates new beg of rnd—8 sts. After completion of Thumb Chart, break yarn, leaving 6" tail. Pass tail through rem sts, and pull tightly to close thumb.

RIGHT MITTEN

CO 42 sts; divide sts evenly over 3 or 4 dpns; pm for beg of rnd. Join, being careful not to twist sts. Purl 1 rnd to marker, remove

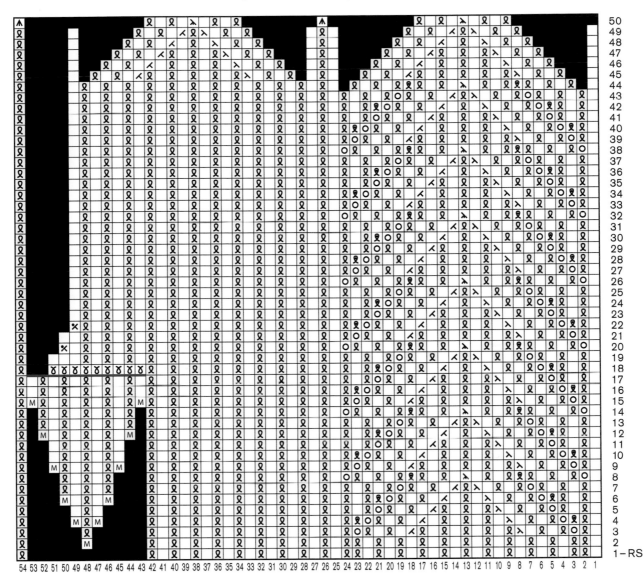

marker, slip 1 st purlwise wyib, replace marker. Knit 1 rnd. Rep previous 2 rnds once more, establishing Circular Gtr st—2 Gtr ridges. Work Set-up Rnd and Rnd 1 from Right Cuff Chart. Marker placement will change on Rnd 2; work as foll. **Rnd 2:** Work in patt to marker. Remove marker, sl 1 st from LH to RH needle, replace marker. This indicates new beg of rnd. Rep Rnds 1 and 2, until pc meas just under 2" from beg. After completion of Right Cuff Chart, cont as foll. Purl 1 rnd to marker, remove marker, sl 1 st purlwise wyib, replace marker. Knit 1 rnd. Purl 1 rnd to marker, remove marker, slip 1 st purlwise wyib, replace marker. **Inc Rnd:** K1, m1, knit to end—43 sts. Work Rnds 1–16 of Right Mitten Chart. After completion of Rnd 16 of Right Mitten Chart, cont as foll:

Divide for Thumb: Work Rnd 17 through 36th st, sl 11 sts just worked (thumb sts) onto waste yarn (these sts are indicated by red bold line in chart); work to end of rnd—43 sts. On Rnd 18, when you reach held sts, use backward loop method to CO 9 sts, as indicated in chart; cont to end of rnd—52 sts. Work Rnds 19–50 of Right Mitten Chart—20 sts. After completion of Right Mitten Chart, finish as for left mitten

RIGHT THUMB

Work as for left thumb.

FINISHING

Weave in all ends. Block mittens; lay flat to dry.

GROVE MITTENS

Right Mitten Chart
(43 sts dec'd to 20 sts; 50 rnds)

Charmed Fingerless Mitts

SKILL LEVEL: INTERMEDIATE

SIZE

One size

FINISHED MEASUREMENTS

7" circumference; 8¼" long

MATERIALS

Charmed by Classic Elite

(85% cashmere, 15% mohair, 50-gram ball = approx 130 yards)

• 1 ball Main Color (MC)—76708 Heathered Rose
• 1 ball Contrast Color (CC)—76709 Heathered Plum

Needles

• One set double-pointed needles size U.S. 9 (5.5 mm) **or size to obtain gauge**
• Stitch marker

GAUGE

18 sts and 28 rnds = 4" in Circular Stockinette stitch. *Take time to save time, check your gauge.*

NOTES

1. If you have difficulty finding the recommended yarn, you may consider using Classic Elite's Kumara as a substitute.
2. Fingerless Mitts can be made with 1 ball of yarn, including Ruffled Edge. 2 balls of yarn will make 2 pairs of gloves. Make 1 pair with MC and CC edge, the other pair with CC and MC edge.

PATTERN STITCH

CIRCULAR STOCKINETTE STITCH (ST ST)

Knit every rnd.

STRAIGHT STOCKINETTE STITCH (ST ST)

Knit on RS, purl on WS.

MITTS (MAKE 2)

With CC, CO 112 sts. Distribute sts evenly onto dpn; join being careful not to twist sts; pm for beg of rnd. *Shape Ruffle: Dec Rnd:* *K2tog; rep from * around—56 sts rem. Rep Dec Rnd 1 time—28 sts rem. Change to MC and Circular St st; work even until piece meas 2" from beg of ruffle. *Inc Rnd:* *Work 7 sts, m1; rep from * 3 times—32 sts. Cont in St st; work even until piece meas 5½" from beg of ruffle; turn.

THUMB OPENING

Est Patt: (WS) Slip 1 st purlwise wyif; work in Straight St st to end. Work as est for ¾", end WS row. Join sts and pm for beg of rnd; work in Circular St st until piece meas 8¼" from beg of ruffle. *Eyelet Rnd:* *K2tog, yo; rep from * around. Work 1 rnd in St st. BO all sts loosely.

FINISHING

Block pieces to finished measurements.

Thicket Mittens

SIZE
One size

FINISHED MEASUREMENTS
7½" circumference; 11½" long

MATERIALS
Woodland by Classic Elite, Verde Collection
(65% wool, 35% nettles; 50-gram ball = approx 131 yards)
• 2 balls 3150 Sunshine
Needles
• One set double-pointed needles (dpns) size U.S. 6 (4 mm) **or size to obtain gauge**
• Stitch markers
• Cable needle
• Stitch holder or waste yarn

GAUGE
20 sts and 29 rows = 4" in Stockinette stitch; 12 sts = 1½" in Right or Left Cable Panel. *Take time to save time, check your gauge.*

NOTE
Mittens are identical and fit either hand.

PATTERN STITCHES

CIRCULAR 2 × 2 RIB (MULTIPLE OF 4 STS)
All rnds: *P1, k2, p1; rep from * around.

RIGHT CABLE PANEL (PANEL OF 12 STS)
Also see chart
Rnd 1: C4B, p4, k2, p2.
Rnd 2: K4, p4, k2, p2.
Rnd 3: K4, p2, T4B, p2.
Rnd 4: K4, p2, k2, p4.
Rnd 5: [C4B] 2 times, p4.
Rnd 6: K8, p4.
Rnd 7: K2, T4B, T4F, p2.
Rnd 8: Rep rnd 2.
Rnd 9: Rep rnd 1.
Rnds 10–12: Rep rnd 2.
Work Rnds 1–12 a total of 4 times, then cont working Rnds 13–20 as follows:

Rnds 13 and 14: Rep Rnds 1 and 2.
Rnd 15: K4, p2, T4B, p2tog—11 sts.
Rnd 16: K4, p2, k2, p3.
Rnd 17: [C4B] 2 times, p2tog, p1—10 sts.
Rnd 18: K8, p2.
Rnd 19: K2, T4B, p2tog, p2—9 sts.
Rnd 20: K4, p5.

LEFT CABLE PANEL (PANEL OF 12 STS)
Also see chart
Rnd 1: P2, k2, p4, C4F.
Rnd 2: P2, k2, p4, k4.
Rnd 3: P2, T4F, p2, k4.
Rnd 4: P4, k2, p2, k4.
Rnd 5: P4, [C4F] 2 times.
Rnd 6: P4, k8.
Rnd 7: P2, T4B, T4F, k2.
Rnd 8: Rep Rnd 2.
Rnd 9: Rep Rnd 1.
Rnds 10–12: Rep Rnd 2.
Work Rnds 1–12 a total of 4 times, then cont working Rnds 13–20 as follows:

Rnds 13 and 14: Rep Rnds 1 and 2.
Rnd 15: P2tog, T4F, p2, k4—11 sts.
Rnd 16: P3, k2, p2, k4.
Rnd 17: P1, p2tog, [C4F] 2 times—10 sts.
Rnd 18: P2, k8.
Rnd 19: P2, p2tog, T4F, k2—9 sts.
Rnd 20: P5, k4

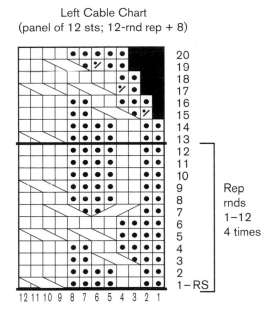

Left Cable Chart
(panel of 12 sts; 12-rnd rep + 8)

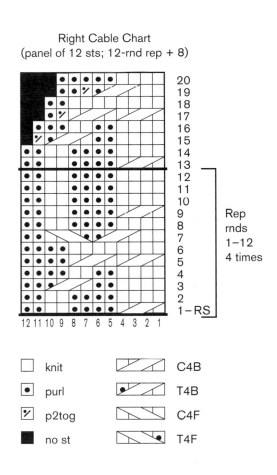

Right Cable Chart
(panel of 12 sts; 12-rnd rep + 8)

Rep rnds 1–12 4 times

☐ knit	▱ C4B
● purl	▱ T4B
✔ p2tog	▱ C4F
■ no st	▱ T4F

MITTENS (MAKE 2)

CO 40 sts. Divide sts evenly over dpn. Join, being careful not to twist sts, pm for beg of rnd. Beg 2 × 2 Rib; work even until pc meas 2½" from beg. *Inc Rnd:* P1, m1p, k2, m1p, p2, m1p, k2, p2, pm for cable panel, [k2, p2] 5 times, k2, pm for cable panel, p2, k2, m1p, p2, m1p, k2, m1p, p1—46 sts. *Est Patt:* Work 12 sts in Right Cable Panel, sl marker, work to next cable panel marker in St st, sl marker, work 12 sts in Left Cable Panel. Work 11 more rnds, ending after Rnd 12 of Cable Panels. *Shape Thumb Gusset: Inc Rnd 1:* Work to first Cable Panel marker as est, work 9 sts, pm for thumb gusset, k1-f/b, k1, k1-f/b, pm for thumb gusset, work to end as est—2 sts inc'd. Work 1 rnd even as est. *Inc Rnd 2:* Work as est to first thumb gusset marker, sl marker, k1-f/b, work to 1 st before next thumb gusset marker, k1-f/b, sl marker, work to end as est—2 sts inc'd. Rep Thumb Gusset Inc Rnd 2, EOR 5 more times—60 sts; 17 sts bet thumb gusset markers. Work 4 rnds even, ending after Rnd 5 of Cable Panels. *Shape Thumb:* Work to first thumb gusset marker as est, rem marker, k1, sl next 16 sts onto st holder or waste yarn for thumb, use Backward Loop Method to CO 2 sts on RH needle, rem marker, work to end as est—46 sts rem. Cont working as est until a total of four 12-rnd reps of Cable Panels have been completed. *Shape Top:* Cont working as est, working Rnds 13–20 of Cable Panels—

40 sts rem. Remove cable panel markers. Pm for side 20 sts from beg-of-rnd marker. *Change to St St and Dec Rnd:* *K1, ssk, work to 3 sts before side marker, k2tog, k1; rep from * once more—4 sts dec'd. Rep dec rnd EOR 2 more times, then every rnd 5 times—8 sts rem. Divide sts evenly onto 2 dpns. Break yarn leaving approx 10" tail. Use Kitchener St to graft rem sts together.

THUMB

Divide sts from holder onto 2 dpns, with empty dpn, pick-up and knit 4 sts over gap—20 sts. Beg St st; work even for 14 rnds or ½" less than desired finished length. *Shape Thumb, Dec Rnd:* K2tog, *k1, k2tog; rep from * around—13 sts rem. Work 1 rnd even. *Dec Rnd 2:* K1 *k2tog; rep from * around—7 sts rem. Break yarn leaving approx 6" tail. Thread tail through rem sts, draw up tightly and fasten off.

FINISHING

Block pcs to required measurements.

Duet Mitts

SKILL LEVEL: INTERMEDIATE

SIZE
One size

FINISHED MEASUREMENTS
7" circumference

MATERIALS
Fresco by Classic Elite
(60% wool, 30% baby alpaca, 10% angora; 50-gram hank = approx 164 yards)
• 1 hank Main Color (MC)—5301 Parchment
• 1 hank Color A—5350 Ginger
• 1 hank Color B—5338 Root Beer
Needles
• One set double-pointed needles size U.S. 2 (2.75 mm) **or size to obtain gauge**
• Stitch marker
• Stitch holder or waste yarn

GAUGE
30 sts = 4" and 19 rows = 2¼" in Color pattern; 20 sts and 30 rows = 4" in Pearl Brioche stitch. *Take time to save time, check your gauge.*

NOTE
Texture-stitch fingerless mitts are worked with a fair isle band at the wrist.

PATTERN STITCHES

PEARL BRIOCHE STITCH (MULTIPLE OF 2 STS)
Rnd 1: *P1, yfsl1yo, rep from *.
Rnd 2: *K1, brk1; rep from *.
Rnd 3: *Yfsl1yo, p1; rep from *.
Rnd 4: *Brk1, k1; rep from *.
Rep Rnds 1–4 for Pearl Brioche St.

COLOR PATTERN (MULTIPLE OF 14 STS)
See chart

LEFT MITT

With 2 strands of MC held together, CO 36 sts. Join, being careful not to twist sts; pm for beg of rnd. Drop 1 strand of MC, cont with 1 strand only. Begin Pearl Brioche St; work even until pc meas 1" from beg, end after an even numbered rnd. **Inc Rnd:** *K1, m1, [k2, m1] 3 times; rep from * 4 more times, k1—56 sts. Change to Color Patt; work 19 rnds. **Change to MC and Dec Rnd:** K1, k2tog, k2, k2tog, k10, k2tog, [k3, k2tog] 7 times, k2—46 sts rem. Change to Pearl Brioche St; work for 2" from Color Patt, end after Rnd 2. **Divide for Thumb:** Work 5 sts as est, sl next 10 sts to st holder or waste yarn, work around—36 sts rem. Cont in Pearl Brioche St for 6 more rnds. Change to Color A; work 2 rnds in Pearl Brioche St. Join a second strand of Color A and BO all sts loosely purlwise, working yo's together with the slipped st.

THUMB

Sl 10 sts from holder onto 2 dpns. With empty dpn and Color A, pick up and knit 4 sts, pm for beg of rnd—14 sts. Begin Pearl Brioche St; work Rnd 1 (work Rnd 3 for right mitt). **Dec Rnd:** Work as est to last 4 sts, cont in patt and at the same time work ssk, k2tog—12 sts. Work rnd 1 of Pearl Brioche St. Join a second strand of Color A. BO all sts loosely purlwise.

RIGHT MITT

Work as for left mitt until Color Patt is complete. **Change to MC and Dec Rnd:** K2tog, k2, [k2tog, k3] 6 times, k2tog, k10, [k2tog, k3] 2 times—46 sts rem. Change to Pearl Brioche St; work for 2½" from Color Patt, end after Rnd 2. **Divide for Thumb:** Work 28 sts as est, sl next 10 sts to st holder or waste yarn, work to end—36 sts rem. Cont as for left mitt.

Color Chart
(multiple of 14 sts; 19 rnds)

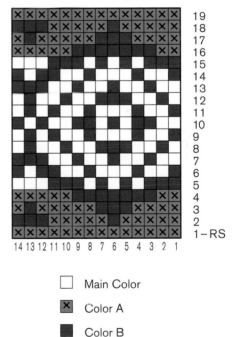

☐ Main Color

☒ Color A

◼ Color B

Anchor Mittens

SKILL LEVEL: INTERMEDIATE

SIZE
One size

FINISHED MEASUREMENTS
8" circumference; 10¼" long from cuff to tip (with a 3" cuff) × 77½" long (including strap)

MATERIALS
Inca Alpaca and Inca Marl by Classic Elite
(100% baby alpaca; 50-gram hank = approx 109 yards)
• 2 hanks Main Color (MC)—1195 Violet (marl)
• 2 hanks Contrast Color (CC)—1179 Santo Grape
Needles
• One set each double-pointed needles each size U.S. 5 and 6 (3.75 and 4 mm) **or size to obtain gauge**
• Stitch markers
• Stitch holder or waste yarn

GAUGE
21 sts and 28 rows= 4" in Stockinette stitch with larger needles.
Take time to save time, check your gauge.

NOTE
A pair of mittens attached with a ribbed strap. A provisional cast on is used to eliminate seaming.

PATTERN STITCH
CIRCULAR 1 × 1 RIB (MULTIPLE OF 2 STS)
All rnds/rows: *K1, p1; rep from *.

FIRST MITTEN

Use MC and Provisional Method to CO 42 sts, divide sts evenly over 3 smaller dpns. Pm for beg of rnd, and join, being careful not to twist sts. Begin 1 × 1 Rib; work even until pc meas 3" from beg. Change to St st; work 1 rnd. ***Change to Larger Dpn and Shape Thumb Gusset, Set-Up Rnd:*** K1- f/b, pm for gusset, work to last st, pm for gusset, k1-f/b—4 sts bet gusset markers; 44 sts total. Work 1 rnd even. ***Gusset Inc Rnd:*** Work to 1 st before first gusset marker, k1-f/b, sl marker, work to next gusset marker, sl marker, k1-f/b, work to end—2 sts inc'd. Rep gusset inc rnd EOR 3 more times—12 sts bet gusset markers; 52 sts total. Work even until pc meas 6" from beg. ***Divide for Fingers:*** Work to second gusset marker, remove marker, sl 12 sts bet gusset markers to holder, removing all markers. Use the Backward Loop Method to CO 1 st, pm for beg of rnd, CO 1 st, join, being careful not to twist sts— 42 sts. Work even until pc meas 9½" from beg. ***Shape Fingers: Set-Up Rnd:*** *K1, k2tog, k15, k2tog, k1, pm; rep from * once more—38 sts rem. ***Dec Rnd:*** *K1, k2tog, work to 3 sts before next marker, k2tog, k1; rep from * once more—4 sts dec'd. Rep finger dec rnd every rnd twice more—26 sts rem. Next Rnd: *K2tog; rep from * around—13 sts rem. Break yarn, leaving a 6" tail. Thread tail onto a tapestry needle and draw through rem sts.

THUMB

Return 12 sts for gusset from holder to larger dpns. Attach MC and pick-up and knit 2 sts from CO sts in mitten—14 sts. Pm for beg of rnd, join, being careful not to twist sts. Beg St st; work even until thumb meas 2" from pick-up rnd. ***Dec Rnd:*** *K2tog; rep from * around—7 sts rem. Break yarn, leaving a 4" tail. Thread tail onto a tapestry needle and draw through rem sts.

STRAP

Carefully remove yarn for Provisional Cast On and divide 42 sts evenly onto smaller dpns. Join MC and work 17 sts in patt, BO rem 25 sts. Turn to beg, working back and forth in rows. Change to CC; (RS) Cont in 1 × 1 Rib as est until pc meas 57" from pick-up row, end after a WS row.

SECOND MITTEN

Change to MC. (RS) Work 17 sts from strap as est. Use Backward Loop Method to CO 25 sts—42 sts. Pm for beg of rnd, and join, being careful not to twist sts. Cont as for first mitten.

FINISHING

Block lightly.

Clickety Clack Mittens

SKILL LEVEL: INTERMEDIATE

SIZE
One size

FINISHED MEASUREMENTS
9¹⁄₂" hand circumference; 10" long

MATERIALS
La Gran by Classic Elite

(78.4% mohair, 17.3% wool, 4.3% nylon; 50-gram ball=
approx 106 yards)

• 2 balls 6516 Natural

Needles

• One set double-pointed needles each size U.S. 6 and 8
  (4 and 5 mm)

OR

• One pair each size U.S. 6 and 8 (4 and 5 mm)

• One set double-pointed needles size U.S. 8 (5 mm) **or size to
  obtain gauge**

• Stitch holder or waste yarn

• Stitch markers

• Tapestry needle

GAUGE
14 sts and 22 rows = 4" in Stockinette stitch with 2 strands of yarn
held together and larger needles. *Take time to save time, check your
gauge.*

NOTE
Simple, doubled-stranded mittens with instructions for knitting in
the round or flat; both versions use double pointed needles for the
thumb.

PATTERN STITCH
CIRCULAR 1 × 1 RIB (MULTIPLE OF 2 STS)

All rnds/rows: *K1, p1; rep from * to end.

FOUR-NEEDLE MITTENS
(KNIT IN THE ROUND)

CUFF

With 2 strands of yarn held tog, CO 28 sts and divide over 3 smaller dpns as follows: 9 sts each on needles 1 and 2; 10 sts on needle 3; pm for beg of rnd, and join to beg working in-the-rnd being careful not to twist sts. Begin 1 × 1 Rib; work even until pc meas 4" from beg. ***Change to Larger Dpn, St St and Inc Rnd:*** Inc 5 sts evenly around as follows: k3, m1, k5, m1, [k6, m1] twice, k5, m1, k3—33 sts. Work even for 3 rnds. ***Arrange Needles for Thumb Gusset:*** With Needle 1, work 15 sts; with Needle 2, work 3 sts; with Needle 3, work 15 sts. ***Shape Thumb Gusset, Inc Rnd:*** On Needle 1, knit; on Needle 2, k1-f/b, work to last st, k1-f/b; on Needle 3, knit—2 sts inc'd. Rep thumb gusset inc rnd EOR 3 more times—41 sts (15 sts each on Needles 1 and 3; 11 sts on Needle 2). Place 11 sts on Needle 2 onto holder for Thumb.

HAND

Next rnd: with Needle 1, k15; with an empty needle (Needle 2) use Backward Loop Method to CO 3 sts; with Needle 3, k15. Redistribute sts evenly over 3 needles—33 sts (11 sts on each needle). Work even until pc meas 10" or 1" less than desired length from beg. ***Shape Fingers:*** K2tog, k1, k2tog, * k2, k2tog; rep from * around—24 sts rem. Work 1 rnd even. Next Rnd: *K1, k2tog; rep from * around—16 sts rem. Work 1 rnd even. Next Rnd: *K2tog; rep from * around—8 sts rem. Break yarn leaving approx 8" tail. Thread tail onto tapestry needle and pull through rem sts twice, pulling tightly.

THUMB

Using 2 strands of yarn held tog and dpn, pick-up and knit 3 sts where 3 sts were CO for hand; with second dpn, work 11 sts from holder for thumb—14 sts. Distribute sts over 3 needles as follows: 4 sts on Needle 1 and 5 sts each on Needles 2 and 3. Begin St st; work even until pc meas 2" (or 1" less than desired finished thumb length) from pick-up rnd. ***Shape Thumb:*** K2tog, *k2tog, k1; rep from * around—9 sts rem. Work 1 rnd even. Next rnd: K1, *k2tog; rep from * around

5 sts rem. Break yarn leaving approx 8" tail. Thread tail onto tapestry needle and pull through rem sts twice, pulling tightly.

TWO-NEEDLE MITTENS
(KNIT FLAT)

CUFF

With 2 strands of yarn held together and smaller needles, CO 28 sts. (RS) Begin 1 × 1 Rib; work even until pc meas 4" from beg, end after a WS row. ***Change to Larger Needles, St St and Inc Row:*** (RS) Inc 5 sts evenly across as follows: K3, m1, k5, m1, [k6, m1] twice, k5, m1, k3—33 sts. Work 2 rows even, ending after a RS row. Work across next row and pm as follows: (WS) P15, pm, p3, pm, p15. ***Shape Thumb Gusset, Inc Row:*** (RS) Work to marker, sl marker, k1-f/b, work to 1 st before next marker in St st, k1-f/b, sl marker, work to end in St st—2 sts inc'd. Rep thumb gusset inc row EOR 3 more times—41 sts; 11 sts bet markers.

HAND

Divide for Thumb: (WS) P15, rem marker, sl next 11 sts onto st holder or waste yarn for thumb, with Backward Loop Method, CO 3 sts, rem marker, purl to end—33 sts. Cont in St st until pc meas 10" (or 1" less than desired finished length) from beg, end after a WS row. ***Shape Fingers:*** (RS) K2tog, k1, k2tog, *k2, k2tog; rep from * across—24 sts rem. (WS) Work 1 Row even. Next Row: (RS) *K1, k2tog; rep from * to end—16 sts rem. (WS) Work 1 row even. Next Row: (RS) *K2tog; rep from * across—8 sts rem. Break yarn, leaving approx 8" tail. Thread tail onto tapestry needle and pull through rem sts twice, pulling tightly.

THUMB

Work as for four-needle mitten thumb.

FINISHING

Sew side seams.

Ripple Mitts

SKILL LEVEL: INTERMEDIATE

SIZE
One size

FINISHED MEASUREMENTS
7¹/₂" circumference; 10³/₄" long

MATERIALS
Moorland by Classic Elite
(42% fine merino, 23% baby alpaca, 19% mohair, 16% acrylic; 50-gram ball = approx 147 yards)
• 1 ball Color A—2595 Perth Purple
• 1 ball Color B—2556 Dusty Lavender
Needles
• One pair size U.S. 6 (4 mm)
• One set double-pointed needles size U.S. 6 (4 mm) **or size to obtain gauge**
• Stitch markers
• Cable needle
• Waste yarn

GAUGE
20 sts and 28 rows = 4" in Stockinette stitch. *Take time to save time, check your gauge.*

NOTE
If you have difficulty finding the recommended yarn, you may consider using Classic Elite's Liberty Wool as a substitute. When working the pattern, carry the unused color along the edge of the work; do not cut.

PATTERN STITCHES

STRAIGHT 2 × 2 RIB (MULTIPLE OF 4 STS + 2)
Row 1: (RS) K2, *p2, k2; rep from * to end.
Row 2: (WS) P2, *k2, p2; rep from * to end.
Rep Rows 1–2 for 2 × 2 Rib.

CABLE/COLOR PANEL (PANEL OF 19 STS)
Also see chart

Rows 1 and 3: (WS) Purl: 1B, 1A, 1B, 2A, 4B 1A, 4B, 2A, 1B, 1A, 1B.
Row 2: (RS) Knit: 1B, 1A, 1B, 2A, 4B 1A, 4B, 2A, 1B, 1A, 1B.
Row 4: (RS) Knit: 1B, 1A, 1B, 2A, C1/3F with B, 1A, C3/1B with B, 2A, 1B,1A, 1B.
Rep Rows 1–4 for Cable/Color Panel.

CIRCULAR 1 × 1 RIB (MULTIPLE OF 2 STS)
All rnds: *K1, p1; rep from * around.

RIGHT MITT

With Color A, CO 66 sts. (RS) Begin 2 × 2 Rib; work 3 rows, ending after a RS row. ***Change to St St and Color B:*** (WS) Work 33 sts, pm for center, work to end. Work 2 rows even, ending after a WS row. ***Shape Sides, Dec Row:*** (RS) K1, ssk, work to marker, sl marker, k2tog, work to last 3 sts, k2tog, k1—3 sts dec'd. *Change to Color A; (WS) work 3 rows, ending after a WS row. (RS) Work side dec row—3 sts dec'd. Rep last 4 rows with Color B. Rep from * 3 more times— 39 sts rem. Rem center marker. ***Change to Color A and Est Patt:*** (WS) Work 17 sts in St st, pm, work 19 sts in Cable/Color Panel, pm, work to end in St st. Work even as est until pc meas 8" from beg, ending after a WS row. ***Divide for Thumb:*** (RS) Work to second marker as est, sl marker, with waste yarn k6, return 6 sts just worked back to LH needle then work them with working yarn, work to end. Work even until pc meas 10¼" from beg, ending after a RS row. ***Change to Color A and Dec Row:*** (WS) P2, p2tog, work to end—38 sts rem. Change to 2 × 2 Rib; (RS) work 3 rows, ending after a RS row. (WS) BO all sts loosely in rib.

LEFT MITT

Work as for right mitten to end of side shaping—39 sts rem. ***Change to Color A and Est Patt:*** (WS) Work 3 sts in St st, pm, work 19 sts in Cable/Color Panel, pm, work to end in St st. Work even as est until pc meas 8" from beg, ending after a WS row. ***Divide for Thumb:*** (RS) Work to 6 sts before first marker, with waste yarn k6, return 6 sts just worked back to LH needle then work them with working yarn, work to end as est. Cont as for right mitt.

THUMB

Carefully remove waste yarn 1 st at a time and sl 6 sts onto 1 dpn and 7 sts onto another dpn—13 sts. Begin Circular St st; beg at inside of hand, join Color A; work 1 rnd, dividing sts as evenly as possible onto 3 dpns, pm for beg of rnd. Work even until pc meas 1¼" from pick-up rnd. ***Change to 1 × 1 Rib and Dec Rnd:*** K2tog, p1, work in 1 × 1 Rib around— 12 sts rem. Work 2 rnds. BO all sts loosely in rib. Rep for second mitten.

FINISHING

Block to measurements. Sew seam, being careful to match up stripes.

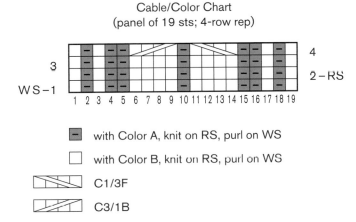

Cable/Color Chart
(panel of 19 sts; 4-row rep)

- with Color A, knit on RS, purl on WS
- with Color B, knit on RS, purl on WS
- C1/3F
- C3/1B

Ann Mitts

SKILL LEVEL: INTERMEDIATE

SIZE

One size

FINISHED MEASUREMENTS

7" around hand; 12½" long

MATERIALS

Princess by Classic Elite

(40% merino, 28% viscose, 15% nylon, 10% cashmere, 7% angora; 50-gram ball = approx 150 yards)

• 2 balls 3471 Keepsake Pink

Needles

• One set double-pointed needles size U.S. 6 (4 mm) **or size to obtain gauge**

• Stitch marker

GAUGE

22 sts and 24 rows = 4" in Wavy Lace pattern.
Take time to save time, check your gauge.

NOTE

Long, lace-stitch fingerless gloves are knit in the round.

PATTERN STITCHES

CIRCULAR RIB PATTERN (MULTIPLE OF 8 STS + 6)

All rnds: P2, *p2, k6 ; rep from * to last 4 sts, p4.

CIRCULAR WAVY LACE PATTERN (MULTIPLE OF 8 STS)

Also see chart

Rnds 1, 2, 4, 6, 8, 9, 10, 12, and 14: *P2, k6; rep from * around.

Rnd 3: *P2, yo, k2, ssk, k2; rep from * around.

Rnd 5: *P2, k1, yo, k2, ssk, k1; rep from * around.

Rnd 7: *P2, k2, yo, k2, ssk; rep from * around.

Rnd 11: *P2, k2, k2tog, k2, yo; rep from * around.

Rnd 13: *P2, k1, k2tog, k2, yo, k1; rep from * around.

Rnd 15: *P2, k2tog, k2, yo, k2; rep from * around.

Rnd 16: Rep Rnd 1.

Rep Rnds 1–16 for Wavy Lace patt.

LEFT MITT

CO 38 sts; pm for beg of rnd. Join, being careful not to twist sts. Begin Rib patt; work even for 4 rnds. *Est Wavy Lace Patt:* Work 2 sts in Rev St st, pm, work Wavy Lace Patt to last 4 sts, pm, work to end in Rev St st. Cont as est until pc meas 4½" from beg, end after an odd numbered rnd. *Wrist Dec Rnd:* P2tog, work in est patt to last 2 sts, p2tog—2 sts dec'd. Rep wrist dec rnd every 6th rnd 1 more time—34 sts rem. Work 4 rnds even. *Wrist Inc Rnd:* P1-f/b, work as est to last st, p1-f/b—2 sts inc'd. Rep wrist inc rnd every 3rd rnd once more—38 sts. Work even until pc meas 8" from beg, end after an odd numbered rnd. *Shape Thumb Gusset:* Work 10 sts as est, pm for beg of gusset, [p1-f/b] twice, pm for end of gusset, work to end—40 sts. Work 1 rnd even, working all sts bet gusset marker's in Rev St st. *Gusset Inc Rnd:* Work to gusset marker, p1-f/b, work to 1 sts before next marker, p1-f/b, work to end—2 sts inc'd bet markers. Rep gusset inc rnd EOR 3 more times—48 sts; 12 sts bet gusset markers. Work 2 rnds even. *BO for Thumb Gusset:* Work to gusset marker, remove marker, p1, BO 10 sts purlwise, p1, remove marker, work to end—38 sts rem. Work even as est until pc meas 2" from Thumb Gusset BO. Change to Rib patt; work 4 rnds even. BO all sts in rib.

RIGHT MITT

Work as for left mitt to thumb gusset shaping, end after an odd numbered rnd. *Shape Thumb Gusset:* Work 26 sts as est, pm for beg of gusset, [p1-f/b] twice, pm for end of gusset, work to end—40 sts. Cont as for left mitt.

FINISHING

Block pcs to measurements.

Wavy Lace Chart
(multiple of 8 sts; 16-rnd rep)

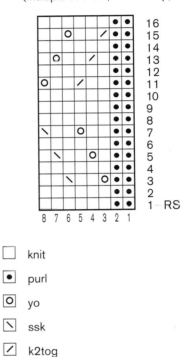

	knit
•	purl
O	yo
\	ssk
/	k2tog

Veritas Mitts

SIZES
S/M (M/L)

FINISHED MEASUREMENTS
6 (6½)" wrist circumference; 8 (8½)" circumference around thumb gusset; 7½" long

MATERIALS
Wool Bam Boo by Classic Elite

(50% wool, 50% bamboo; 50-gram ball = approx 118 yards)

• 1 ball Main Color (MC)—1678 Chestnut
• 1 ball Color A—1615 Ivy
• 1 ball Color B—1672 Artichoke Green
• 1 ball Color C—1660 Treasure
• 1 ball Color D—1691 Bay Blue
• 1 ball Color E—1627 Mulled Wine
• 1 ball Color F—1634 Mulberry

Needles

• One set double-pointed needles each size U.S. 3 and 4 (3.25 and 3.5 mm) **or size to obtain gauge**
• Stitch markers
• Stitch holder or waste yarn

GAUGE
27 sts and 30 rows = 4" in Fair Isle Chart with larger needles. *Take time to save time, check your gauge.*

NOTE
Mittens will grow significantly in length when blocked, but the fit will remain true to gauge.

PATTERN STITCHES

CIRCULAR 3 × 2 RIB (MULTIPLE OF 5 STS)
All rnds: *K3, p2; rep from *.

CIRCULAR 2 × 1 RIB (MULTIPLE OF 3 STS)
All rnds: *K2, p1; rep from *.

Also see charts

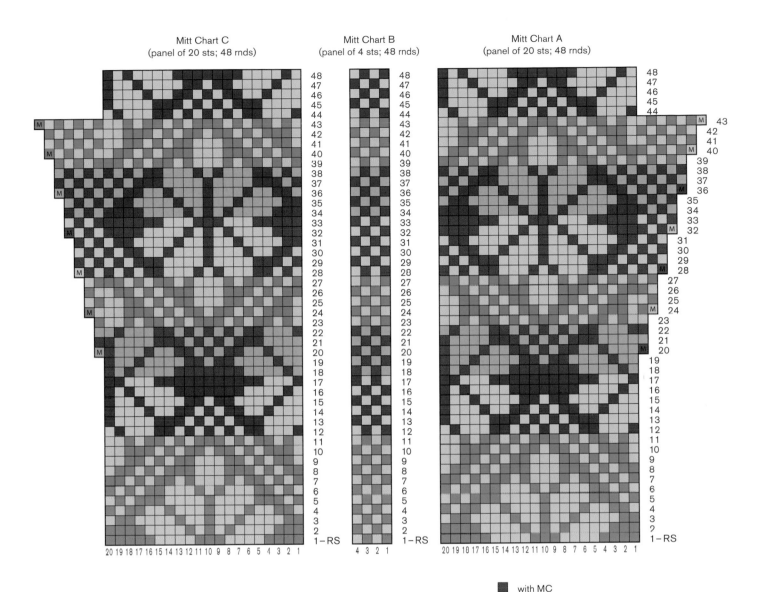

Mitt Chart C
(panel of 20 sts; 48 rnds)

Mitt Chart B
(panel of 4 sts; 48 rnds)

Mitt Chart A
(panel of 20 sts; 48 rnds)

■ with MC
■ with Color A
□ with Color B
■ with Color C
□ with Color D
■ with Color E
■ with Color F
Ⓜ m1

MITTS

With MC and smaller dpn, CO 39 (42) sts; pm for beg of rnd.
Join, being careful not to twist sts. Begin 2 × 1 Rib; work 6
rnds. *Inc Rnd: S/M Only:* K1-f/b, k18, pm, k20—40 sts. *M/L
Only:* K1-f/b, k18, pm, k1-f/b, k22—44 sts. *All Sizes, Change
to Larger Dpn and Est Mitt Patt:* Work 20 sts in Mitt Chart A,
sl marker, work 0 (4) sts in Mitt Chart B, work 20 sts in Mitt
Chart C. Work 18 more rnds, end after Rnd 19 of Mitt Chart.
Shape Thumb Gusset, Inc Rnd: M1 in patt, work to end of
Mitt Chart C, m1 in patt—2 sts inc'd. Rep Thumb Gusset Inc
Rnd every fourth rnd 5 more times, then every third rnd once,
end after Rnd 43 of Mitt Chart—54 (58) sts rem. Break yarn.
Sl the 7 sts before the beg-of-rnd marker, and the 7 sts after
the beg-of-rnd marker to a st holder or waste yarn for thumb
gusset—40 (44) sts rem. Rejoin yarn and cont as est for 5 more
rnds, ending after Rnd 48 of Mitt Chart. *Change to Smaller
Dpns, MC, St St and Dec Rnd. Size S/M Only:* Work to last
2 sts, k2tog—39 sts rem. *Size M/L Only:* *K20, k2tog; rep from

* once more—42 sts rem. *All sizes:* Change to 2 × 1 Rib; work
4 rnds. BO all sts in rib.

THUMB

Sl 14 sts from st holder or waste yarn onto smaller dpns.
With MC, pick up and knit 1 st from hand fabric near thumb
gusset—15 sts. Begin 2 × 1 Rib; work 4 rnds. BO all sts in rib.

FINISHING

Block pcs to measurements.

Socks

contents

Avery Socks

SIZE

One size Women's Medium

FINISHED MEASUREMENTS LEG LENGTH:

Leg length: 10½"; foot length: 10" or desired size; foot and ankle circumference: approx 7"

MATERIALS

Alpaca Sox by Classic Elite

(60% alpaca, 20% merino, 20% nylon; 100-gram hank = approx 450 yards)

• 1 hank 1825 Rose

Needles

• One set of 5 double-pointed needles size U.S. 2 (2.75 mm) **or size to obtain gauge**

• Stitch marker

• Cable needle

• Stitch holder

• Tapestry needle

GAUGE

32 sts and 42 rnds = 4" in Circular Stockinette stitch. *Take time to save time, check your gauge.*

PATTERN STITCHES

CIRCULAR STOCKINETTE STITCH (ST ST):

Knit every rnd.

CIRCULAR CORDED RIB (MULTIPLE OF 4 STS + 2)

Also see chart.

Rnd 1: P2, *ssk, m1, p2; rep from * around.

Rnd 2: P2, *k2, p2; rep from * around.

Rep Rnds 1 and 2 for Circular Corded Rib.

STRAIGHT CORDED RIB (MULTIPLE OF 4 STS + 2)

Row 1: (RS) P2, *ssk, m1, p2; rep from * to end.

Row 2: K2, *p2, k2; rep from * to end.

Rep Rows 1 and 2 for Straight Corded Rib.

CIRCULAR PANEL A (PANEL OF 6 STS)

Also see chart

Rnd 1: K2, p2, k2.

Rnd 2 and all even-numbered rnds: Ssk, m1, p2, ssk, m1.

Rnds 3, 5, 7, 9, 13, and 15: Rep Rnd 1.

Rnd 11: T6F.

Rnd 16: Rep Rnd 2.

Rep Rnds 1–16 for Circular Panel A.

STRAIGHT PANEL A (PANEL OF 6 STS)

Row 1: (RS) K2, p2, k2.

Row 2 and all WS rows: M1p, ssp, k2, m1p, ssp.

Rows 3, 5, 7, 9, 13, and 15: Rep Row 1.

Row 11: T6F.

Row 16: Rep Row 2.

Rep Rows 1–16 for Straight Panel A.

CIRCULAR PANEL B (PANEL OF 6 STS)

Also see chart

Rnd 1: K2, p2, k2.

Rnd 2 and all even-numbered rnds: Ssk, m1, p2, ssk, m1.

Rnds 3, 5, 7, 9, 13, and 15: Rep Rnd 1.

Rnd 11: T6B.

Rnd 16: Rep Rnd 2.

Rep Rnds 1–16 for Circular Panel B.

STRAIGHT PANEL B (PANEL OF 6 STS)

Row 1: (RS) K2, p2, k2.

Row 2 and all WS rows: M1p, ssp, k2, m1p, ssp.

Rows 3, 5, 7, 9, 13, and 15: Rep Row 1.

Row 11: T6B.

Row 16: Rep Row 2.

Rep Rows 1–16 for Straight Panel B.

KITCHENER STITCH

Step 1: Bring threaded tapestry needle through first st on front needle as if to knit and slip this st off needle.

Step 2: Bring threaded tapestry needle through next st on front needle as if to purl and leave st on needle.

Step 3: Bring threaded tapestry needle through first st on back needle as if to purl and slip this st off needle.

Step 4: Bring threaded tapestry needle through next st on back needle as if to knit and leave st on needle.

Rep Steps 1–4 until no sts rem on needles.

For more information, visit our website: www.classiceliteyarns.com/WebLetter/Stitches/Grafting/Grafting.php

NOTES

Gusset decrease stitch On Needle 1, knit to last 2 sts, k2tog; on Needles 2 and 3, work instep sts as est; on Needle 4, ssk, knit to end.

Toe decrease stitch On Needle 1, knit to last 3 sts, k2tog, k1; on Needle 2, k1, ssk, knit to end; on Needle 3, k to last 3 sts, k2tog, k1; on Needle 4, k1, ssk, knit to end.

LEG

CO 64 sts. Divide sts evenly over 4 dpn, pm for beg of rnd. Join, being careful not to twist sts. Begin St st; work 9 rnds. *Picot Turning Rnd:* *K2tog, yo; rep from * around. Change to St st; work 8 rnds. Purl 1 rnd. *Est Patt:* *P1, work 6 sts in Panel A, 18 sts in Corded Rib, 6 sts in Panel B, p1; rep from * 1 time. Work even as est until pc meas 8" from picot turning rnd, end even numbered rnd. Make note of rnd number worked last.

HEEL FLAP

Heel flap is worked back and forth in rows on first 32 sts; slip the rem 32 sts onto a holder to work later for instep; instep sts will beg and end with p1. *Est Patt:* (RS) Slip 1 st knitwise wyib (edge st, sl knitwisc wyib on RS, p on WS), work 6 sts in Panel A as est, 18 sts in Corded Rib, 6 sts in Panel B, k1 (edge st, k on RS, sl purlwise wyif on WS). Work 31 rows, end WS row (16 chain edge sts along each selvedge edge).

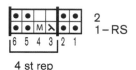

AVERY SOCKS

Corded Rib Chart
(multiple of 4 sts + 2; 2-rnd rep)

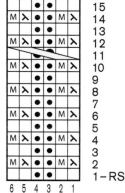

4 st rep

Panel A Chart
(panel of 6 sts; 16-rnd rep)

Panel B Chart
(panel of 6 sts; 16-rnd rep)

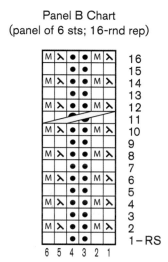

☐ knit on RS, purl on WS

• purl on RS, knit on WS

⅄ ssk on RS, ssp on WS

Ⓜ m1 on RS, m1p on WS

▱ sl 4 sts to cn and hold in front; k2;
replace last 2 sts on cn to LH needle
and p2; k2 from cn.

HEEL TURN

Change to St St and Shape Heel with Short Rows: (RS) Slip
1 st knitwise wyib, k18, ssk, k1, turn—31 sts. Next Row: (WS)
Slip 1 st purlwise wyif, p7, p2tog, p1, turn—30 sts. *Next Row:
(RS) Slip 1 st purlwise wyib, knit to 1 st before gap formed
on previous row, ssk (1 st from each side of gap), k1, turn.
Next Row: (WS) Slip 1 st purlwise wyif, purl to 1 st before gap
formed on previous row, p2tog (1 st from each side of gap),
p1, turn. Rep from * 4 times—20 sts rem.

GUSSETS

Pick up sts along selvedge edges of heel flap and rejoin for
working in rnds as follows: (RS) With Needle 1, k20 heel
sts, then with the same needle pick up and knit 16 sts along
selvedge edge of heel flap (pick up 1 st in each chain edge st);
with Needles 2 and 3, work 32 instep sts from holder in patt as
est beg with next rnd from number marked at end of leg; with
Needle 4, pick up and knit 16 sts along selvedge edge of heel
flap (pick up 1 st in each chain edge st), then knit the first
10 sts from Needle 1 again—84 sts total; 26 sts each on Needles
1 and 4, and 16 sts each on Needles 2 and 3. Pm for beg of rnd;
rnd begins at back of heel. ***Shape Gusset:*** Dec 2 sts this rnd
(see Pattern Stitches), then EOR 9 times—64 sts rem.

FOOT

Work even as est until pc meas approx 8" from back of heel, or
2" less than desired finished length from back of heel. Change
to St st; work 4 rnds. ***Shape Toe:*** Dec 4 sts this rnd (see Pattern
Stitches), EOR 7 times, then every row 4 times—16 sts rem.
With Needle 4, knit the sts from Needle 1 and sl sts from
Needle 2 to Needle 3 (8 sts each on 2 needles).

FINISHING

Cut yarn, leaving a 10" tail. Thread tail on a tapestry needle
and use the Kitchener st to graft rem sts tog. Block lightly.

Child's Striped Socks

SKILL LEVEL: INTERMEDIATE

SIZE

One size

FINISHED MEASUREMENTS

7½" long

MATERIALS

Star by Classic Elite

(99% cotton, 1% lyrca; 50-gram hank = approx 112 yards)

- 1 hank Color A—5147 Aquarium
- 1 hank Color B—5102 Arizona Sun
- 1 hank Color C—5172 Lime Sherbert
- 1 hank Color D—5120 Purple Rain

Needles

- One set double-pointed needles size U.S. 8 (5 mm) **or size to obtain gauge**
- Stitch marker

GAUGE

22 sts and 40 rnds = 4" in Stockinette stitch after washing. *Take time to save time, check your gauge.*

NOTES

1. If you have difficulty finding the recommended yarn, you may consider using Classic Elite's Seedling as a substitute.

2. Star is a lycra product; the pattern allows for yarn to contract. Machine wash and dry flat.

PATTERN STITCHES

CIRCULAR 1 × 1 RIB (MULTIPLE OF 2 STS)

Rnd 1: *K1, p1; rep from * around.

Rnd 2: Knit the knit sts and purl the purl sts as they face you.

Rep Rnd 2 for 1 x 1 Rib.

CIRCULAR STOCKINETTE STITCH (ST ST)

Knit every rnd.

CIRCULAR STOCKINETTE AND GARTER STRIPES

Rnds 1 and 3: With Color B, knit.

Rnds 2 and 4: With Color B, purl.

Rnds 5–8: With Color C, knit.

Rnds 9–12: With Color D, knit.

Rnds 13–16: Rep Rnds 5–8.

Rnds 17–20: With Color B, rep Rnds 1–4.

Rnds 21–24: With Color D, knit.

Rnds 25–28: With Color A, knit.

Rnds 29–32: Rep Rnds 21–24.

Rnds 33–36: WIth Color B, rep Rnds 1–4.

Rnds 37–40: With Color A, knit.

Rnds 41–44: With Color C, knit.

Rnds 45–48: Rep Rounds 37–40.

Work Rnds 1–48 for Stripe patt.

THREE-NEEDLE BIND-OFF METHOD

Sl the sts from holders onto each of 2 dpn; with the RS of garment pieces tog (to form ridge on inside of garment), hold the needles parallel. With a third dpn knit the first st of front and back needles tog, *knit next st from each needle tog., (2 sts on RH needle), BO 1 st; rep from * until all sts are BO.

TUBE SOCKS

Beg at cuff, using dpn and Color A, CO 28 sts; divide sts evenly on dpn; join, being careful not to twist sts, pm for beg of rnd. (RS) Begin St st; work even until piece meas 1" from beg. Change to 1 × 1 Rib; work even for 1". Change to Stripe patt; work even until piece meas 4½" from end of rib. **Shape Toe:** Divide sts evenly on 2 needles (14 sts each needle). Using Color B, work back and forth across one set of 14 sts as follows: Row 1: (RS) K1, k2tog, k8, k2tog, k1—12 sts rem. Row 2 and all WS rows: Purl. Row 3: K1, k2tog, k6, k2tog, k1—10 sts rem. Row 5: K1, k2tog, k4, k2tog, k1—8 sts rem. Row 7: K1, k2tog, k2, k2tog, k1—6 sts rem. Row 8: Purl. Place sts on holder, or leave on spare dpn. Rep Rows 1–8 over rem 14 sts; do not place rem sts on holder.

FINISHING

Join rem sts using Three Needle Bind Off Method. Sew sides of toes together.

Fluffy Booties

SIZE

6 months

FINISHED MEASUREMENT

4" foot length

MATERIALS

Princess by Classic Elite

(40% merino, 28% viscose, 10% cashmere, 7% angora, 15% nylon; 50-gram ball = approx 150 yards)

• 1 ball Main Color (MC)—3419 Precious Pink

La Gran by Classic Elite

• (76$\frac{1}{2}$% mohair, 17$\frac{1}{2}$% wool, 6% nylon; 42-gram ball = approx 90 yards)

• 1 ball Contrast Color (CC)—61532 Positively Pink

Needles

• One pair size U.S. 6 (4 mm) **or size to obtain gauge**

• Two 3" pieces of cardboard for making pom-poms, or pom-pom maker.

GAUGE

22 sts and 28 rows = 4" in Stockinette stitch

Take time to save time, check your gauge.

PATTERN STITCHES

1 × 1 RIB (MULTIPLE OF 2 STS + 1)

Row 1: K1, *p1, k1; rep from * across.

Row 2: Knit the knit sts and purl the purl sts as they face you.

Rep Row 2 for 1 × 1 Rib.

STOCKINETTE STITCH (ST ST)

Knit on RS, purl on WS.

GARTER STITCH (GRT ST)

Knit every row.

THREE-NEEDLE BIND-OFF METHOD

Sl the sts from holders onto each of 2 dpn; with the RS of garment pieces tog (to form ridge on inside of garment), hold the needles parallel. With a third dpn knit the first st of front and back needles tog, *knit next st from each needle tog, (2 sts on RH needle), BO 1 st; rep from * until all sts are BO.

BOOTIE

Cuff: Using CC, CO 27 sts loosely. (WS) Change to MC and Begin 1 × 1 Rib; work even for 13 rows, end WS row. Change to St st; (RS) work even for 4 rows, end WS row. Instep: Row 1: (RS) K18, turn. Row 2: (WS) P9, turn. Row 3: (RS) K9, turn. Rep Rows 2 and 3 for 13 more rows, end WS row. Next row: (RS) K1, k2tog, k3, ssk, k1—7 toe sts rem. Break yarn. With RS facing, rejoin yarn at cuff edge, knit 9 sts from needle, pick up and knit 12 sts along right side of instep, knit 7 toe sts, pick up and knit 12 sts along left side of instep, knit 9 cuff sts—49 sts. Work 5 rows in St st, end WS row. **Change to Gtr St and Shape Sole:** Row 1: (RS) K1, ssk, k18, k2tog, k3, ssk, k18, k2tog, k1—45 sts rem. Row 2 and all WS rows: Knit. Row 3: K1, ssk, k16, k2tog, k3, ssk, k16, k2tog, k1—41 sts rem. Row 5: K1, ssk, k14, k2tog, k3, ssk, k14, k2tog, k1—37 sts rem. Row 7: K1, ssk, k12, k2tog, k3, ssk, k12, k2tog, k1—33 sts rem. Row 8: K16, k2tog, k15—32 sts rem. Divide sts evenly onto two needles and join using Three-Needle Bind-Off Method.

FINISHING

Sew up back of Bootie. **Pom-Poms:** Cut two circular pieces of cardboard 3" in diameter. Cut a pie-shape wedge out of each circle, then a smaller (1¼" diameter) circle into the center of each circle or use a pom-pom maker. Using CC and holding the two circles together, wrap the yarn tightly around the cardboard circles approx 60 times. Carefully cut the yarn around the circumference of the cardboard. Tie a piece of yarn (at least 8" long) tightly between the two pieces of cardboard. Remove the cardboard and trim the pom-pom. Rep to make two. Attach a pom-pom to the center of each instep.

Baby Cable Socks

SIZES

Child's Medium (Women's Medium)

FINISHED MEASUREMENTS

7½ (9)" foot length; 3½ (5)" leg length.

MATERIALS

Alpaca Sox by Classic Elite

(60% alpaca, 20% merino wool, 20% nylon; 100-gram hank = approx 450 yards)

• 1 hank 1871 Candy Hearts

Needles

• One set double-pointed needles size U.S. 1 (2.25 mm) **or size to obtain gauge**

• 2 stitch holders

• Stitch marker

• Tapestry needle

GAUGE

34 sts and 44 rows = 4" in Stockinette stitch. *Take time to save time, check your gauge.*

PATTERN STITCHES

CIRCULAR 2 × 2 RIB (MULTIPLE OF 4 STS)

Rnd 1: *P1, k2, p1; rep from * around.

Rnd 2: Knit the knit sts and purl the purl sts as they face you.

Rep Rnd 2 for 2 × 2 Rib.

CIRCULAR BABY CABLE RIB (MULTIPLE OF 4 STS)

Rnds 1, 2, and 4: *P1, k2, p1; rep from * around.

Rnd 3: *P1, BC, p1; rep from * around.

Rep Rnds 1–4 for Baby Cable Rib.

KITCHENER STITCH

Step 1: Bring threaded tapestry needle through first st on front needle as if to purl and leave st on needle.

Step 2: Bring threaded tapestry needle through first st on back needle as if to knit and leave st on needle.

Step 3: Bring threaded tapestry needle through first st on front needle as if to knit and slip this st off needle.

Step 4: Bring threaded tapestry needle through next st on front needle as if to purl and leave st on needle.

Step 5: Bring threaded tapestry needle through first st on back needle as if to purl and slip this st off needle.

Step 6: Bring threaded tapestry needle through next st on back needle as if to knit and leave st on needle. Rep Steps 3 –6 until no sts rem on needles.

NOTE

When slipping sts, slip purlwise.

SOCK (MAKE 2)

CO 52 (64) sts. Divide sts evenly onto 3 dpn; join, being careful not to twist sts and pm for beg of rnd. Beg 2 × 2 Rib; work even until piece meas ¾ (1)" from beg. Change to Baby Cable Rib; work even until piece meas 3½ (5)" or desired length from beg. ***Divide for Heel Flap:*** Place next 26 (32) sts on 1 needle for heel sts. Divide rem 26 (32) sts evenly onto 2 st holders for instep sts. ***Heel Flap:*** Row 1: (RS) *Slip 1 st purlwise wyib, k1; rep from * across. Row 2: Slip 1 st purlwise wyif, purl across. Rep Rows 1 and 2, 12 (14) times. ***Turn the Heel:*** Row 1: (RS) Slip 1 wyib, k18 (20), ssk, k1, turn. ***Note:*** Not all heel flap sts are worked—4 (8) heel flap sts rem unworked; 25 (31) sts rem. Row 2: Slip 1 st wyif, p13 (11), p2tog, p1, turn—24 (30) sts rem. Row 3: Slip 1 wyib, k14 (12), ssk, k1, turn—23 (29) sts rem. Row 4: Slip 1 st wyif, p15 (13), p2tog, p1, turn—22 (28) sts rem. Row 5: Slip 1 wyib, k16 (14), ssk, k0 (1), sl 1 (0) wyib, turn—21 (27) sts rem. Row 6: Slip 1 st wyif, p17 (15), p2tog, p0 (1), slip 1 (0) wyif, turn—20 (26) sts rem. ***Women's Size Only:*** Row 7: Slip 1 st wyib, k(16), ssk, k1, turn—(25) sts rem. Row 8: Slip 1 st wyif, p(17), p2tog, p1, turn—(24) sts rem. Row 9: Slip 1 st wyib, k(18), ssk, slip 1 wyib, turn—(23) sts rem. Row 10: Slip 1 st wyif, p(19), p2tog, slip 1 st wyif, turn—(22) sts rem. ***Both Sizes: Shape Gusset:*** With RS facing and free needle, slip 1 st wyib, knit across all heel sts, then pick up and knit 13 (15) sts along right edge of heel flap, skipping the first slip st (Needle 1); on next free needle work in patt across sts on holders (Needle 2); on last needle pick up and knit 13 (15) along left edge of heel skipping the last slip st (Needle 3); knit first 10 (11) sts of heel onto same needle; slip rem 10 (11) sts of heel onto beg of needle 1—72 (84) sts. Rnd 1: Knit across needle 1 to last 2 sts, k2tog. Work in patt on needle 2. Ssk first 2 sts of needle 3, knit to end—70 (82) sts rem. Rnd 2: Work even as est. Rep Rnds 1 and 2 nine times—52 (64) sts rem.

FOOT

Cont in patt as est until piece meas 5½ (7)" or desired length from heel. ***Shape Toe:*** Rnd 1: *K1, ssk k20 (26) sts, k2tog, k1; rep from * 1 time—4 sts dec'd. Rnd 2: Knit. Rep Rnds 1 and 2, 8 (9) times—16 (24) sts rem. Slip 8 (12) sts onto 1 dpn; slip rem 8 (12) sts onto a second dpn. Graft the toe sts together using Kitchener st.

Harmony Socks

SIZE

One size

FINISHED MEASUREMENTS

8½" foot circumference; 9½" or desired foot length

MATERIALS

Waterlily by Classic Elite

(100% extrafine merino; 50-gram ball = approx 90 yards)

• 3 balls 1924 Blueberry

Needles

• One set double-pointed needles size U.S. 9 (5.5 mm) **or size to obtain gauge**

• Stitch marker

GAUGE

17 sts and 23 rnds in Circular Stockinette stitch. *Take time to save time, check your gauge.*

PATTERN STITCHES

CIRCULAR GARTER STITCH

Rnd 1: Purl.

Rnd 2: Knit.

Rep Rnds 1–2 for Gtr st.

CIRCULAR CABLE PATTERN (MULTIPLE OF 16 STS)

Also see chart

Rnd 1: *K8, C8B; rep from * around.

Rnds 2, 3, and 4: Knit.

Rnd 5: *C8F, k8; rep from * around.

Rnds 6, 7, and 8: Knit.

Rep Rnds 1–8 for Cable Patt.

SOCK

CO 36 sts. Join to beg working in-the-rnd, being careful not to twist sts; pm for beg of rnd. Begin Gtr St; work 4 rnds, end after a knit rnd. *Inc Rnd:* *K3, m1; rep from * around—48 sts. Change to Cable Patt; work 37 rnds even, end after rnd 5. *Dec Rnd:* K2, k2tog; rep from * around—36 sts rem. Change to St st; work even until pc meas 7½" from dec rnd or 2" less than desired length. *Shape Toe, Dec Rnd 1:* *K7, k2tog, pm; rep from * around—32 sts rem. Work 1 rnd even. *Dec Rnd 2:* Work to 2 sts before marker, k2tog, sl marker—4 sts dec'd. Rep Dec Rnd 2 EOR 2 more times, then every rnd 4 times— 4 sts rem. Break yarn, leaving approx 8" tail. Thread tail onto tapestry needle and pull through rem 4 sts 2 times tightly.

Cable Chart
(multiple of 16 sts; 8-rnd rep)

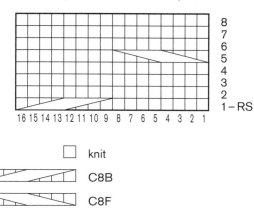

8
7
6
5
4
3
2
1 – RS

16 15 14 13 12 11 10 9 8 7 6 5 4 3 2 1

☐ knit

C8B

C8F

Legwarmers

SIZE

One size

FINISHED MEASUREMENTS

8" circumference at ankle unstretched; 9¼" circumference at upper leg unstretched; 16¼" long

MATERIALS

Alpaca Sox by Classic Elite

(60% alpaca, 20% merino wool, 20% nylon; 100-gram hank = approx 450 yards)

• 1 hank 1809 Celadon

Needles

• One set double-pointed needles size U.S. 3 (3 mm) **or size to obtain gauge**

• Stitch markers

GAUGE

30 sts and 46 rnds = 4" in Eyelet Rib. *Take time to save time, check your gauge.*

PATTERN STITCHES

CIRCULAR 1 × 1 RIB (MULTIPLE OF 2 STS)

Rnd 1: *K1, p1; rep from * around.

Rnd 2: Knit the knit sts and purl the purl sts as they face you.

Rep Rnd 2 for 1 × 1 Rib.

CIRCULAR EYELET RIB (MULTIPLE OF 12 STS)

Also see chart

Rnd 1: *K2tog, yo, k1, yo, ssk, p1, k2, slip 1 st purlwise wyib, k2, p1; rep from * around.

Rnd 2: Knit.

Rnd 3: *K5, p1, k2, slip 1 st purlwise wyib, k2, p1; rep from * around.

Rnd 4: Knit.

Rep Rnds 1–4 for Eyelet Rib.

CIRCULAR ONE INCREASE EYELET RIB (MULTIPLE OF 13 STS)

Also see chart

Rnd 1: *K5, p1, k3, slip 1 st purlwise wyib, k2, p1; rep from * around.

Rnd 2: *K6, p1, k6; rep from * around.

Rnd 3: *K2tog, yo, k1, yo, ssk, p1, k3, slip 1 st purlwise wyib, k2, p1; rep from * around.

Rnd 4: Rep Rnd 2.

Rep Rnds 1–4 for One Inc Eyelet Rib.

CIRCULAR TWO INCREASE EYELET RIB (MULTIPLE OF 14 STS)

Also see chart

Rnd 1: *K5, p1, k3, slip 1 st purlwise wyib, k2, p1, k1; rep from * around.

Rnd 2: *P1, k6; rep from * around.

Rnd 3: *K2tog, yo, k1, yo, ssk, p1, k3, slip 1 st purlwise wyib, k2, p1, k1; rep from * around.

Rnd 4: Rep Rnd 2.

Rep Rnds 1–4 for Two Inc Eyelet Rib

LEGWARMERS

Eyelet Rib Chart
(multiple of 12 sts; 4-rnd rep)

```
                              4
                              3
                              2
                            1 – RS
12 11 10 9 8 7 6 5 4 3 2 1
```

One Inc Eyelet Rib Chart
(multiple of 13 sts; 4-rnd rep)

```
                              4
                              3
                              2
                            1 – RS
13 12 11 10 9 8 7 6 5 4 3 2 1
```

Two Inc Eyelet Rib Chart
(multiple of 14 sts; 4-rnd rep)

```
                              4
                              3
                              2
                            1 – RS
14 13 12 11 10 9 8 7 6 5 4 3 2 1
```

☐ knit	◉ purl	🄺 k2tog
Ⓞ yo	⅄ ssk		sl1p wyib

LEGWARMER

CO 60 sts. Divide evenly over 3 dpn. Join, being careful not to twist sts; pm for beg of rnd. (RS) Begin 1 × 1 Rib; work even until pc meas 1¼" from beg. Change to Eyelet Rib; work even until pc meas approx 5" from beg, end Rnd 1 of Eyelet Rib. *Inc Rnd 1:* Inc 5 sts as follows: Work 5 sts as est, k1-f/b, *work 11 sts as est, k1-f/b; rep from * to last 6 sts, work to end as est—65 sts. Change to One Inc Eyelet Rib; work even until pc meas 10" from beg, end Rnd 3 of One Inc Eyelet Rib. *Inc Rnd 2:* Inc 5 sts as follows: *Work 12 sts as est, k1-f/b; rep from * around—70 sts. Change to Two Inc Eyelet Rib; work even until pc meas 15" from beg, end Row 3 of Two Inc Eyelet Rib. Change to 1 × 1 Rib; work even for 1¼". BO all sts loosely in rib.

FINISHING

Block pc to measurements.

Dorm Socks

SKILL LEVEL: INTERMEDIATE

SIZE

One size (Women's Medium)

FINISHED MEASUREMENTS

Leg length: 6½"; foot length: 9" or desired length; foot and ankle circumference: approx 9" stretched

MATERIALS

Waterlily by Classic Elite

(100% extra fine merino; 50-gram ball = approx 100 yards)

• 3 balls 1915 Eucalyptus or 1988 Goldfish

Needles

• One set of 5 double-pointed needles each size U.S. 7 and 8 (4.5 and 5 mm) **or size to obtain gauge**

• Cable needle

• Stitch markers

GAUGE

18 sts and 26 rows = 4" in Stockinette stitch with larger needles. *Take time to save time, check your gauge.*

PATTERN STITCHES

CIRCULAR 2 × 2 RIB (MULTIPLE OF 4 STS)

Rnd 1: *k1, p2, k1; rep from * around.

Rnd 2: Knit the knit sts and purl the purl sts as they face you.

Rep Rnd 2 for 2 × 2 Rib.

CIRCULAR RIB BRAID PANEL (PANEL OF 16 STS)

Also see chart

Rnds 1, 3, 5, and 7: P1, *k2, p2; rep from * 2 times, k2, p1.

Rnds 2 and all even-numbered rnds: Knit the knit sts and purl the purl sts as they face you.

Rnd 9: P1, k2, p2, C2B, p2, C2F, p2, k2, p1.

Rnds 11 and 19: P1, k2, p2, [T2B, T2F] 2 times, p1, k2, p1.

Rnd 13: P1, k2, p1, k1, p2, C2F, p2, k1, p1, k2, p1.

Rnds 15 and 23: P1, k2, p1, [T2F, T2B] 2 times, p1, k2, p1.

Rnd 17: P1, k2, p2, C2B, p2, C2F, p2, k2, p1.

Rnd 21: P1, k2, p1, k1, p2, C2B, p2, k1, p1, k2, p1.

Rnd 25: Rep Rnd 9.

Rep Rnds 1–25 for Rib Braid Panel.

CIRCULAR CABLE PANEL (PANEL OF 6 STS)

Also see chart

Rnds 1–4: Knit.

Rnd 5: C6B.

Rnd 6: Knit.

Rep Rnds 1–6 for Cable Panel.

CIRCULAR STOCKINETTE STITCH (ST ST)

Knit every rnd.

STRAIGHT STOCKINETTE STITCH (ST ST)

Knit on RS, purl on WS.

KITCHENER STITCH

Step 1: Bring threaded tapestry needle through first st on front needle as if to knit and sl this st off needle.

Step 2: Bring threaded tapestry needle through next st on front needle as if to purl and leave st on needle.

Step 3: Bring threaded tapestry needle through first st on back needle as if to purl and sl this st off needle.

Step 4: Bring threaded tapestry needle through next st on back needle as if to knit and leave st on needle.

Rep Steps 1–4 until no sts rem on needles.

For more information, visit our website: www.classiceliteyarns.com/WebLetter/Stitches/Grafting/Grafting.php

WRAP AND TURN

Knit row Slip next st purlwise onto RH needle, bring yarn to front of work, return slipped st to LH needle, bring yarn to back of work, then turn work.

Purl row Slip next st purlwise onto RH needle, bring yarn to back of work, return slipped st to LH needle, bring yarn to front of work, then turn work.

HIDE WRAPS

Knit row Pick up the wrap from the front with the RH needle and knit tog with the st it wraps.

Purl row Pick up the wrap through back of loop with RH needle and purl tog with the st it wraps.

DORM SOCKS

Rib Braid Panel Chart
(panel of 16 sts; 25-rnd rep)

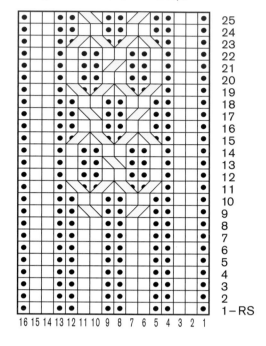

25 24 23 22 21 20 19 18 17 16 15 14 13 12 11 10 9 8 7 6 5 4 3 2 1–RS

16 15 14 13 12 11 10 9 8 7 6 5 4 3 2 1

Cable Panel Chart
(panel of 6 sts; 6-rnd rep)

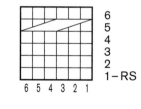

6 5 4 3 2 1–RS

6 5 4 3 2 1

▢ knit

▣ purl

◺ sl 1 st to cn, hold in back; k1; k1 from cn

◹ sl 1 st to cn, hold in front; k1; k1 from cn

◺ sl 1 st to cn, hold in back; k1; p1 from cn

◹ sl 1 st to cn, hold in front; p1; k1 from cn

◳ sl 3 sts to cn, hold in back; k3; k3 from cn

LEG

With smaller needles, CO 44 sts. Divide over 4 dpn as follows: 16 sts each on Needles 1 and 3; 6 sts each on Needles 2 and 4. Join, being careful not to twist sts; pm for beg of rnd. Rnd beg at side of leg. Begin 2 × 2 Rib; work even until pc meas 1½" from beg. ***Change to Larger Needles and Est Patt:*** With Needle 1, work 16 sts in Rib Braid Panel; with Needle 2, work 6 sts in Cable Panel; with Needle 3, work 16 sts in Rib Braid Panel; with Needle 4, work 6 sts in Cable Panel. Work even for 32 more rows, end Rnd 8 of Rib Braid Panel.

HEEL

Heel is worked back and forth in rows. Sl 3 sts from end of Needle 4 to empty dpn, slip next 19 sts to same dpn; divide rem 22 sts evenly over 2 dpn for instep. ***Change to Straight St St and Shape Heel:*** Working back and forth on 22 heel sts only, (RS) work to last st, wrap and turn. (WS) P20, wrap and turn. (RS) K19 sts, wrap and turn. *Work to 1 st before wrapped st, wrap and turn; rep from * 12 more times, end WS row. (RS) **Work to first wrapped st, hide wrap(s), wrap and turn (1 st double wrapped); rep from ** 13 more times, end WS row.

FOOT

Divide over 3 dpn as foll: With Needle 1, k22 heel sts, hiding wraps, k3 from next needle; with Needle 2, work 16 instep sts in Rib Braid Panel as est, beg with Rnd 9; with Needle 3, k3 sts, then k11 from Needle 1—44 sts total; 14 sts each on Needles 1 and 3; 16 sts on Needle 2. Rnd beg at bottom of foot. Work even as est until pc meas 7" from back of heel, or 2" shorter than desired finished length from back of heel. Change to Circular St st; work 1 rnd even. Rearrange sts on dpns as follows: sl 3 sts from Needle 1 to beg of Needle 2, sl 3 sts from Needle 3 to end of Needle 2—11 sts each on Needles 1 and 3; 22 sts on Needle 2.

TOE

Rnd 1: On Needle 1, knit to last 3 sts, k2tog, k1; on Needle 2, k1, ssk, knit to last 3 sts, k2tog, k1; on Needle 3, k1, ssk, knit to end of rnd—4 sts dec'd. Rnd 2: Knit. Rep these 2 rnds 4 times—24 sts rem. Work 3 times Rnd 1 only—12 sts rem. Work sts on Needle 1 with Needle 3—6 sts on each of 2 dpn.

FINISHING

Cut yarn, leaving a 12" tail. Thread tail on a tapestry needle and use the Kitchener st to graft rem sts together. Block lightly.

Twisted Lace Socks

SKILL LEVEL: INTERMEDIATE

SIZES

Women's Medium (Large)

FINISHED MEASUREMENTS

Leg length: 7"; foot length: 8½ (9½)" or desired size; foot and ankle circumference: approx 7¾ (8½)"

MATERIALS

Alpaca Sox by Classic Elite

(60% alpaca, 20% merino, 20% nylon; 100-gram hank = approx 450 yards)

• 1 hank 1872 Dried Herbs

Needles

• One set double-pointed needles size U.S. 2 (2.75 mm) **or size to obtain gauge**

• Stitch marker

• Tapestry needle

GAUGE

28 sts and 42 rnds = 4" in Circular Stockinette stitch.
Take time to save time, check your gauge.

PATTERN STITCHES

CIRCULAR 3 × 3 RIB (MULTIPLE OF 6 STS)

Rnd 1: *K3, p3; rep from * around.

Rnd 2: Knit the knit sts and purl the purl sts as they face you.

Rep Rnd 2 for 3 × 3 Rib.

CIRCULAR EYELET RIB (MULTIPLE OF 6 STS)

Also see chart

Rnds 1, 2, and 4: *K3, [k1-tbl] 3 times; rep from * around.

Rnd 3: Yo, sk2p, yo, [k1-tbl] 3 times; rep from * around.

Rep Rnds 1–4 for Eyelet Rib.

CIRCULAR STOCKINETTE STITCH (ST ST)

Knit every rnd.

KITCHENER STITCH

Step 1: Bring threaded tapestry needle through first st on front needle as if to knit and slip this st off needle.

Step 2: Bring threaded tapestry needle through next st on front needle as if to purl and leave st on needle.

Step 3: Bring threaded tapestry needle through first st on back needle as if to purl and slip this st off needle.

Step 4: Bring threaded tapestry needle through next st on back needle as if to knit and leave st on needle.

Rep Steps 1–4 until no sts rem on needles.

For more information, visit our website: www.classiceliteyarns.com/WebLetter/Stitches/Grafting/Grafting.php

LEG

CO 54 (60) sts. Divide sts over 3 dpn as foll: 14 (15) sts on Needle 1, 13 (15) sts on Needle 2, and 27 (30) sts on Needle 3. Pm for beg of rnd, and join, being careful not to twist sts. Rnd beg at side of leg. Begin 3 × 3 Rib; work even until pc meas 1½" from beg. Change to Eyelet Rib; work even until pc meas approx 7" from beg, ending Rnd 4 of Eyelet Rib.

HEEL FLAP

Slip 13 (15) sts from Needle 2 to Needle 1—27 (30) sts on Needle 1. Work heel flap back and forth in rows on Needle 1 only; rem 27 (30) sts will be worked later for instep. Size M only: (RS) Sl 1 st purlwise wyib, k1, m1, k1, *slip 1 st purlwise wyib, k1; rep from * to end of Needle 1—28 sts. Next Row: (WS) Sl 1 st purlwise wyif, purl to end. Both Sizes: Row 1: (RS) *Sl 1 st purlwise wyib, k1; rep from * to end. Row 2: (WS) Sl 1 st purlwise wyif, purl to end. Rep Rows 1 and 2 thirteen (fifteen) more times; flap meas approx 2"—15 (16) selvedge edge sts.

HEEL TURN

Row 1: (RS) Slip 1 st purlwise wyib, k15 (16), ssk, k1, turn. Row 2: Slip 1 st purlwise wyif, p5, p2tog, p1, turn. Row 3: Slip 1 st purlwise wyib, work to 1 st before gap created on previous row, ssk (1 st from each side of gap), k1, turn. Row 4: Slip 1 st purlwise wyif, work to 1 st before gap created on previous row, p2tog (1 st from each side of gap), p1, turn. Rep Rows 3 and 4 until all sts have been worked. On last 2 rows the knit and purl st after the dec st may need to be omitted—16 (18) sts rem.

GUSSETS

Pick up and knit sts along selvedge edges of heel flap and rejoin for working in rnds as foll: **Set-Up Rnd:** With Needle 1, k16 (18) heel sts, then with the same needle pick up and knit 15 (16) sts along selvedge edge of heel flap (pick up 1 st in each selvedge edge st). With Needle 2, work 27 (30) instep sts in Eyelet Rib as est. With Needle 3, pick up and knit 15 (16) sts along selvedge edge of heel flap, then knit the first 8 (9)

sts from Needle 1 again—73 (80) sts total; 23 (25) sts on each Needles 1 and 3; 27 (30) instep sts on Needle 2. Pm for beg of rnd; rnd beg at center of heel. Rnd 1, dec: On Needle 1, knit to last 3 sts, k2tog, k1; on Needle 2, work instep sts in Eyelet Rib as est; on Needle 3, k1, ssk, knit to end—2 sts dec'd. Rnd 2: On Needle 1, knit; on Needle 2, work as est; on Needle 3, knit. Rep Rnds 1 and 2 eight (nine) more times—55 (60) sts rem,

FOOT

Size M only: Next Rnd: K2tog, work to end of rnd as est—54 sts rem. Both Sizes: Cont even, working Eyelet Rib on Needle 2 and St st on Needles 1 and 3, until pc meas approx 7 (7¾)" from back of heel, or about 1½ (1¾)" less than desired total length.

TOE

Change to St St on All Needles: Rnd 1: On Needle 1, knit to last 3 sts, k2tog, k1; on Needle 2: k1, ssk, knit to last 3 sts, k2tog, k1; on Needle 3: k1, ssk, knit to end—4 sts dec'd. Rnd 2: Knit. Rep Rnds 1 and 2 five (six) times—30 (32) sts rem. Rep Rnd 1 only 4 (5) times—14 (12) sts rem. Knit all sts from Needle 1 onto Needle 3—7 (6) sts rem on each of 2 needles.

FINISHING

Cut yarn, leaving a 10" tail. Thread tail on a tapestry needle and use the Kitchener st to graft rem sts tog. Block lightly.

Eyelet Rib Chart
(multiple of 6 sts; 4-rnd rep)

6	5	4	3	2	1	
k1-tbl	k1-tbl	k1-tbl				4
k1-tbl	k1-tbl	k1-tbl	yo	sk2p	yo	3
k1-tbl	k1-tbl	k1-tbl				2
k1-tbl	k1-tbl	k1-tbl				1

☒ k1-tbl

☒ sk2p

○ yo

Wavy Lace Socks

SIZE

One size

FINISHED MEASUREMENTS

8" leg circumference; 8" foot circumference; foot length as desired

MATERIALS

Summer Sox by Classic Elite

(40% cotton, 40% superwash merino, 20% nylon; 50-gram ball = approx 175 yards)

• 2 balls 5578 Hickory

Needles

• One set double-pointed needles each size U.S. 1 and 2 (2.25 and 2.75 mm) **or size to obtain gauge**

• Stitch markers

• Waste yarn

GAUGE

30 sts and 42 rows = 4" in Circular Stockinette stitch and Lace pattern with larger needles. *Take time to save time, check your gauge.*

PATTERN STITCHES

CIRCULAR LACE PATTERN (MULTIPLE OF 10 STS)

Also see chart

Rnds 1, 3, 5 and 7: Knit.

Rnds 2 and 4: *K1, yo, k2, k2tog, k1, ssk, k2, yo; rep from * around.

Rnds 6 and 8: *K1, ssk, k2, yo, k1, yo, k2, k2tog; rep from * around.

Rep Rnds 1–8 for Lace Patt.

LEG

With larger dpn, waste yarn and Provisional Method, CO 60 sts. Divide sts evenly over 3 dpn. Join, being careful not to twist sts, pm for beg of rnd. ***Beg Circular St St:*** With working yarn, work even until pc meas 1" from beg. ***Turning Rnd:*** * K2tog, yo; rep from * around. Cont in St st until pc meas 2" from beg. ***Joining Rnd:*** Remove the waste yarn and place the provisional CO sts onto smaller dpns; *k2tog (1 leg st with 1 CO st); rep from * around—60 sts. Change to Lace patt; work even until pc meas approx 4" from turning rnd, end after Rnd 1 or 5 of Lace patt.

HEEL (UPPER SIDE)

The first 30 sts are worked back and forth in St st on 1 needle for the heel; place rem 30 sts on holder or waste yarn for instep to be worked later. ***Change to Straight St St:*** Row 1: (RS) K29, wrap and turn. Row 2: P28, wrap and turn. Row 3: Work to 1 st before wrapped st on previous row, wrap and turn. Rep Row 3 fifteen more times, end after a WS row—12 sts rem unwrapped in the center; 9 sts are wrapped on each side.

HEEL (LOWER SIDE)

Row 1: (RS) K12, wrap and turn (this st has now been wrapped 2 times). Row 2: P13 hiding wrap; wrap and turn (this st has now been wrapped 2 times). Row 3: Work to first wrapped st, work that st hiding wraps, wrap and turn (this st has now been wrapped 2 times). Rep Row 3 fourteen more times, end after a RS row. Next Row: (WS) Purl to last wrapped st, work that st, hiding the wrap, turn—30 sts; the st at the end of LH needle is still wrapped.

FOOT

Est Patt: With heel needle (Needle 1), k15; with Needle 2, knit rem 15 heel sts hiding wrap; with Needle 3, work 30 instep sts in Lace patt as est. Work even until pc meas approx 2" less than desired length from back of heel, end after Rnd 1 or 5 of Lace patt. ***Note:*** If after ending on Rnd 1 or 5 your sock does not meas 2" less than desired length, work even in Circular St st until it does.

TOE

Rnd 1: On Needle 1, k1, ssk, knit to end; on Needle 2, knit to last 3 sts, k2tog, k1; on Needle 3, k1, ssk, knit to last 3 sts, k2tog, k1—4 sts dec'd. Rnd 2: Knit. Rep Rnds 1 and 2 five more times—36 sts rem. Rep Rnd 1 only 2 times—28 sts rem. Sl sts from Needle 2 to Needle 1; 14 sts on each of 2 needles. To prevent "ears," pull the outside st of each end of both needles over the adjacent stitch—24 sts rem; 12 sts on each of 2 needles.

FINISHING

Using Kitchener st, graft sts tog. Block socks.

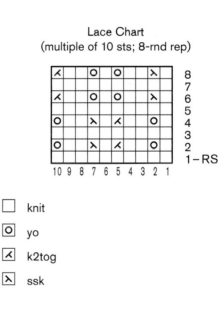

Lace Chart
(multiple of 10 sts; 8-rnd rep)

knit
yo
k2tog
ssk

Fresco Legwarmers

SKILL LEVEL: INTERMEDIATE

SIZES

Extra Small/Small (Medium/Large)

FINISHED MEASUREMENTS

10½ (13¼)" circumference; 16" long

MATERIALS

Fresco by Classic Elite

(60% wool, 30% baby alpaca, 10% angora; 50-gram hank = approx 164 yards)

• 2 (3) hanks Color A—5358 Tomato
• 2 (3) hanks Color B—5367 Blue Turquoise

Needles

• One set double-pointed needles each size U.S. 3, 4, and 5 (3, 3.5, and 3.75 mm) **or size to obtain gauge**
• Stitch marker

GAUGE

24 sts and 28 rows = 4" in Snowflake pattern with larger needles; 24 sts and 34 rows = 4" in Circular Stockinette stitch with middle size needle. *Take time to save time, check your gauge.*

PATTERN STITCHES

CIRCULAR STOCKINETTE STITCH (ST ST)

Knit every rnd.

CIRCULAR 2 × 2 RIB (MULTIPLE OF 4 STS)

Rnd 1: *K2, p2; rep from * around.

Rnd 2: Knit the knit sts and purl the purl sts as they face you.

Rep Rnd 2 for 2 × 2 Rib.

SNOWFLAKE PATTERN (MULTIPLE OF 16 STS)

See chart

CIRCULAR STRIPE SEQUENCE

Rnds 1–2: Color A

Rnds 3–4: Color B

Rep Rnds 1–4 for Stripe Sequence.

LEGWARMER

With smallest needles CO 64 (80) sts. Divide sts evenly onto dpn. Join, being careful not to twist sts; pm for beg of rnd. *Beg Circular 2 × 2 Rib and Work in Circular Stripe Sequence* for 8 rnds. *Change to Largest Needles and Est Snowflake Patt:* Work 3 full reps of Snowflake patt. Then work only Rnds 1–4 of chart. *Change to Middle Needles and Beg St St and Circular Stripe Sequence.* Work in Circular Stripe Sequence until pc meas approx 15" from beg, ending with Rnd 2. *Change to smallest needles and beg 2 × 2 Rib;* work 2 rnds in Color B, then 2 rnds in Color A. Rep last 4 rnds once more. BO all sts.

FINISHING

Block pcs to measurements.

Snowflake Chart
(multiple of 16 sts; 19-rnd rep)

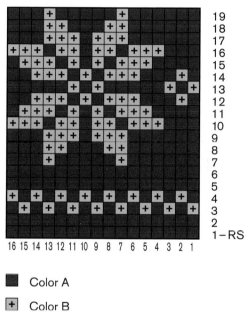

19
18
17
16
15
14
13
12
11
10
9
8
7
6
5
4
3
2
1–RS

16 15 14 13 12 11 10 9 8 7 6 5 4 3 2 1

■ Color A

[+] Color B

Fresco
Legwarmer

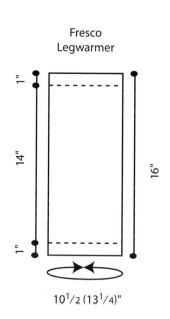

1"

14"

1"

16"

10¹/₂ (13¹/₄)"

Bohus Socks

SIZE

One size (Women's Medium)

FINISHED MEASUREMENTS

Leg length: 4¾"; foot length: 9½" or desired length; foot and ankle circumference: 8"

MATERIALS

Alpaca Sox by Classic Elite

(60% alpaca, 20% merino wool, 20% nylon; 100-gram hank = approx 450 yards)

• 1 hank Color A—1854 Amethyst
• 1 hank Color B—1827 Bordeaux
• 1 hank Color C—1809 Celadon

Needles

• One set of 5 double-pointed needles size U.S. 1 (2.25 mm) **or size to obtain gauge**
• Stitch marker
• Tapestry needle

GAUGE

32 sts and 40 rnds = 4" in Color patt. *Take time to save time, check your gauge.*

PATTERN STITCHES

CIRCULAR 1 × 1 RIB (MULTIPLE OF 2 STS)

Rnd 1: *K1, p1; rep from * around.

Rnd 2: Knit the knit sts and purl the purl sts as they face you.

Rep Rnd 2 for 1 × 1 Rib.

CIRCULAR COLOR PATTERN (MULTIPLE OF 4 STS)

Also see chart

Rnd 1: With Color A, knit.

Rnd 2: *With Color A, k2; with Color B, k1; with Color A, k1; rep from * around.

Rnd 3: *With Color A, k1; with Color B, k1; with Color C, k1; with Color B, k1; rep from * around.

Rnd 4: *With Color B p1, k1; with Color C, k1; with Color B, k1; rep from * around.

Rnd 5: *With Color B, k1; with Color C, k1; with Color B, p1; with Color C, k1; rep from * around.

Rnd 6: *With Color B, k1; with Color C, k1; with Color A, k1; with Color C, k1; rep from * around.

Rnds 7 and 8: *With Color B, k2; with Color C, k1; with Color B, k1; rep from * around.

Rnd 9: With Color B, knit.

Rnd 10: *With Color B, k1; with Color A, p3; rep from * around.

Rnd 11: *With Color A, k1, p1; with Color B, p1; with Color A, p1; rep from * around

Rnd 12: *With Color A, k1; with Color B, k3; rep from * around.

Rnd 13: With Color B, purl.

Rnd 14: *With Color C, p1; with Color B, k1; rep from * around.

Rnd 15: *With Color C, k1; with Color B, k1; rep from * around.

Rnd 16: With Color C, knit.

Rnd 17: *With Color B, k1, p1; rep from * around.

Rnd 18: With Color B, knit.

Rnd 19: *With Color B, k1; with Color A, p1; rep from * around.

Rep Rnds 1–19 for Color patt.

STOCKINETTE STITCH (ST ST)

Knit on RS, purl on WS.

WRAP AND TURN

Knit row Slip next st purlwise onto RH needle, bring yarn to front of work, return slipped st to LH needle, bring yarn to back of work, then turn work.

Purl row Slip next st purlwise onto RH needle, bring yarn to back of work, return slipped st to LH needle, bring yarn to front of work, then turn work.

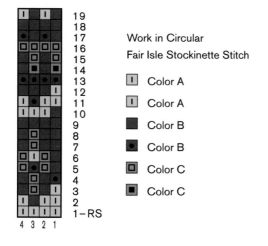

Color Chart
(multiple of 4 sts; 19-rnd rep)

Work in Circular
Fair Isle Stockinette Stitch

☐ Color A
☐ Color A
■ Color B
● Color B
▣ Color C
▣ Color C

HIDE WRAPS

Knit row Pick up the wrap from the front with the RH needle and knit tog with the st it wraps.

Purl row Pick up the wrap through back of loop with RH needle and purl tog with the st it wraps.

KITCHENER STITCH

Step 1: Bring threaded tapestry needle through first st on front needle as if to knit and slip this st off needle.

Step 2: Bring threaded tapestry needle through next st on front needle as if to purl and leave st on needle.

Step 3: Bring threaded tapestry needle through first st on back needle as if to purl and slip this st off needle.

Step 4: Bring threaded tapestry needle through next st on back needle as if to knit and leave st on needle.

Rep Steps 1–4 until no sts rem on needles.

For more information, visit our website: http://www.classiceliteyarns .com/WebLetter/Stitches/Grafting/Grafting.php.

NOTE

When changing colors, carry the unused colors up the inside of the sock securing it in every few rounds as needed. This will eliminate the need to weave in lots of ends when the sock is complete.

LEG

With Color B, CO 64 sts, divide over 4 dpn as foll: 16 sts on Needle 1, 17 sts on Needle 2, 16 sts on Needle 3, 15 sts on Needle 4. Join, being careful not to twist sts; pm for beg of rnd. Change to Color A and 1 × 1 Rib; work even until pc meas 1" from beg. Change to Color patt; work even for 38 rnds, end Rnd 19 of Color patt. Change to Color A and St st; slip next 33 sts onto a single dpn and cont working heel back and forth in rows over these sts.

HEEL

Heel Turn: Row 1: (RS) Work 32 sts, wrap and turn. Row 2: (WS) Work 31 sts, wrap and turn. Row 3: (RS) Work 30 sts, wrap and turn. Row 4: (WS) Work 29 sts, wrap and turn. Row 5: Work to 1 st before st wrapped st, wrap and turn. Rep Row 5 seventeen times, end WS row. Row 23: (RS) Work 11 sts, hide wrap on next st, turn. Row 24: Slip 1 st purlwise, work 11 sts, hide wrap on next st, turn. Row 25: Slip 1 st purlwise, work 12 sts, hide wrap on next st, turn. Row 26: Slip 1 st purlwise, work 13 sts, hide wrap on next st, turn. Row 27: Slip 1 st purlwise, work to next wrapped st, hide wrap on next st, turn. Rep Row 27 seventeen times, end WS row. Divide sts just worked back over 2 dpn as foll: 16 sts on Needle 1, 17 sts on Needle 2.

FOOT

Change to Color patt; beg working on all needles in the rnd; hide the last wrapped heel st on the first rnd, cont to work even for 38 rnds, end Rnd 19 of Color patt. If your foot is 9" or longer, work 9 more rnds in Color patt.

TOE

Change to Color A and St st; work even until foot meas 2" less than desired finished length from back of heel. ***Shape Toe:*** K1, ssk, work to last 3 sts on Needle 2, k2tog, k1, work across Needles 3 and 4—62 sts rem. Work 1 rnd even. ****Dec Rnd:*** K1, ssk, knit to last 3 sts on Needle 2, k2tog, k2, ssk, knit to last 3 sts on Needle 4, k2tog, k1—4 sts dec'd. Work 1 rnd even. Rep from * 11 times—14 sts rem. Sl sts from Needle 2 to Needle 1, then sts from Needle 4 to Needle 3—7 sts rem on each needle. Break yarn leaving 14" tail. Graft sts tog using Kitchener st.

FINISHING

Block pcs lightly to measurements.

Scarves, Cowls, Wraps, Shrugs, Capelets

contents

Aspen Capelet

SKILL LEVEL: INTERMEDIATE

SIZE
One size

FINISHED MEASUREMENTS
30" circumference, 8³/₄" long

MATERIALS
Aspen by Classic Elite
(50% alpaca, 50% wool; 100-gram hank = approx 51 yards)
• 3 hanks 1503 Mogul
Needles
• One 29" circular U.S. size 17 (12.75 mm) **or size to obtain gauge**
• Stitch marker

GAUGE
8 sts and 11 rows = 4" in Stockinette stitch. *Take time to save time, check your gauge.*

NOTE
If you have difficulty finding the recommended yarn, you may consider using Classic Elite's Ariosa doubled as a substitute.

STITCH PATTERNS

CIRCULAR CABLE RIB (MULTIPLE OF 6 STS)
Also see chart
Rnds 1, 2, and 3: *K4, p2; rep from * around.
Rnd 4: *C4F, p2; rep from * around.
Rnd 5: Rep Rnd 1.
Rnd 6: *K2, MB, k1, p2; rep from * around.
Rep Rnds 1–6 for Cable Rib

CAPELET

CO 60 sts. Join, being careful not to twist sts, pm for beg of rnd. (BOR). *Foundation Rnd:* * [K2, p2] 3 times, [k4, p2] 3 times; rep from * around. *Est Patt:* *Work 12 sts in rib as est, beg Rnd 1 work 18 sts in Cable Rib; rep from * around. Work as est for 22 rnds, end Rnd 5 of Cable Rib. Work 1 more rnd as est, working Rnd 1 of Cable Rib. BO all sts.

FINISHING

Block pc to measurements.

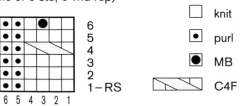

Aspen Capelet

10"

30"

Cable Rib Chart
(multiple of 6 sts; 6-rnd rep)

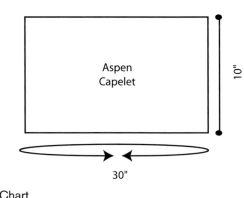

☐ knit

• purl

● MB

C4F

Aspen Scarf

SKILL LEVEL: INTERMEDIATE

SIZE
One size

FINISHED MEASUREMENTS
72" long × 8" wide

MATERIALS
Aspen by Classic Elite
(50% alpaca, 50% wool; 100-gram hank = approx 51 yards)
• 4 hanks 1593 Après Ski
Needles
• One pair size U.S. 17 (12.75 mm) **or size to obtain gauge**

GAUGE
8 sts and 12 rows = 4" in Stockinette stitch. *Take time to save time, check your gauge.*

NOTE
If you have difficulty finding the recommended yarn, you may consider using Classic Elite's Ariosa doubled as a substitute.

PATTERN STITCHES

STOCKINETTE STITCH (ST ST)
Knit on RS; purl on WS.

KNITTED CAST-ON METHOD
*Insert RH needle knitwise into first st of LH needle, wrap the yarn around the needle and pull through as to make a knit st, leave the first st on LH needle and slip st just made to LH needle (1 st CO); rep from * to required number of sts.

LACE RIB PATTERN (MULTIPLE OF 5 STS + 2)
Also see chart
Row 1: (RS) K1, *p1, [k1, p1] 2 times; rep from * to last st, k1.
Row 2: K1, *k1, [p1, k1] 2 times; rep from * to last st, k1.
Row 3: K1, *p1, yo, k3tog, yo, p1; rep from * to last st, k1.
Row 4: Rep Row 2.

SCARF
With Knitted Cast-On Method, CO 17 sts. (RS) Begin Lace Rib Patt; work even until pc meas approx 72" from beg, end WS Row 3 of Lace Rib Patt. (WS) BO all sts loosely in rib.

FINISHING
Block pc to finished measurements.

Lace Rib Chart
(multiple of 5 sts + 2; 4 row rep)

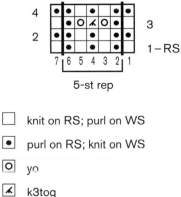

□ knit on RS; purl on WS

⊡ purl on RS; knit on WS

Ο yo

☒ k3tog

Turtle Scarf

SIZE
One size

FINISHED MEASUREMENTS
24" around neck opening, 46" long

MATERIALS
Commotion 2 by Classic Elite
(86% wool, 14% nylon; 50-gram ball = approx 200 yards)
• 3 balls 4258 Heat Wave
Needles
• One pair size U.S. 9 (5.5mm)
• One 16" circular size U.S. 9 (5.5 mm) **or size to obtain gauge**
• Stitch markers

GAUGE
14 sts and 32 rows = 4" in Garter stitch.
Take time to save time, check your gauge.

NOTE
If you have difficulty finding the recommended yarn, you may consider using Classic Elite's Alpaca Sox and Giselle, held together, as a substitute.

PATTERN STITCHES

CIRCULAR GARTER STITCH (GTR ST)
Rnd 1: Knit every st.
Rnd 2: Purl every st.
Rep Rnds 1 and 2 for Circular Gtr St.

STRAIGHT GARTER STITCH (GTR ST)
Knit every row.

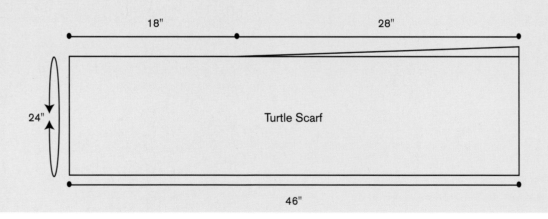

Turtle Scarf

SCARF NECK

Using circular needle, CO 84 sts. PM for beg of rnd and join, being careful not to twist sts. Beg Circular Gtr St; work even until piece meas 18" from beg, end on a purl round.

SCARF TIE ENDS

Divide sts in half and work both Scarf Tie Ends at the same time, each in straight Gtr St. Rem stitch marker and knit 42 sts, join second ball of yarn and knit rem 42 sts. Work even until pieces meas 28" from divide. BO all sts.

FINISHING

Block pc to measurements.

Button-Up Shrug

SKILL LEVEL: INTERMEDIATE

SIZES

Small (Medium, Large, Extra Large)

FINISHED MEASUREMENTS

12½ (14, 15¼, 16½)" wide × 57 (58, 59, 60)"

MATERIALS

Soft Linen by Classic Elite

(35% linen, 35% wool, 30% baby alpaca; 50-gram ball = approx 137 yards)

• 5 (6, 6, 7) balls 2248 Blue Grotto

Needles

• One pair each size U.S. 5 and 6 (3.75 and 4 mm) **or size to obtain gauge**

• Ten ½" buttons

GAUGE

21 sts and 30 rows = 4" in Chevron Rib with larger needles.
Take time to save time, check your gauge.

PATTERN STITCHES

GARTER STITCH (GTR ST)

Knit every row.

CHEVRON RIB (MULTIPLE OF 7 STS)

Also see chart

Row 1: (RS) *K1, k2tog, yo, k1, yo, ssk, k1; rep from * across.

Row 2: Purl.

Row 3: *K2tog, yo, k3, yo, ssk; rep from * across.

Row 4: Rep Row 2.

Rep Rows 1–4 for Chevron Rib.

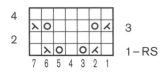

BUTTON-UP SHRUG

Chevron Rib Chart
(multiple of 7 sts; 4-row rep)

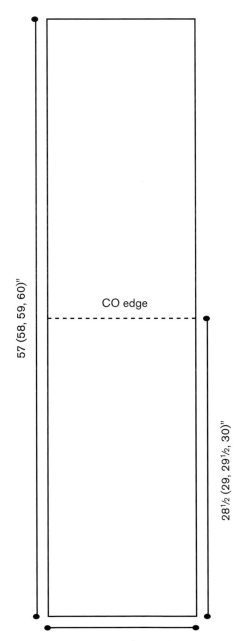

☐ knit on RS, purl on WS

☒ k2tog

☒ yo

☒ ssk

NOTE

When meas for buttonhole placement, meas along the Gtr st with rows stretched.

SHAWL

With larger needles, and Provisional CO , CO 66 (73, 80, 87) sts. *Est Patt:* Work 5 sts in Gtr St, 56 (63, 70, 77) sts in Chevron Rib, 5 sts in Gtr st. Work as est until pc meas 11½ (12, 12½, 13)" from beg, end WS row. *Buttonhole Row:* (RS) Work as est to last 5 sts, k2, yo, k2tog, k1. *Work as est for 4" from Buttonhole Row, end WS row. Work Buttonhole Row; rep from * 3 times for a total of 5 holes. Work even until pc meas 27½ (28, 28½ , 29)" from CO edge, end RS row. Change to smaller needles and Gtr St; (WS) work even for 8 rows, end RS row. (WS) BO all sts knitwise. *Second Side:* Pick up 66 (73, 80, 87) sts from CO edge. Work as before until pc meas 11½ (12, 12½, 13)" from CO row, end WS row. *Buttonhole Row:* (RS) K1, ssk, yo, k2, work to end as est. *Work as est for 4" from Buttonhole Row, end WS row. Work Buttonhole Row; rep from * 3 times for a total of 5 holes. Work even until pc meas 27½ (28, 28½, 29)" from CO row, end RS row. *Change to Smaller Needles and Gtr St:* (WS) Work even for 8 rows, end RS row. (WS) BO all sts knitwise.

FINISHING

Block pc to measurements. Sew buttons on RS of garment, opposite buttonholes.

Little Leaf Scarf

SKILL LEVEL: INTERMEDIATE

SIZE
One size

FINISHED MEASUREMENTS
27" long × 1½" wide

MATERIALS
Soft Linen by Classic Elite

(35% linen, 35% wool, 30% baby alpaca; 50-gram ball = approx 137 yards)

• 1 ball 2281 New Fern

Needles

• One pair size U.S. 6 (4 mm) **or size to obtain gauge**

• Stitch markers

GAUGE
22 sts and 32 rows = 4" in Stockinette stitch
Take time to save time, check your gauge.

PATTERN STITCHES

STOCKINETTE STITCH (ST ST)
Knit on RS, purl on WS.

2 × 2 RIB (MULTIPLE OF 4 STS + 2)
Row 1: (RS) K2, *p2, k2; rep from * across.
Row 2: Knit the knit sts and purl the purl sts as they face you.
Rep Row 2 for 2 × 2 Rib.

GARTER STITCH (GTR ST)
Knit every row.

SEED STITCH (MULTIPLE OF 2 STS + 1)
Row 1: (WS) P1, *k1, p1; rep from * across.
Row 2: Knit the purl sts and purl the knit sts as they face you.
Rep Row 2 for Seed st.

1 × 1 RIB (MULTIPLE OF 2 STS + 1)
Row 1: (WS) K1, *p1, k1; rep from * across.
Row 2: Knit the knit sts and purl the purl sts as they face you.
Rep Row 2 for 1 × 1 Rib.

SCARF (SEED LEAF SIDE)

Using Provisional Method, CO 20 sts. ***Est 2 × 2 Rib:*** (RS) K1 (edge st, keep in St st throughout), work across 18 sts in 2 × 2 Rib, k1 (edge st, keep in St st throughout). Work even until pc meas 8¼" from beg, end WS row. ***Shape Scarf:*** Row 1: (RS) K3, ssp, [k2, p2] 2 times, k2, p2tog, k3—18 sts rem. Work 1 row even. Row 3: (RS) K3, p1, k2, ssp, k2, p2tog, k2, p1, k3—16 sts rem. Work 1 row even. Row 5: (RS) K3, p1, ssk, p1, k2, p1, k2tog, p1, k3—14 sts rem. Work 1 row even. Row 7: (RS) K1, ssk, p1, k1, p1, k2, p1, k1, p1, k2tog, k1—12 sts rem. Work 1 row even. Row 9: (RS) K2, p1, k1, p1, k2tog, p1, k1, p1, k2—11 sts rem. Work 1 row even. Row 11: (RS) K2, p1, k1, p3tog, k1, p1, k2—9 sts rem. Work 3 rows even, end WS row. Row 15: (RS) K2, p1, sk2p, p1, k2—7 sts rem. Work even until pc meas 11" from beg, end RS row. ***Est Seed St:*** (WS) K2 (edge sts, keep in Gtr st throughout), work 1 st in Seed st, pm, p1, pm, work

1 st in Seed St, k2 (edge sts, keep in Gtr St throughout). ***Shape Leaf, Inc:*** (RS) Beg this row, inc 2 sts EOR 7 times working inc sts in Seed st as they become available as foll: K2 (edge sts), work to marker in Seed St, yo, sl m, k1, sl m, yo, work to last 2 sts in Seed st, k2 (edge sts)—21 sts. Work 3 rows even, end WS row. ***Shape Leaf, Dec:*** (RS) Beg this row, dec 2 sts EOR 8 times as foll: K2 (edge sts), work in Seed st to 1 st before marker, replace marker, sk2p, replace marker, work to last 2 sts in Seed st, k2 (edge sts)—5 sts rem. Next Row: K1, sk2p, k1—3 sts rem. Work 1 row even. (RS) Sk2p—1 st rem. Fasten off.

SCARF (RIB LEAF SIDE)

Sl 20 CO sts to working needle, work as for Seed Leaf Side until pc meas 5" from CO row, end WS row. ***Shape Scarf:*** (RS) Work Rows 1–11 of Seed Leaf Side—9 sts rem. ***Shape Slit:*** Work 4 sts as est, join second ball of yarn, BO 1 st, work rem 4 sts—4 sts each side. Working both sides at the same time, work even as est until slit meas 1", end WS row. ***Join Slit:*** (RS) K2, p1, ssk (the last and the first st), p1, k2—7 sts rem. Work even until pc meas 8" from CO row, end RS row. ***Est 1 × 1 Rib:*** (WS): K2 (edge sts, keep in Gtr St throughout), work 1 st in 1 × 1 Rib, pm, p1, pm, work 1 st in 1 × 1 Rib, k2 (edge sts, keep in Gtr st throughout). ***Shape Leaf, Inc:*** (RS) As for Seed Leaf Side working inc sts in 1 × 1 Rib as they become available—21 sts. Work 3 rows even, end WS row. ***Shape Leaf, Dec:*** (RS) As for Seed Leaf Side working sts in 1 × 1 Rib—1 st rem. Fasten off.

FINISHING

Block pc to measurements.

Wrap Skirt

SKILL LEVEL: INTERMEDIATE

SIZES
Extra Small (Small, Medium, Large, Extra Large, 2X Large)

FINISHED MEASUREMENTS
Waist: 28 (30¼, 32½, 35¼, 37¼, 39½)";
length: 12 (12½, 13, 13½, 14, 14½)"

MATERIALS
Bam Boo by Classic Elite
(100% bamboo; 50-gram hank = approx 77 yards)
• 4 (5, 5, 6, 6, 6) balls 4915 Bamboo Leaf
Needles
• One each 24" circular size U.S. 5 and 8 (3.75 and 5 mm)
  or size to obtain gauge

GAUGE
14 sts and 18 rows = 4" in Lace Pattern with larger needles; 18 sts and 36 rows = 4" in Seed stitch with smaller needles. *Take time to save time, check your gauge.*

NOTE
If you have difficulty finding the recommended yarn, you may consider using Classic Elite's Cotton Bam Boo, doubled, as a substitute.

PATTERN STITCHES

SEED STITCH (MULTIPLE OF 2 STS)
Row 1: (WS) *K1, p1, rep from * across.
Row 2: Knit the purl sts and purl the knit sts as they face you.
Rep Row 2 for Seed st.

LACE PATTERN (MULTIPLE OF 2 STS)
Also see chart
Row 1: (RS) *K2tog, yo; rep from * across.
Row 2: Purl.
Rep Rows 1–2 for Lace patt.

Lace Chart
(multiple of 2 sts; 2-row rep)

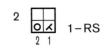

☐ knit on RS, purl on WS

☒ k2tog

◎ yo

NOTE

Garment is worked on circular needles to accommodate large number of sts.

SKIRT

With larger needle, CO 126 (136, 146, 158, 168, 178) sts. (WS) Begin Seed St; work even for 3 rows, end WS row. *Est Lace Patt:* (RS) Work 3 sts in Seed St as est (edge sts, keep in Seed St throughout), work in Lace Patt across center 120 (130, 140, 152, 162, 172) sts, work 3 sts in Seed St as est (edge sts, keep in Seed St throughout). Work as est until piece meas 12 (12½, 13, 13½, 14, 14½)" from beg, end WS row.

TIES

CO 62 sts at end of previous row—188 (198, 208, 220, 230, 240) sts. Change to smaller needle and Begin Seed St; (RS) beg with p1, work 1 row; CO 140 (150, 160, 170, 182, 192) sts at end of row—328 (348, 368, 390, 412, 432) sts. Next Row: (WS) Work across in Seed St, beg with k1. *Tie Hole Row:* (RS) Work across 89 sts, k2tog, yo, *work across 4 sts, k2tog, yo; rep from * 11 (13, 15, 17, 18, 20) times, work to end. (WS) Work 1 row even. (RS) BO all sts loosely in patt using larger needle if necessary.

FINISHING

Block pc to measurements.

WRAP SKIRT

31¼ (33¼, 35½, 37¾, 40½, 42½)"

28 (30¼, 32½, 35¼, 37¼, 39½)"

13¾"

12 (12½, 13, 13½, 14, 14½)"

36 (38¾, 41¾, 45¼, 48, 50¾)"

Ruched Shawl

SIZES
Small/Medium (Large/Extra Large)

FINISHED MEASUREMENTS
30" wide × 78" long (30" wide × 92" long)

MATERIALS
Classic Silk by Classic Elite
(50% cotton, 30% silk, 20% nylon; 50-gram ball = approx 135 yards)
• 16 (18) balls 6905 Old Lilac
Needles
• One pair size U.S. 7 (4.5 mm) **or size to obtain gauge**

GAUGE
18 sts and 26 rows = 4" in Stockinette stitch.
Take time to save time, check your gauge.

PATTERN STITCHES

GARTER STITCH (GTR ST)
Knit every row.

RUCHING (MULTIPLE OF 2 STS)
Row 1: (RS) Knit.
Row 2 and all WS rows: Purl.
Rows 3 and 5: (RS) *K1, k1-f/b; rep from * to end.
Rows 7 and 9: Knit.
Row 11 and 13: (RS) *K1, k2tog; rep from * to end.
Row 15: Knit.
Row 16: Purl.
Work Rows 1–16 for Ruching.

LACE PATTERN (MULTIPLE OF 2 STS)
Also see chart
Rows 1 and 5: (RS) *K2tog, yo; rep from * across.
Row 2 and all WS rows: Purl.
Row 3: *Yo, ssk; rep from * across.
Row 6: Purl.
Work Rows 1–6 for Lace Patt.

STOCKINETTE STITCH (ST ST)
Knit on RS, purl on WS.

NOTE
If you are interested in making the Classic Silk and Premier Ruched Tank shown above, please refer to Curvy Knits (9089) by Classic Elite.

SHAWL

CO 136 sts. (RS) Beg Gtr st; work 4 rows even, end WS row. Change to Ruching; (RS) work 16 rows, end WS Row. ****Est Patt:** (RS) K3 (edge sts, keep in Gtr st until Ruching), work in St st across to last 3 sts, k3 (edge sts, keep in Gtr st until Ruching). (WS) Work 9 rows even as est, end WS row. ***Est Lace Patt:** (RS) K3 (edge sts), work across center 130 sts in Lace Patt, k3 (edge sts). Work even as est for 5 rows, end WS row. **Est St St:** (RS) K3 (edge sts) work in St st across to last

3 sts, k3 (edge sts). Work even for 9 rows, end WS row; rep from * 2 times. Change to Ruching; (RS) work 16 rows, end WS row. Rep from ** 6 (7) times. Change to Gtr st; (RS) work 5 rows even, end RS row. (WS) BO all sts loosely knitwise.

FINISHING

Block pc to measurements.

RUCHED SHAWL

Lace Chart
(multiple of 2 sts; 6 rows)

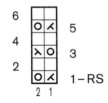

☐ knit on RS, purl on WS

⬛O⬛ yo

⬛↗⬛ k2tog

⬛↘⬛ ssk

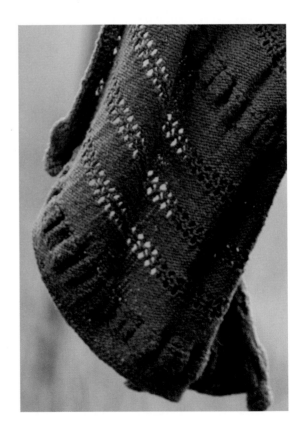

Wavy Scarf

SIZES
Small (Large)

FINISHED MEASUREMENTS
7" wide × 60" long (7" wide × 100" long)

MATERIALS
Sinful by Classic Elite
(100% cashmere; 50-gram hank = approx 65 yards)
• 3 (6) hanks 92026 Wisteria
Needles
• One pair size U.S. 10¹/₂ (6.5 mm) **or size to obtain gauge**

GAUGE
21 sts and 18 rows = 4" in Flame Rib. *Take time to save time, check your gauge.*

NOTE
If you have difficulty finding the recommended yarn, you may consider using Classic Elite's Ariosa as a substitute.

PATTERN STITCHES

1 × 1 RIB (MULTIPLE OF 2 STS + 1)
Row 1: (WS) Slip 1 st purlwise wyif, *k1, p1; rep from * to end.
Work Row 1 for 1 × 1 Rib.

FLAME RIB (PANEL OF 23 STS; VARIABLE ST COUNT)
Also see chart
Stitch count does not remain consistent.
Row 1: (RS) Slip 1 st purlwise wyib, p1, sk2p, [p1, k1] 6 times, p1, m2, [p1, k1] 2 times.
Row 2 and all WS rows: Slip 1 st purlwise wyif, *k1, p1; rep from * to end.
Row 3: Slip 1 st purlwise wyib, p1, sk2p, [p1, k1] 5 times, p1, m2, [p1, k1] 3 times.
Row 5: Slip 1 st purlwise wyib, p1, sk2p, [p1, k1] 4 times, p1, m2, [p1, k1] 4 times.
Row 7: Slip 1 st purlwise wyib, p1, sk2p, [p1, k1] 3 times, p1, m2, [p1, k1] 5 times.
Row 9: Slip 1 st purlwise wyib, p1, sk2p, [p1, k1] 2 times, p1, m2, [p1, k1] 6 times.
Row 11: Slip 1 st purlwise wyib, p1, sk2p, p1, k1, p1, m2, [p1, k1] 7 times.
Row 13: Slip 1 st purlwise wyib, p1, sk2p, p1, m2, [p1, k1] 8 times.
Row 15: Slip 1 st purlwise wyib, p1, sk2p, [p1, k1] 9 times—21 sts.
Row 17: Slip 1 st purlwise wyib, p1, m2, [p1, k1] 9 times—23 sts.
Row 19: Slip 1 st purlwise wyib, p1, k1, p1, m2, [p1, k1] 6 times, p1, srp, p1, k1.
Row 21: Slip 1 st purlwise wyib, [p1, k1] 2 times, p1, m2, [p1, k1] 5 times, p1, srp, p1, k1.
Row 23: Slip 1 st purlwise wyib , [p1, k1] 3 times, p1, m2, [p1, k1] 4 times, p1, srp, p1, k1.
Row 25: Slip 1 st purlwise wyib , [p1, k1] 4 times, p1, m2, [p1, k1] 3 times, p1, srp, p1, k1.
Row 27: Slip 1 st purlwise wyib , [p1, k1] 5 times, p1, m2, [p1, k1] 2 times, p1, srp, p1, k1.
Row 29: Slip 1 st purlwise wyib , [p1, k1] 6 times, p1, m2, p1, k1, p1, srp, p1, k1.
Row 31: Slip 1 st purlwise wyib , [p1, k1] 7 times, p1, m2, p1, srp, p1, k1.
Row 32: Rep Row 2.
Rep Rows 1–32 for Flame Rib.

SCARF

CO 23 sts. (WS) Beg 1 × 1 Rib; work 1 row. (RS) Change to Flame Rib; beg Row 1 of Flame Rib, work even until piece meas approx 60 (100)" from beg, end WS Row 16 or 32 of Flame Rib. (RS) BO all sts in Rib.

FINISHING

Block pc lightly to measurements being careful not to flatten texture.

WAVY SCARF

Flame Rib Chart
(panel of 23 sts; 32-row rep)

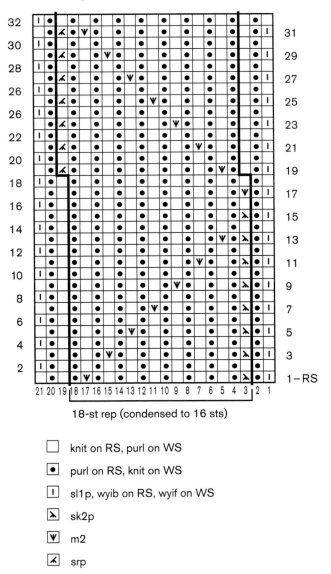

18-st rep (condensed to 16 sts)

☐ knit on RS, purl on WS

• purl on RS, knit on WS

1 sl1p, wyib on RS, wyif on WS

⅄ sk2p

V m2

⅄ srp

Berry Scarf

SKILL LEVEL: INTERMEDIATE

SIZE

One size

FINISHED MEASUREMENTS

7¼" wide × 80" long

MATERIALS

Inca Alpaca by Classic Elite

(100% alpaca; 50-gram hank = approx 109 yards)

• 4 hanks 1142 Cajamaica Maroon

Needles

• One pair size U.S. 7 (4.5 mm) **or size to obtain gauge**

• Stitch holder

GAUGE

18 sts and 30 rows = 4" in Scarf Berry stitch. *Take time to save time, check your gauge.*

PATTERN STITCHES

GARTER STITCH (GTR ST)

Knit every row.

BERRY STITCH (MULTIPLE OF 4 STS + 1)

Also see chart

Row 1: (RS) [K1, k1-tbl, k1] into next st, *p3, [k1, k1-tbl, k1] into next st; rep from * across—multiple of 6 sts + 3.

Row 2: K3, *p3tog, k3; rep from * across—multiple of 4 sts + 3.

Row 3: P3, *[k1, k1-tbl, k1] into next st, p3; rep from * across—multiple of 6 sts + 3.

Row 4: P3tog, *k3, p3tog; rep from * across—multiple of 4 sts + 1.

Rep Rows 1–4 for Berry St.

NOTE

For Berry st, st count does not rem consistent; count sts after Row 4.

Berry Chart
(multiple of 4 sts + 1; 4-row rep)

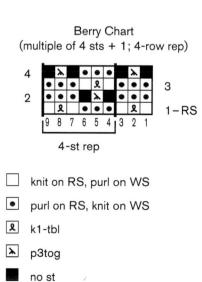

4-st rep

☐ knit on RS, purl on WS

⊡ purl on RS, knit on WS

🅇 k1-tbl

🅇 p3tog

■ no st

SCARF

CO 33 sts. (WS) Beg Gtr St; work 3 rows. *Est Berry St:* (RS) K4 (edge sts, keep in Gtr St throughout), work 25 sts in Berry St, k4 (edge sts, keep in Gtr St throughout). Work even until pc meas approx 79½" from beg, end WS Row 4 of Berry St. Change to Gtr St; (RS) work 3 rows. (WS) BO all sts knitwise.

FINISHING

Block pc to measurements.

Aspen
Airy Scarf

SKILL LEVEL: INTERMEDIATE

SIZE
One size

FINISHED MEASUREMENTS
11" wide × 69" long

MATERIALS
Aspen by Classic Elite
(50% alpaca, 50% wool; 100-gram hank = approx 51 yards)
• 5 hanks 1555 Ski Ticket
Needles
• One pair size U.S. 17 (12.75 mm) **or size to obtain gauge**

GAUGE
10 sts and 5 rows = 4" in Hole Patt. *Take time to save time, check your gauge.*

NOTE
If you have difficulty finding the recommended yarn, you may consider using Classic Elite's Ariosa dbld as a substitute. To make the Airy Hat, see p. 13.

PATTERN STITCHES

SINGLE CAST-ON METHOD
Make a slip knot at the end of your yarn leaving a short tail. Place the slip knot on the RH needle. * Wrap the yarn from the ball around your left thumb from the inside, around the back of your thumb, securing it in your palm with your other fingers. Insert the needle upward through the strand on your thumb. Slip this loop from your thumb onto the needle, pulling the yarn to tighten it. Rep from * as many times as indicated.

HOLE PATTERN (MULTIPLE OF 6 STS + 1)
Row 1: (RS) K1, *BO 5, k1; rep from * across. [K1 equals the rem st on RH needle after the last BO; 1 st rem bet each set of BOs]

Row 2: P1, *CO 5, p1; rep from * across.

Row 3: K1, BO 2, k1, *BO 5, k1; rep from * across to last 3 sts, BO 2, k1.

Row 4: P1, CO 2, p1, *CO 5, p1; rep from * across to last st, CO 2, p1.

Rep Rows 1–4 for Hole patt.

NOTE
St count does not rem consistent. Count sts after Rows 2 or 4 of Hole patt.

SCARF
Using Single Cast-on Method, CO 31 sts. (RS) Beg Hole patt; work even until piece meas 69" from beg, end WS Row 2 of Hole Patt. BO all sts knitwise.

FINISHING
Block pc to measurements.

Aspen Wrap

SKILL LEVEL: INTERMEDIATE

SIZES

Small (Medium, Large)

FINISHED MEASUREMENTS

46 (51³/₄, 58¹/₂)"

MATERIALS

Aspen by Classic Elite

(50% alpaca, 50% wool; 100-gram hank = approx 51 yards)

• 5 (6, 8) hanks 1578 Elk

Needles

• One each 16", 24" and 40" circular size U.S. 17 (12.75 mm) **or size to obtain gauge**

• Stitch markers (1 a different color for beg of round)

GAUGE

8¹/₂ sts and 12 rows = 4" in Stockinette stitch. *Take time to save time, check your gauge.*

NOTE

If you have difficulty finding the recommended yarn, you may consider using Classic Elite's Ariosa dbld as a substitute.

PATTERN STITCHES

CIRCULAR 1 × 1 RIB (MULTIPLE OF 2 STS)

Rnd 1: *K1, p1; rep from * around.

Rnd 2: Knit the knit sts and purl the purl sts as they face you.

Rep Rnd 2 for 1 × 1 Rib.

CIRCULAR 2 × 2 RIB (MULTIPLE OF 4 STS)

Rnd 1: *K2, p2; rep from * around.

Rnd 2: Knit the knit sts and purl the purl sts as they face you.

Rep Rnd 2 for 2 × 2 Rib.

CIRCULAR STOCKINETTE STITCH (ST ST)

Knit every rnd.

NOTES

1. Wrap was photographed off center. The shaping on the body actually forms vertical lines in the front and back.

2. Wrap is worked in the round from the top down.

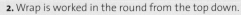

WRAP

Using shortest circular needle, CO 34 (38, 42) sts. Join, being careful not to twist sts; pm for beg of rnd. Beg 1 × 1 Rib; work even until piece meas 2½" from beg. On last rnd, pm as follows: Sl BOR marker, work 2 sts, pm, work 15 (17, 19) sts, pm, work 2 sts, pm, work 15 (17, 19) sts to end of rnd. *Inc Rnd:* Cont in 1 × 1 Rib, *sl marker, [m1, work 1] 2 times, m1, sl marker, work to next marker; rep from * 1 time—40 (44, 48) sts. Change to 2 × 2 Rib; work even until piece meas 5" from beg. *Change to St St and Shape Wrap:* Inc 4 sts, every rnd 6 (10, 14) times—64 (84, 104) sts; then EOR 7 (5, 3) times as follows: *Sl marker, m1, work to next marker, m1, sl marker, work to next marker; rep from * 1 time—92 (104, 116) sts. Work even until piece meas 13½ (14½, 15½)" from beg of St st. *Inc Rnd:* Inc 6 (6, 8) sts evenly around—98 (110, 124) sts. Begin 1 × 1 Rib; work even for 1". BO all sts loosely in rib.

FINISHING

Block pc to measurements.

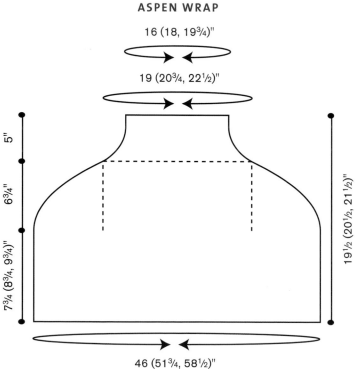

ASPEN WRAP

16 (18, 19¾)"

19 (20¾, 22½)"

5"

6¾"

7¾ (8¾, 9¾)"

19½ (20½, 21½)"

46 (51¾, 58½)"

Mock Wrap Pullover

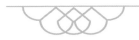

SKILL LEVEL: INTERMEDIATE

SIZES

Small (Medium, Large, Extra Large)

FINISHED MEASUREMENTS

36 (40, 44, 48)"

MATERIALS

Inca Marl by Classic Elite

(100% alpaca; 50-gram hank = approx 109 yards)

• 9 (10, 11, 13) hanks 1138 Tobacco Road

Needles

• One pair each size U.S. 5 and 7 (3.75 and 4.5 mm)

• 3 double-pointed needles size U.S. 6 (4 mm) **or size to obtain gauge**

GAUGE

20 sts and 25 rows = 4" in Stockinette stitch using largest needles.
Take time to save time, check your gauge.

PATTERN STITCHES

STOCKINETTE STITCH (ST ST)

Knit on RS, purl on WS.

1 × 1 RIB (MULTIPLE OF 2 STS + 1)

Row 1: (WS) P1, *k1, p1; rep from * across.

Row 2: Knit the knit sts and purl the purl sts as they face you.

Rep Row 2 for 1 × 1 Rib.

LARGE I-CORD EDGING

Using dpn, CO 5 sts. Pick up and knit 1 st along edge—6 sts. *Without turning the work, sl all sts to the RH end of dpn. Pull yarn tightly from the end of the row, k4 sts, k2tog-tbl—5 sts rem. Pick up and knit 1 st along edge—6 sts; rep from * for length desired.

SMALL I-CORD EDGING

Using dpn and 3 sts from large I-Cord Edging (see Finishing), pick up and knit 1 st along edge—4 sts. *Without turning the work, sl all sts to the RH end of dpn. Pull yarn tightly from the end of the row, k2 sts, k2tog-tbl—3 sts rem. Pick up and knit 1 st along edge—4 sts; rep from * for length desired.

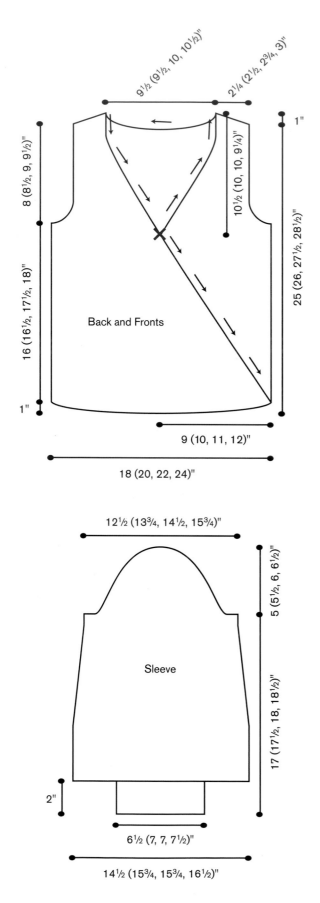

9½ (9½, 10, 10½)"

2¼ (2½, 2¾, 3)"

1"

8 (8½, 9, 9½)"

10½ (10, 10, 9¼)"

25 (26, 27½, 28½)"

16 (16½, 17½, 18)"

Back and Fronts

1"

9 (10, 11, 12)"

18 (20, 22, 24)"

12½ (13¾, 14½, 15¾)"

5 (5½, 6, 6½)"

Sleeve

17 (17½, 18, 18½)"

2"

6½ (7, 7, 7½)"

14½ (15¾, 15¾, 16½)"

NOTE

Work all dec sts 1 st in from each edge as follows: (RS) K1, k2tog, work across to last 3 sts, ssk, k1; (WS) p1, ssp, work across to last 3 sts, p2tog, p1.

BACK

Using larger needles, CO 56 (60, 64, 68) sts. *Beg St St and Shape Lower Edge:* (WS) Work across, CO 9 (10, 11, 12) sts at end of this and next row, then 4 (5, 6, 7) sts at end of next 4 rows—90 (100, 110, 120) sts. Work even until piece meas 16 (16½, 17½, 18)" from last CO row, end WS row. *Shape Armholes:* (RS) BO 5 (6, 5, 6) sts at beg of next 2 rows, then dec 1 st each side EOR 5 (7, 11, 13) times—70 (74, 78, 82) sts rem. Work even until armholes meas 7 (7½, 8, 8½)" from beg of shaping, end WS row. PM each side of center 28 (28, 30, 32) sts. *Shape Neck:* (RS) Work across to first marker, join second ball of yarn, BO center sts and work to end—21 (23, 24, 25) sts rem each side. At each neck edge, BO 5 sts 2 times—11 (13, 14, 15) sts rem each side for shoulder. Work even until armholes meas 8 (8½, 9, 9½)" from beg of shaping, end WS row. *Shape Shoulders:* (RS) BO 5 sts at beg of next 0 (2, 4, 6) rows, 4 sts at beg of next 4 (4, 2, 0) rows, then 3 sts at beg of next 2 (0, 0, 0) rows.

LEFT FRONT

Using larger needles, CO 1 st. *Beg St St and Shape Front Edge:* (WS) Beg this row, inc 1 st at center Front edge (beg of WS rows) EOR 44 (49, 54, 59) times as foll: (WS) K1-f/b, work to end—45 (50, 55, 60) sts. Work 2 rows even, end WS row. *Shape Neck:* (RS) Dec 1 st at neck edge (end of RS rows) EOR 15 (17, 20, 23) times, then every 4 rows 9 (7, 5, 3) times; *and At the Same Time,* when piece meas 16 (16½, 17½, 18)" from beg, end WS row. *Shape Armhole:* (RS) BO 5 (6, 5, 6) sts, work to end. Work 1 row even. (RS) At armhole edge, dec 1 st EOR 5 (7, 11, 13) times—11 (13, 14, 15) sts rem after all shaping. Work even until armhole meas 8 (8½, 9, 9½)" from beg of shaping, end WS row. *Shape Shoulder:* (RS) At armhole edge, BO 5 sts 0 (1, 2, 3) times, 4 sts 2 (2, 1, 0) times, then 3 sts 1 (0, 0, 0) time.

RIGHT FRONT

Using larger needles, CO 56 (60, 64, 68) sts. **Beg St St and Shape Lower Edge:** (WS) Work across, CO 9 (10, 11, 12) sts at end of this and next row, then 4 (5, 6, 7) sts at end of next 4 rows, end WS row—90 (100, 110, 120) sts. **Shape Front Edge:** (RS) Beg this row, dec 1 st at front edge (beg of RS rows) EOR 60 (67, 75, 83) times then every 4 rows 9 (7, 5, 3) times as foll: (RS) K1, k2tog, work to end; **and At the Same Time,** when piece same as back to armholes, end RS row. **Shape Armhole:** (WS) BO 5 (6, 5, 6) sts at beg of next row, work across. Next Row: (RS) Dec 1 st at end of row EOR 5 (7, 11, 13) times— 11 (13, 14, 15) sts rem after all shaping. Work even until armhole meas 8 (8½, 9, 9½)" from beg of armhole shaping, end RS row. **Shape Shoulder:** (WS) At armhole edge, BO 5 sts 0 (1, 2, 3) times, 4 sts 2 (2, 1, 0) times, then 3 sts 1 (0, 0, 0) time.

SLEEVE

Using smaller needles, CO 45 (49, 49, 51) sts. (WS) Begin 1 × 1 Rib; work even until piece meas 2" from beg, end WS row. **Change to Larger Needles and Increase Row:** (RS) Inc 28 (30, 30, 32) sts evenly across row as foll: K1 (2, 2, 1), k1-f/b, k1, *[k1-f/b] 2 times, k1; rep from * across to last 3 sts, k1-f/b, k2—73 (79, 79, 83) sts. Work even until piece meas 5" from beg, end WS row. **Shape Sleeve:** (RS) Beg this row, dec 1 st each side every 14 (14, 26, 42) rows 3 (1, 2, 2) times, then every 16 (16, 28, 0) rows 2 (4, 1, 0) times—63 (69, 73, 79) sts rem. Work even until piece meas 17 (17½, 18, 18½)" from beg, end WS row. **Shape Cap:** (RS) BO 5 (6, 5, 6) sts at beg of next 2 rows, dec 1 st each side EOR 13 (15, 17, 18) times, BO 3 sts at beg of next 4 rows—15 (15, 17, 19) sts rem. BO rem sts.

FINISHING

Block pieces to measurements. Sew shoulder seams. Set in sleeves; sew side and sleeve seams. **I-Cord Neck Trim: Note:** When picking up sts, hide the inc and dec sts whenever possible. Using dpn, CO 5 sts. With WS facing, beg at left front center point (see red X on schematic), work Large I-Cord edging up left front neck (see arrows on schematic), around

back neck, down right front to the bottom left side seam. **Bottom Trim:** Divide the 6 sts evenly onto 2 dpn (3 sts each). **Note:** You are working the 3 edging sts closest to the back along the front edge, then crossing the 3 front edging sts rem at the left side seam *over* the front edge trim to avoid a large gap or stretched st from splitting the trim, then working across the back edge. Change to Small I-Cord Edging; using the 3 sts closest to the back work along right front lower edge to side seam. Break yarn, place sts on holder. Attach yarn to rem 3 sts at other seam (the ones closest to the front). Work Small I-Cord Edging along back lower edge to side seam. Join to sts on holder from front lower edge using Kitchener st. On WS, sew center edge of left front along I-Cord edging of right front.

Fresco Shrug

SIZES

Extra Small (Small, Medium, Large, Extra Large)

FINISHED MEASUREMENTS

38 (40, 42, 44, 46)" around opening

MATERIALS

Fresco by Classic Elite

(60% wool, 30% baby alpaca, 10% angora; 50-gram hank = approx 164 yards)

• 5 (5, 6, 6, 6) hanks 5336 Oatmeal

Needles

• One pair size U.S. 6 (4 mm)

• One 32" circular each size U.S. 6 and 7 (4 and 4.5 mm) **or size to obtain gauge**

• Stitch markers

GAUGE

21 sts and 36 rows = 4" in Seed stitch with smaller needles. *Take time to save time, check your gauge.*

PATTERN STITCHES

STOCKINETTE STITCH (ST ST)

Knit on RS, purl on WS.

SEED STITCH (MULTIPLE OF 2 STS + 1)

Row 1: K1, *p1, k1; rep from * across.

Row 2: Knit the purl sts and purl the knit sts as they face you.

Rep Row 2 for Seed st.

STRAIGHT DIAMOND SEED PATTERN
(MULTIPLE OF 8 STS + 9)

Also see chart

Row 1: K1, *yo, ssk, k3, k2tog, yo, k1; rep from * across.

Rows 2, 4, 6, 12, 14, and 16: Purl.

Row 3: K1, *k1, yo, ssk, k1, k2tog, yo, k2; rep from * across.

Row 5: K1, *k2, yo, sk2p, yo, k3; rep from * across.

Rows 7–10: K1, *p1, k1; rep from * across.

Row 11: K1, *k1, k2tog, yo, k1, yo, ssk, k2; rep from * across.

Row 13: K1, *k2tog, yo, k3, yo, ssk, k1; rep from * across.

Row 15: K2tog, yo, k5, *yo, sk2p, yo, k5; rep from * to last 2 sts, yo, ssk.

Rows 17–20: Rep Rows 7–10.

Work Rows 1–20 for Diamond Seed patt.

CIRCULAR DIAMOND SEED PATTERN
(MULTIPLE OF 8 STS)

Rnd 1: *Yo, ssk, k3, k2tog, yo, k1; rep from * around.

Rnds 2, 4, 6, 12, 14, and 16: Knit.

Rnd 3: *K1, yo, ssk, k1, k2tog, yo, k2; rep from * around.

Rnd 5: *K2, yo, sk2p, yo, k3; rep from * around.

Rnds 7 and 9: *P1, k1; rep from * around.

Rnds 8 and 10: *K1, p1; rep from * around.

Rnd 11: *K1, k2tog, yo, k1, yo, ssk, k2; rep from * around.

Rnd 13: *K2tog, yo, k3, yo, ssk, k1; rep from * around.

Rnd 15: K1, *yo, k5, yo, sk2p; rep from * to end borrowing the first st of the rnd to complete last sk2p.

Rnds 17–20: Rep Rnds 7–10.

Work Rnds 1–20 for Diamond Seed patt.

NOTE

Work Sleeve dec sts as follows: (RS) Ssk, work to last 2 sts, k2tog.

FIRST SLEEVE

Using Provisional Method, CO 69 (73, 77, 81, 85) sts. *Est Seed St:* (RS) K1 (edge st, keep in St st throughout), work to last st in Seed st, k1 (edge st, keep in St st throughout). Work even as est until pc meas 9½ (10, 10½, 11, 11½)" from beg, end WS row. *Shape Sleeve:* (RS) Dec 1 st each side this row, every 34th row 0 (0, 1, 0, 1) time, every 28th row 2 (0, 1, 0, 1) times, every 24th row 1 (1, 1, 1, 2) times, every 20th row 2 (2, 2, 2, 1) times, then every 16th row 0 (4, 0, 4, 0) times—57 (57, 65, 65, 73) sts rem. Work even until pc meas 25½ (26½, 27, 28, 28½)" from beg, end WS row. (RS) Change to Diamond Seed Patt; work even for 20 rows end WS row. (RS) BO all sts loosely in Seed st.

SECOND SLEEVE

Sl sts from Provisional CO to working needle preparing to work a WS row. *Est Seed St:* (WS) P1 (edge st, keep in St st throughout), work to last st in Seed st, p1 (edge st, keep in St st throughout). Cont as for first sleeve.

FRESCO SHRUG

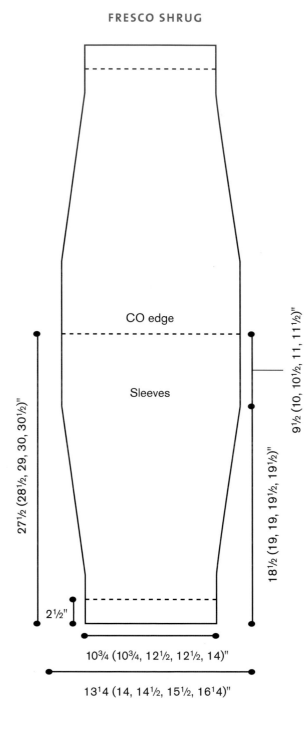

27½ (28½, 29, 30, 30½)"

18½ (19, 19, 19½, 19½)"

9½ (10, 10½, 11, 11½)"

CO edge

Sleeves

2½"

10¾ (10¾, 12½, 12½, 14)"

13¹4 (14, 14½, 15½, 16¹4)"

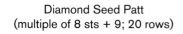

FINISHING

Block pc to measurements. PM 18½ (19, 19, 19½, 19½)" from the BO edge for sleeves. Seam both sleeves from cuff to marker.
Body Trim: With smaller circular needle and RS facing, beg at Provisional CO, pick up and knit 50 (52, 56, 58, 60) sts along open edge to marker, 100 (104, 112, 116, 120) sts bet markers, 50 (52, 56, 58, 60) sts to beg of rnd; pm—200 (208, 224, 232, 240) sts rem. Begin Circular Diamond Seed Patt; work for 10 rnds. Change to larger circular needle; work 10 more rnds, end Rnd 20 of Diamond Seed Patt. BO all sts loosely in Seed st.

Diamond Seed Patt
(multiple of 8 sts + 9; 20 rows)

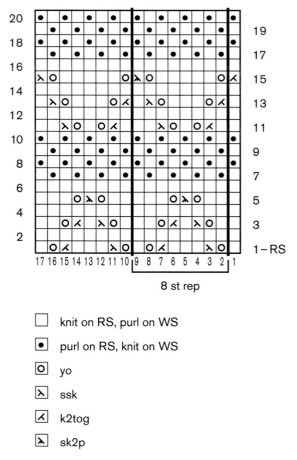

8 st rep

	knit on RS, purl on WS
	purl on RS, knit on WS
O	yo
	ssk
	k2tog
	sk2p

136

Montera Shawl

SIZES

One size

FINISHED MEASUREMENTS

58" wide × 27" long

MATERIALS

Montera by Classic Elite

(50% llama, 50% wool; 100-gram hank = approx 127 yards)

• 11 hanks 3877 Smoke

Needles

• One 40" circular size U.S. 11 (8 mm) **or size to obtain gauge**

GAUGE

11 sts and 18 rows = 4" in Leaf Lace pattern stretched. *Take time to save time, check your gauge.*

PATTERN STITCHES

GARTER STITCH (GTR ST)

Knit every row.

FOUNDATION PATT (PANEL OF 10 STS; INC'D TO 38 STS)

Also see chart

Row 1: (RS) *K2, yo, k1, yo, k2, pm; rep from * 1 time—14 sts.

Row 2 and all WS rows: K2, p to 2 sts before marker, k2, sl marker, k2, p to last 2 sts, k2.

Row 3: *K2, yo, k3, yo, k2; rep from * 1 time—18 sts.

Row 5: *K2, yo, k5, yo, k2; rep from * 1 time—22 sts.

Row 7: *K2, yo, k1, k2tog, yo, k1, yo, ssk, k1, yo, k2; rep from * 1 time—26 sts.

Row 9: *K2, yo, k1, k2tog, [k1, yo] 2 times, k1, ssk, k1, yo, k2; rep from * 1 time—30 sts.

Row 11: *K2, yo, k1, k2tog, k2, yo, k1, yo, k2, ssk, k1, yo, k2; rep from * 1 time—34 sts.

Row 13: *K2, yo, k1, k2tog, k3, yo, k1, yo, k3, ssk, k1, yo, k2; rep from * 1 time—38 sts.

Row 14: Rep Row 2.

Work Rows 1–14 for Foundation patt.

LEAF LACE PATTERN (MULTIPLE OF 10 STS + 18; INC'D TO MULTIPLE OF 10 STS + 38)

Also see chart

Row 1: (RS) **[K2, yo] 2 times, k1, yo, *ssk, k5, k2tog, yo, k1, yo; rep from * to 4 sts before marker, k2, yo, k2, sl marker; rep from ** 1 time—8 sts inc'd.

Row 2 and all WS rows: K2, p to 2 sts before marker, k2, sl marker, k2, p to last 2 sts, k2.

Row 3: **K2, yo, k1, k2tog, k1, [yo, k1] 2 times, ssk, *k3, k2tog, [k1, yo] 2 times, k1, ssk; rep from * to 3 sts before marker, k1, yo, k2, sl marker; rep from ** 1 time—4 sts inc'd.

Row 5: **K2, yo, k1, k2tog, k2, yo, k1, yo, k2, ssk, *k1, k2tog, k2, yo, k1, yo, k2, ssk; rep from * to last 3 sts, k1, yo, k2; rep from ** 1 time—4 sts inc'd.

Row 7: **K2, yo, k1, k2tog, k3, yo, k1, yo, k3, *sk2p, k3, yo, k1, yo, k3; rep from * to 5 sts before marker, ssk, k1, yo, k2; rep from ** 1 time—4 sts inc'd.

Row 8: Rep Row 2.

Rep Rows 1–8 for Leaf Lace patt.

SHAWL

CO 10 sts. (RS) Begin Gtr St; work 2 rows even. Change to Foundation patt; work for 14 rows—38 sts. Change to Leaf Lace Patt; work until pc meas approx 27" from beg, end RS Row 7 of Leaf Lace Patt—298 sts (WS) BO all sts knitwise.

FRINGE

Cut 150 40" strands. Fold 1 strand in half, then pull halfway through edge st on shawl. Twist both 2-plied ends separately in clockwise direction. Then align both ends and twist counter-clockwise to form the 4-plied fringe. Tie a knot at approx 5½" from garment edge to fasten the twist. Rep for a total of 150 8" fringes. Trim if desired.

MONTERA SHAWL

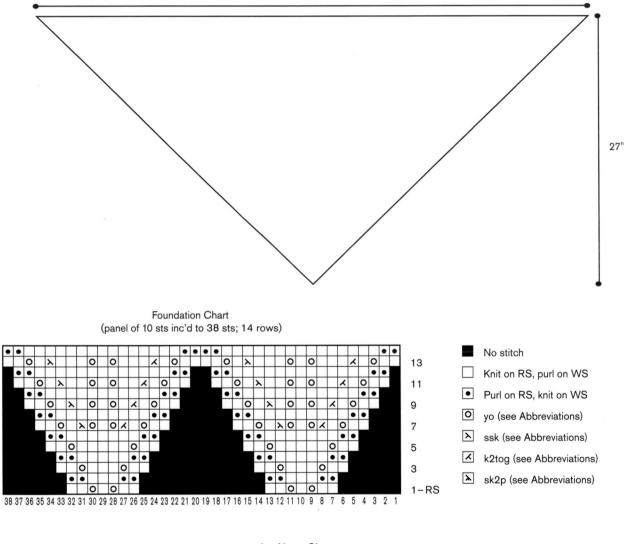

Foundation Chart
(panel of 10 sts inc'd to 38 sts; 14 rows)

	No stitch
	Knit on RS, purl on WS
•	Purl on RS, knit on WS
O	yo (see Abbreviations)
⋋	ssk (see Abbreviations)
⋌	k2tog (see Abbreviations)
⋏	sk2p (see Abbreviations)

Leaf Lace Chart
(multiple of 10 sts + 18 inc'd to multiple of 10 sts + 38; 8 row rep)

10 st rep   10 st rep

Lace Tube Scarf

SKILL LEVEL: INTERMEDIATE

SIZE
One size

FINISHED MEASUREMENTS
60" around × 7¾" wide

MATERIALS
Silky Alpaca Lace by Classic Elite
(70% alpaca, 30% silk; 50-gram ball = approx 460 yards)
• 1 ball Color A—2403 Cloud Gray
• 1 ball Color B—2416 French Vanilla
Needles
• One pair size U.S. 4 (3.5 mm) **or size to obtain gauge**
• Stitch markers

GAUGE
32 sts and 33 rows = 4" in Stockinette stitch; 35 sts and 31 rows = 4" in Lace stitch. *Take time to save time, check your gauge.*

PATTERN STITCHES

STOCKINETTE STITCH (ST ST)
Knit on RS, purl on WS.

LACE STITCH (MULTIPLE OF 14 STS + 1)
Also see chart
Row 1 and all WS rows: Purl.
Rows 2, 4, 6, 8, and 10: K1, *yo, k3, sk2p, yo, k1, yo, k3tog, k3, yo, k1; rep from * across.
Rows 12, 14, 16, 18, and 20: K1, *yo, k3tog, k3, yo, k1, yo, k3, sk2p, yo, k1; rep from * across.
Rep Rows 1–20 for Lace st.

SCARF

LACE STITCH SCARF
CO 47 sts. **Est Lace St:** (WS) P2 (edge sts, keep in St st throughout), pm, beg Row 1, work 43 sts in Lace st, pm, p2 (edge sts, keep in St st throughout). Work as est until pc meas approx 60" from beg, end WS Row 1 of Lace st. BO all sts.

STOCKINETTE STITCH SCARF
CO 55 sts. (WS) Begin St st; work even until pc meas same as Lace st scarf from beg, end WS row. (RS) BO all sts loosely.

FINISHING
Block pieces to measurements. With WS's of each scarf facing each other, sew edges together lengthwise to form tube. Sew short edge to the short edge at the other end of the scarf to form a ring.

Lace Stitch Chart
(multiple of 14 sts + 1; 20-row rep)

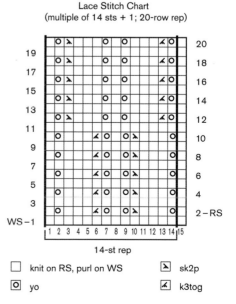

14-st rep

☐ knit on RS, purl on WS   ☒ sk2p
⊡ yo   ☒ k3tog

La Gran Lace Shawl

SKILL LEVEL: INTERMEDIATE

SIZE
One size

FINISHED MEASUREMENTS
32" wide × 90½" long

MATERIALS
La Gran by Classic Elite

(76½% mohair, 17½% wool, 6% nylon; 42-gram ball = approx 90 yards)

• 7 balls 63520 Winter Sky

Needles

• One pair size U.S. 13 (9 mm) **or size to obtain gauge**

GAUGE
8 sts and 10 rows = 4" in Lace stitch. *Take time to save time, check your gauge.*

PATTERN STITCHES

GARTER STITCH (GTR ST)
Knit every row.

LACE PATTERN (MULTIPLE OF 6 STS + 7)
Also see chart

Row 1: (RS) K1, *yo, p1, p3tog, p1, yo, p1; rep from * across.

Row 2 and all WS rows: Purl.

Row 3: K1, *k1, yo, sk2p, yo, k2; rep from * across.

Row 5: P2tog, p1, yo, k1, yo, p1, *p3tog, p1, yo, k1, yo, p1; rep from * to last 2 sts, p2tog.

Row 7: K2tog, yo, k3, yo, *sk2p, yo, k3, yo; rep from * to last 2 sts, ssk.

Row 8: Purl.

Rep Rows 1–8 for Lace patt.

SHAWL

CO 65 sts. (RS) Begin Gtr st; work 2 rows, end WS row. *Est Lace Patt:* (RS) K2 (edge sts, keep in Gtr st throughout), work 61 sts in Lace Patt, k2 (edge sts, keep in Gtr st throughout). Work even as est until pc meas approx 90" from beg, end WS Row 8 of Lace Patt. Change to Gtr st; (RS) work 3 rows, end RS row. (WS) BO all sts knitwise.

FINISHING

Block pc to measurements.

Lace Chart
(multiple of 6 sts + 7; 8-row rep)

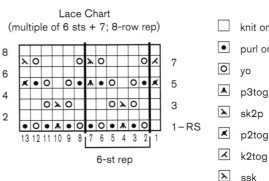

6-st rep

☐ knit on RS, purl on WS

● purl on RS, knit on WS

⊙ yo

⟑ p3tog

⟍ sk2p

⟋ p2tog

⟍ k2tog

⟍ ssk

Allegoro Kerchief

SIZE
One size

FINISHED MEASUREMENTS
11" long × 15½" wide, excluding ties; 28½" wide including ties

MATERIALS
Allegoro by Classic Elite
(70% organic cotton, 30% linen; 50-gram ball = approx 152 yards)
• 1 ball 5619 Lupine Pink
Needles
• One pair size U.S. 5 (3.75 mm) **or size to obtain gauge**
• Stitch markers

GAUGE
21 sts and 37 rows = 4" in Seed stitch; 13 sts in Lace Panel = 2¼".
Take time to save time, check your gauge.

PATTERN STITCHES

SEED STITCH (MULTIPLE OF 2 STS)
Row 1: (WS) *P1, k1; rep from * to end.
Row 2: Knit the purl sts and purl the knit sts as they face you.
Rep Row 2 for Seed st.

LACE PANEL (PANEL OF 13 STS)
Also see chart
Rows 1 and 3: (WS) Purl.
Row 2: K3, yo, k2, ssk, k2tog, k2, yo, k2.
Row 4: K2, yo , k2, ssk, k2tog, k2, yo, k3.
Rep Rows 1–4 for Lace Panel.

1 × 1 RIB (MULTIPLE OF 2 STS + 1)
Row 1: (RS) K1, *p1, k1; rep from * to end.
Row 2: Knit the knit sts and purl the purl sts as they face you.
Rep Row 2 for 1 × 1 Rib.

PICOT BIND-OFF METHOD (MULTIPLE OF 2 STS + 1)
Row 1: (RS) BO 2 sts, *sl st on RH needle to LH needle, use Cable Cast-On method to CO 2 sts, BO 4 sts; rep from * to end.
Work Row 1 for Picot Bind-Off Method.

NOTE

Work inc sts as follows: (RS) K1-f/b, work as est to last st, k1-f/b.

KERCHIEF

CO 15 sts. **Est Patt:** (WS) Work 1 st in Seed st, pm, work 13 sts in Lace Panel, pm, work 1 st in Seed st. **Shape Kerchief:** (RS) Inc 1 st each side this row, then EOR 20 more times, then every fourth row 12 times—81 sts. (WS) Work 1 row even as est.

TIES

(RS) Change to 1 × 1 Rib; with Cable Cast-On Method, CO 34 sts at the beg of the next 2 rows—149 sts. Work 2 rows even, end after a WS row. Next row: (RS) BO 34 sts in rib, work to end. (WS) BO rem sts in rib.

FINISHING

Block pc to measurements. **Picot Trim:** With RS facing, beg where indicated on schematic, pick up and knit 82 sts along side edge, 15 sts along CO edge, and 82 sts along side edge—179 sts. (WS) Purl all sts. (RS) Begin Picot Bind-Off Method; work 1 row.

ALLEGORO KERCHIEF

Lace Chart
(panel of 13 sts; 4-row rep)

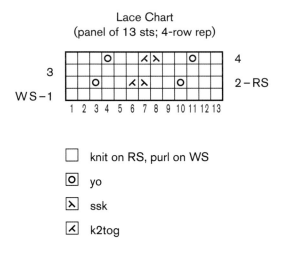

knit on RS, purl on WS

O yo

ssk

k2tog

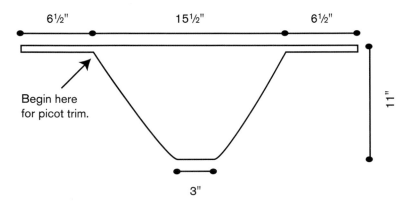

Begin here for picot trim.

6½"   15½"   6½"

11"

3"

Interlude Lace Shrug

SKILL LEVEL: INTERMEDIATE

SIZES

Extra Small (Small, Medium, Large, Extra Large)

FINISHED MEASUREMENTS

41½ (44½, 46½, 49½, 51½)" around opening without trim;
39½ (42¾, 44¾, 47, 49)" with trim

MATERIALS

Interlude by Classic Elite

(70% linen, 30% silk; 50-gram hank = approx 82 yards)

• 3 (4, 4, 5, 6) hanks 20286 Lilac Ice

Needles

• One pair size U.S. 7 (4.5 mm)

• One 32" circular size U.S. 7 (4.5 mm) **or size to obtain gauge**

• Stitch markers

GAUGE

18 sts and 24 rows = 4" in Arrow Lace pattern. *Take time to save time, check your gauge.*

NOTES

1. If you have difficulty finding the recommended yarn, you may consider using Classic Elite's Solstice as a substitute.

2. Shrug is shown in size small.

PATTERN STITCHES

ARROW PANEL (PANEL OF 15 STS)

Also see chart

Row 1: (RS) K5, k2tog, yo, k1, yo, ssk, k5.

Row 2 and all WS rows: Purl.

Row 3: K4, k2tog [k1, yo] 2 times, k1, ssk, k4.

Row 5: K3, k2tog, k1, yo, k3, yo, k1, ssk, k3.

Rows 7, 9, 11, and 13: K2, k2tog, k1, yo, k5, yo, k1, ssk, k2.

Row 14: Rep Row 2.

Rep Rows 1–14 for Arrow Panel.

STRAIGHT GARTER STITCH (GTR ST)

Knit every row.

CIRCULAR GARTER STITCH (GTR ST)

Rnd 1: Purl.

Rnd 2 Knit.

Rep Rnds 1 and 2 for Circular Gtr st.

ARROW LACE PATTERN (MULTIPLE OF 14 STS + 3)

Also see chart

Row 1: (RS) K3, *k3, k2tog, yo, k1, yo, ssk, k6; rep from * to end.

Row 2 and all WS rows: Purl.

Row 3: K3, *k2, k2tog, k1, [yo, k1] 2 times, ssk, k5; rep from * to end.

Row 5: K3, *k1, k2tog, k1, yo, k3, yo, k1, ssk, k4; rep from * to end.

Rows 7, 9, 11, and 13: K3, *k2tog, k1, yo, k5, yo, k1, ssk, k3; rep from * to end.

Row 15: K2, *yo, ssk, k9, k2tog, yo, k1; rep from * to last st, k1.

Row 17: K2, *yo, k1, ssk, k7, k2tog, k1, yo, k1; rep from * to last st, k1.

Row 19: K3, *yo, k1, ssk, k5, k2tog, k1, yo, k3; rep from * to end.

Rows 21, 23, 25, and 27: K3, *k1, yo, k1, ssk, k3, k2tog, k1, yo, k4; rep from * to end.

Row 28: Rep Row 2.

Rep Rows 1–28 for Arrow Lace patt.

INTERLUDE LACE SHRUG

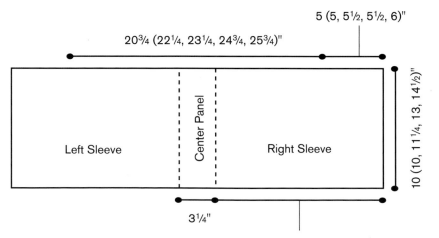

5 (5, 5½, 5½, 6)"

20¾ (22¼, 23¼, 24¾, 25¾)"

Left Sleeve

Center Panel

Right Sleeve

10 (10, 11¼, 13, 14½)"

3¼"

13¾ (14½, 15½, 16¼, 17¼)"

CENTER PANEL

With straight needles, CO 15 sts. (WS) Purl 1 row. (RS) Begin Arrow Panel; work even until pc meas approx 9 (9, 10¾, 11¾, 13½)" from beg, end after any WS row bet Rows 8 and 14; rep Rows 13 and 14 until pc meas 10 (10, 11¼, 13, 14½)" from beg, end after WS Row 14 of Arrow Panel. (RS) BO all sts loosely knitwise.

SLEEVES

CO 45 (45, 51, 59, 65) sts. (RS) Beg Gtr St; work even for 5 rows, end after a RS row. (WS) Purl 1 row. **Est Arrow Lace Patt:** (RS) Work 0 (0, 3, 0, 3) sts in St st, work 45 (45, 45, 59, 59) sts in Arrow Lace Patt, work 0 (0, 3, 0, 3) sts in St st. Work even until pc meas approx 12¾ (14, 14½, 15, 16¼)" from beg, end after any WS row bet 8 and 14 or 22 and 28. If you ended bet rows 8 and 14, rep Rows 13 and 14 until pc meas 13¾ (14½, 15½, 16¼, 17¼)" from beg; if you ended bet rows 22 and 28, rep Rows 27 and 28 until pc meas 13¾ (14½, 15½, 16¼, 17¼)" from beg, end after WS Row 14 or 28 of Arrow Lace Patt. (RS) BO all sts loosely knitwise.

FINISHING

Seam BO edges of sleeves to each side of center panel. PM on each edge of sleeve 5 (5, 5½, 5½, 6)" up from cuff. Fold pc in half lengthwise and seam each sleeve from the cuff to the marker. **Trim:** With circular needle and RS facing, beg in center of center panel at the CO edge, pick up and knit 37 (40, 42, 44, 46) sts evenly to the sleeve seam, pm, pick up and knit 74 (80, 84, 88, 92) sts evenly to the next sleeve seam, pm, pick up and knit 37 (40, 42, 44, 46) sts; pm for beg of rnd— 148 (160, 168, 176, 184) sts. **Begin Circular Gtr St and Dec Rnd:** * Work to 1 st before marker, p2tog, removing marker; rep from * 1 time, work to end—146 (158, 166, 174, 182) sts rem. Work even for 3 more rnds, end after a knit rnd. BO all sts loosely purlwise.

INTERLUDE LACE SHRUG

Arrow Panel Chart
(panel of 15 sts; 14-row rep)

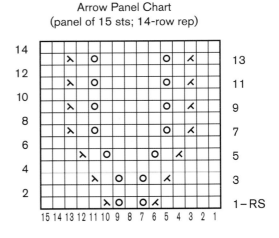

Arrow Lace Chart
(multiple of 14 sts + 3; 28-row rep)

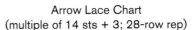

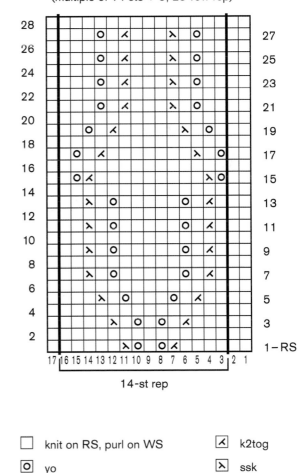

14-st rep

☐ knit on RS, purl on WS   ⤢ k2tog

◉ yo   ⤡ ssk

Silky Alpaca Lacy Scarf

SKILL LEVEL: INTERMEDIATE

SIZE

One size

FINISHED MEASUREMENTS

10" wide × 70" long

MATERIALS

Silky Alpaca Lace by Classic Elite

(70% alpaca, 30% silk; 50-gram ball = approx 460 yards)

• 2 balls 2425 Rosa Rugosa

Needles

• One pair size U.S. 4 (3.5 mm) **or size to obtain gauge**

• Tapestry needle

• Cable needle

GAUGE

19 sts and 35 rows = 4" in Lacy Cable pattern. *Take time to save time, check your gauge.*

PATTERN STITCHES

LACY CABLE PATTERN (MULTIPLE OF 16 STS)

Also, see chart

Rows 1, 5, and 9: (RS) Slip 1 st purlwise wyib, k2, yo, k2tog, k1, k2tog, [yo] 2 times, k2tog, k2, yo, *k2tog, k5, yo, k2tog, k1, k2tog, [yo] 2 times, k2tog, k2, yo; rep from * to last 4 sts, k2tog, k2.

Rows 2, 6, and 10: (WS) Slip 1 st purlwise wyif, k2, yo, k2tog, p2, (p1, k1) into double yo, p3, yo, k2tog, *p5, yo, k2tog, p2 (p1, k1) into double yo, p3, yo, k2tog; rep from * to last 2 sts, k2.

Row 3 and 7: Slip 1 st purlwise wyib, k2, yo, k2tog, k7, yo, *k2tog, k5, yo, k2tog, k7, yo; rep from * to last 4 sts, k2tog, k2.

Rows 4 and 8: Slip 1 st purlwise wyif, k2, yo, k2tog, p7, yo, k2tog, *p5, yo, k2tog, p7, yo, k2tog; rep from * to last 2 sts, k2.

Row 11: Slip 1 st purlwise wyib, k2, yo, k2tog, k7, yo, *k2tog, C4F, k1, yo, k2tog, k7, yo; rep from * to last 4 sts, k2tog, k2.

Row 12: Rep Row 4

Rep Rows 1–12 for Lacy Cable patt.

NOTE

One ball of yarn yields approx 46 reps of patt (552 rows).

GARTER STITCH (GTR ST)

Knit every row.

SCARF

Loosely CO 48 sts. **Beg Gtr St**: (RS) work 4 rows, end WS row. Change to Lacy Cable patt; work Rows 1–12 of Lacy Cable patt 50 times (600 rows), then Rows 1–10 once, end after WS Row 10 of Lacy Cable patt. Change to Gtr st; (RS) work 3 rows, end RS row. (WS) BO all sts loosely knitwise.

FINISHING

Wet block scarf to measurements.

Lacy Cable Chart
(multiple of 16 sts; 12-row rep)

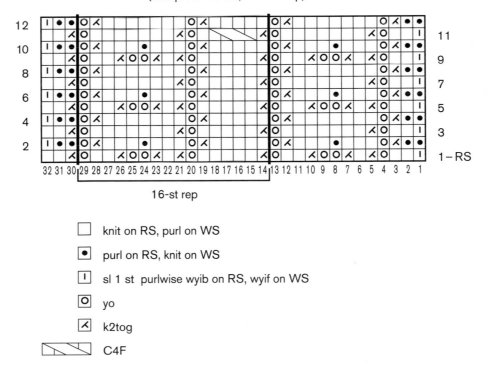

16-st rep

	knit on RS, purl on WS
•	purl on RS, knit on WS
I	sl 1 st purlwise wyib on RS, wyif on WS
O	yo
⋋	k2tog
⟋⟋	C4F

Fresco Lace Cowl

SIZE
One size

FINISHED MEASUREMENTS
11" wide; 44½" circumference

MATERIALS
Fresco by Classic Elite
(60% wool, 30% baby alpaca, 10% angora; 50-gram hank = approx 164 yards)
• 3 hanks 5322 Port Royale
Needles
• One 29" circular U.S. size 6 (4 mm) **or size to obtain gauge**
• Stitch marker

GAUGE
24 sts and 29 rows = 4" in Circular Lace pattern. *Take time to save time, check your gauge.*

PATTERN STITCH

CIRCULAR LACE PATTERN (MULTIPLE OF 16 STS)
Also see chart
Rnds 1–3: Knit
Rnd 4: (K1, yo) 3 times, (ssk) twice, s2kp, (k2tog) twice, yo, (k1, yo) twice.
Rnds 5–8: Rep Rnds 1–4.
Rnds 9–12: Rep Rnds 1–4.
Rnds 13–16; Rep Rnds 1–4.
Rnds 17–19: Knit
Rnd 20: S2kp, (k2tog) twice, yo, (k1, yo) 5 times, (ssk) twice.
Rnds 21–24: Rep Rnds 17–20.
Rnds 25–28: Rep Rnds 17–20.
Rnds 29–32: Rep Rnds 17–20.
Rep Rnds 1–32 for Circular Lace patt.

Circular Lace Chart
(multiple of 16 sts; 32-rnd rep)

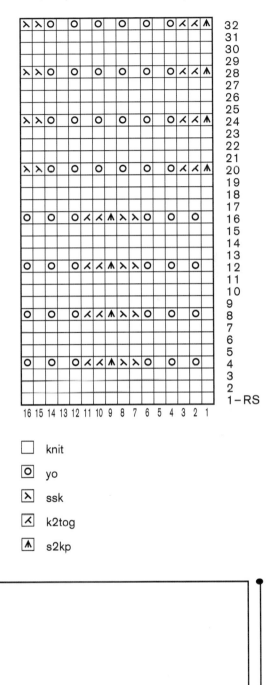

knit

☐ yo

ㅅ ssk

ㅅ k2tog

ㅅ s2kp

COWL

CO 256 sts. Join to work in-the-rnd being careful not to twist sts; pm for beg of rnd. *Beg Circular Lace Patt:* Work even until piece meas 11" from beg, end after even numbered rnd. BO all sts loosely in patt.

FINISHING

Block pc to required measurements.

11"

44½"

Princess Ascot

SIZE
One size

FINISHED MEASUREMENTS
34" long × 5" wide (at center back neck)

MATERIALS
Princess by Classic Elite
(40% merino, 28% viscose, 10% cashmere, 7% angora, 15% nylon; 50-gram hank = approx 150 yards)
- 1 hank Color A—3416 Natural
- 1 hank Color B—3468 Orange Attitude
- 1 hank Color C—3419 Precious Pink
- 1 hank Color D—3458 Royal Red
- 1 hank Color E—3428 Major Grey

Needles
- One pair each size U.S. 5 and 7 (3.75 and 4.5 mm)
- One set double-pointed needles size U.S. 5 (3.75 mm) **or size to obtain gauge**
- Stitch holder

GAUGE
20 sts and 28 rows = 4" in Garter Rib Patt using larger needles; 19 sts and 26 rows = 4" in Fair Isle Patt using larger needles. *Take time to save time, check your gauge.*

PATTERN STITCHES

GARTER ST (GTR ST)
Knit every row.

STOCKINETTE STITCH (ST ST)
Knit on the RS, purl on the WS.

FAIR ISLE PATTERN (MULTIPLE OF 6 STS + 3)
See chart.

1×1 RIB (MULTIPLE OF 2 STS + 3)
Row 1: (RS) K1, * k1, p1; rep from * to last 2 sts, k2.
Row 2: Knit the knits and purl the purls as they face you.
Rep Row 2 for 1 × 1 Rib.

GARTER RIB PATTERN
Row 1: (WS) P3, * k2, p2; rep from * to last 3 sts, p3.
Row 2: Knit
Rep Rows 1–2 for Garter Rib patt.

ASCOT

With Larger Needles and Color A, CO 27 sts. ***Beg Gtr St:***
Work 2 rows with Color A, 2 rows with Color B, 2 rows with
Color C. Change to St st and Color A, work 3 rows, end RS
row. Change to Fair Isle Patt and St st; Work 22 rows of Fair
Isle Patt, then work Rows 1–8 one more time. ***With Color A,
Work Dec Row (WS):*** P3tog, *p2tog; rep from * to end—13 sts
rem. ***Front of Casing:*** Change to smaller needles and 1 × 1 Rib;
work 18 rows. Place sts on holder. ***Back of Casing:*** With WS
facing, using smaller needles and Color A, starting 1 st in from
right edge and ending 1 st in from left edge, pick up and knit
11 sts in back of first row of rib sts. Change to 1 × 1 Rib;
work 17 rows.

Place sts on dpn. ***Casing Join:*** Return first set of sts to smaller
needle, ready to work a RS row. Hold both sides of casing, WS's
together, with dpn sts in back, RS of pc facing you, ready to
work a RS row. Join Row: (RS) K1, *k2tog (1 from needle and
1 from dpn held in back); rep from * to last st, end k1. ***Change
to Larger Needles and Work Inc Rows:*** (WS) *P1-f/b; rep
from * to end—26 sts on needles. Next row: (RS) K1-f/b, k24,
k1-f/b—28 sts. ***Begin Gtr Rib Patt:*** Work even in patt until pc
meas 15" from beg, end WS row. ***Dec row:*** (RS) * K2tog; rep
from * to end—14 sts rem. Change to smaller needles and dec
for rib; p2tog, *p1, k1; rep from * to last 2 sts, p2—13 sts rem.
Change to 1 × 1 Rib; work 16 rows. ***Change to Larger Needles
and Work Inc Rows:*** Next row (RS): * k1-f/b; rep from * to
end—26 sts. (WS) P12, p1-f/b, p13—27 sts. Change to St st;
work 3 rows. ***Begin Fair Isle Patt as Foll:*** Work Rows 19–22 of
chart, then work rows 1–22, then work Rows 1–4 once more.
Change to Gtr st; work 2 rows with Color C, work 2 rows with
Color B, work 2 rows with Color A. BO loosely in patt.

FINISHING

Block pc to measurements.

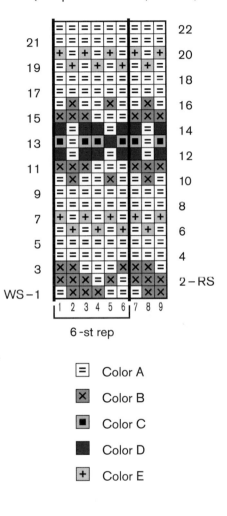

Fair Isle Chart
(multiple of 6 sts + 3; 22 rows)

6-st rep

=	Color A
✕	Color B
■	Color C
■	Color D
+	Color E

PRINCESS ASCOT

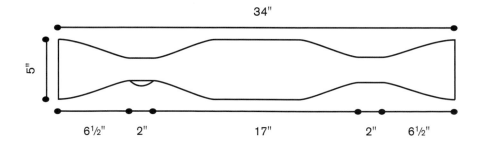

34"

5"

6½" 2" 17" 2" 6½"

ASCOT

With Larger Needles and Color A, CO 27 sts. **Beg Gtr St:**
Work 2 rows with Color A, 2 rows with Color B, 2 rows with
Color C. Change to St st and Color A, work 3 rows, end RS
row. Change to Fair Isle Patt and St st; Work 22 rows of Fair
Isle Patt, then work Rows 1–8 one more time. **With Color A,**
Work Dec Row (WS): P3tog, *p2tog; rep from * to end—13 sts
rem. **Front of Casing:** Change to smaller needles and 1 × 1 Rib;
work 18 rows. Place sts on holder. **Back of Casing:** With WS
facing, using smaller needles and Color A, starting 1 st in from
right edge and ending 1 st in from left edge, pick up and knit
11 sts in back of first row of rib sts. Change to 1 × 1 Rib;
work 17 rows.

Place sts on dpn. **Casing Join:** Return first set of sts to smaller
needle, ready to work a RS row. Hold both sides of casing, WS's
together, with dpn sts in back, RS of pc facing you, ready to
work a RS row. Join Row: (RS) K1, *k2tog (1 from needle and
1 from dpn held in back); rep from * to last st, end k1. **Change**
to Larger Needles and Work Inc Rows: (WS) *P1-f/b; rep
from * to end—26 sts on needles. Next row: (RS) K1-f/b, k24,
k1-f/b—28 sts. **Begin Gtr Rib Patt:** Work even in patt until pc
meas 15" from beg, end WS row. **Dec row:** (RS) * K2tog; rep
from * to end—14 sts rem. Change to smaller needles and dec
for rib; p2tog, *p1, k1; rep from * to last 2 sts, p2—13 sts rem.
Change to 1 × 1 Rib; work 16 rows. **Change to Larger Needles**
and Work Inc Rows: Next row (RS): * k1-f/b; rep from * to
end—26 sts. (WS) P12, p1-f/b, p13—27 sts. Change to St st;
work 3 rows. **Begin Fair Isle Patt as Foll:** Work Rows 19–22 of
chart, then work rows 1–22, then work Rows 1–4 once more.
Change to Gtr st; work 2 rows with Color C, work 2 rows with
Color B, work 2 rows with Color A. BO loosely in patt.

FINISHING

Block pc to measurements.

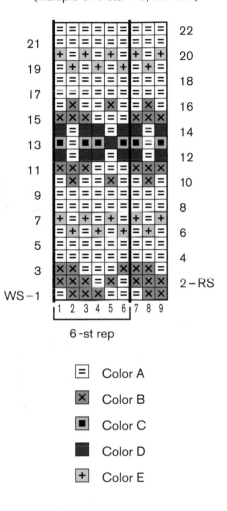

Fair Isle Chart
(multiple of 6 sts + 3; 22 rows)

6-st rep

☐ = Color A

☒ = Color B

◼ = Color C

⬛ = Color D

⊞ = Color E

PRINCESS ASCOT

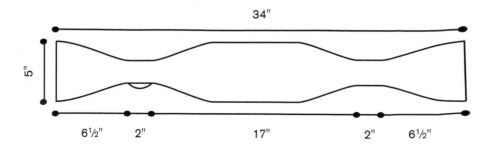

34"

5"

6½"   2"   17"   2"   6½"

ASCOT

With Larger Needles and Color A, CO 27 sts. **Beg Gtr St:**
Work 2 rows with Color A, 2 rows with Color B, 2 rows with
Color C. Change to St st and Color A, work 3 rows, end RS
row. Change to Fair Isle Patt and St st; Work 22 rows of Fair
Isle Patt, then work Rows 1–8 one more time. **With Color A,**
Work Dec Row (WS): P3tog, *p2tog; rep from * to end—13 sts
rem. **Front of Casing:** Change to smaller needles and 1 × 1 Rib;
work 18 rows. Place sts on holder. **Back of Casing:** With WS
facing, using smaller needles and Color A, starting 1 st in from
right edge and ending 1 st in from left edge, pick up and knit
11 sts in back of first row of rib sts. Change to 1 × 1 Rib;
work 17 rows.

Place sts on dpn. **Casing Join:** Return first set of sts to smaller
needle, ready to work a RS row. Hold both sides of casing, WS's
together, with dpn sts in back, RS of pc facing you, ready to
work a RS row. Join Row: (RS) K1, *k2tog (1 from needle and
1 from dpn held in back); rep from * to last st, end k1. **Change**
to Larger Needles and Work Inc Rows: (WS) *P1-f/b; rep
from * to end—26 sts on needles. Next row: (RS) K1-f/b, k24,
k1-f/b—28 sts. **Begin Gtr Rib Patt:** Work even in patt until pc
meas 15" from beg, end WS row. **Dec row:** (RS) * K2tog; rep
from * to end—14 sts rem. Change to smaller needles and dec
for rib; p2tog, *p1, k1; rep from * to last 2 sts, p2—13 sts rem.
Change to 1 × 1 Rib; work 16 rows. **Change to Larger Needles**
and Work Inc Rows: Next row (RS): * k1-f/b; rep from * to
end—26 sts. (WS) P12, p1-f/b, p13—27 sts. Change to St st;
work 3 rows. **Begin Fair Isle Patt as Foll:** Work Rows 19–22 of
chart, then work rows 1–22, then work Rows 1–4 once more.
Change to Gtr st; work 2 rows with Color C, work 2 rows with
Color B, work 2 rows with Color A. BO loosely in patt.

FINISHING

Block pc to measurements.

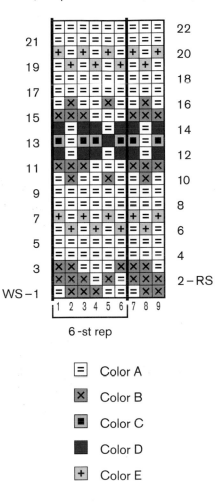

Fair Isle Chart
(multiple of 6 sts + 3; 22 rows)

6-st rep

☐= Color A

☒ Color B

▣ Color C

■ Color D

+ Color E

PRINCESS ASCOT

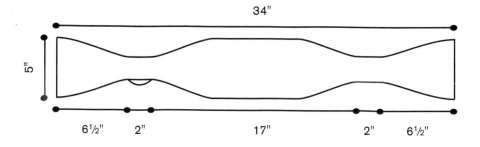

34"

5"

6½"   2"   17"   2"   6½"

Willoughby

SKILL LEVEL: INTERMEDIATE

SIZES
Average (Long)

FINISHED MEASUREMENTS
Approx 13" × 60 (72)" after blocking

MATERIALS
Marly by Classic Elite
(100% cashmere; 50-gram hank = approx 190 yards)
• 3 (4) balls 36 Khaki
Needles
• One pair size U.S. 8 (5 mm) **or size to obtain gauge**
• Blunt tapestry needle
• Waste yarn
• Blocking wires or T-pins

GAUGE
10 sts and 10 rows = 2" in Stole Lace pattern after blocking.
Take time to save time, check your gauge.

NOTES

1. This stole is worked as two separate halves—the first half is started from the center with a Provisional Cast-On, worked toward the edge, then trimmed with a knitted-on edging. The second half is worked directly from the Provisional Cast-On sts at center, for the same length as the first and then the knitted-on edging is added to this half.

2. If you have difficulty finding the recommended yarn, you may consider using Classic Elite's Fresco as a substitute.

PATTERN STITCHES

See charts

STOLE

Using Provisional Method, CO 57 sts. *Set-Up Row:* (RS) K6, k2tog, k2, yo, k1, yo, k1, ssk, k1, p1, k2tog, yo, k1, p1, k3, k2tog, ssk, [yo, k1] 3 times, yo, k2tog, ssk, k3, p1, k2tog, yo, k1, p1, k1, k2tog, k2, yo, k1, yo, k1, ssk, k1, yo, ssk, [yo] 2 times, k2tog, k1—58 sts. *Work Rows 2–8 of Stole Chart.* Rep rows 1–8 of Stole Chart 16 (20) more times. *Work Rows 1–8 of Corner Chart as Foll:* Chart is worked back and forth and joins to the live sts at end of shawl by knitting 1 edging st tog with

1 live stole st at the end of RS Rows 3 and 7. ***Work rows 1–8 of Edging Chart as Foll:*** Chart is worked back and forth and joins to the live sts at end of shawl by knitting 1 edging st tog with 1 live stole st at the end of every RS row. Work Rows 1–8 of Edging Chart 10 times total—18 sts; [18 sts rem; 9 live stole sts and 9 edging sts]. ***Work rows 1–8 of Corner Chart as Foll:*** Chart is worked back and forth and joins to the live sts at end of shawl slightly differently from before. At end of row 3, knit

1 edging st tog with 2 live stole sts by working a k3tog. Work all other rows as before—15 sts. ***Cont as foll:*** BO 3 edging sts—12 sts. Divide sts evenly onto 2 needles. Use Kitchener st to graft 6 live sts from edging to 6 rem live sts in row. To begin second half of stole, carefully remove Provisional Cast-On and place live sts on needle. Beg with Set-Up Row, working second half in the same manner as for first. Block stole to measurements.

WILLOUGHBY

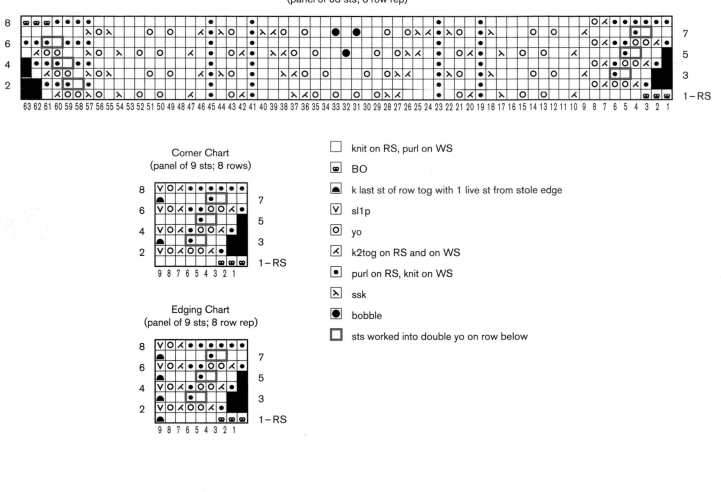

Stole Chart
(panel of 63 sts; 8 row rep)

Corner Chart
(panel of 9 sts; 8 rows)

Edging Chart
(panel of 9 sts; 8 row rep)

☐	knit on RS, purl on WS
⊠	BO
◣	k last st of row tog with 1 live st from stole edge
V	sl1p
O	yo
⌿	k2tog on RS and on WS
•	purl on RS, knit on WS
⟍	ssk
●	bobble
☐	sts worked into double yo on row below

Bridgewater

SIZE
One size

FINISHED MEASUREMENTS
42½" × 42½" after blocking

MATERIALS
Silky Alpaca Lace by Classic Elite
(70% alpaca, 30% silk; 50-gram ball = approx 460 yards)
• 4 balls 2403 Cloud Gray
Needles
• One 32" circular needle in size U.S. 5 (3.75 mm) **or size to obtain gauge**
• 8 stitch markers (1 in a different color for beg of rnd)
• Tapestry needle

GAUGE
21 sts and 21 ridges (42 rows) to 4" in Garter st after blocking. *Take time to save time, check your gauge.*

PATTERN STITCHES
See chart

NOTES
1. The Bridgewater Shawl is a simple, central square of Garter stitch knit on the bias, creating long diagonals across the center section, which is trimmed by a frame of horseshoe lace and finished off with a lacy knitted-on edge.

2. Starting from just one cast-on stitch, the biased square of Garter stitch is shaped through the use of simple increases and decreases at the beginning of each row. After the square is complete, stitches are picked up along the outer edge as you begin working in the round on the main lace motif, working simple increases at the four corners to continue a regular rate of growth. The shawl is finished with a knitted-on edging, worked sideways, which consumes one stitch from the circumference of shawl on every other round, slowly but steadily finishing off each side and eliminating any need for a bound-off edge.

SHAWL

With circular needle, CO 1 st. First Row: K1-f/b—2 sts. *Inc Row:* K1-f/b, knit to end of row—1 st inc'd. Rep inc row until 205 sts are on needle—102 Gtr ridges on RS. *Dec Row:* K2tog, knit to end of row—1 st dec'd. Rep Dec Row until 1 st rem on needle—102 Gtr ridges along each edge of square.

HORSESHOE LACE EDGING

With single live stitch on needle, begin picking up sts down 1 side of square by picking up and knitting 3 sts for every 2 ridges as follows: * pick up and knit 1 st from first ridge, pick up and knit 1 st each in the front and back of next ridge; rep from * to end. You will pick up 153 sts along first side of square.

After picking up 153 sts from first side of square, pm and rep along rem 3 sides; pm at each corner bet sets of 153 sts.

Use a marker in an alternate color to indicate beg of rnd— 612 sts on needle. Work Rnds 1–39 of Horseshoe Lace Chart.

EDGING

Note: Bracketed 10-st motif reps 15 times on each side of shawl. Lace Chart reps a total of 4 times on each rnd—1 time for each side of square. Inc'd sts at beg and end of Lace Chart occur EOR at the 4 corners of square—768 sts on needle after completion of Lace Chart; 192 sts bet each marked corner.

Remove beg-of-round marker. Slip next 2 sts purlwise wyib, replace marker, this indicates new BOR. *Set-Up Rnd:* * Knit until 2 sts rem before next marker, place new marker, k2, remove corner marker, k2, place new marker; rep from * 2 more times, knit until 4 sts rem before new beg of round, pm, k4.

There are now 4 sections of 4 sts indicated with pairs of markers at each corner of the square; 188 sts bet these sections. With dpn, use the Provisional Method to CO 13 sts. *Set-Up Row:* With needle holding the live Edging sts, p13 sts from

BRIDGEWATER

Horsehoe Lace Chart
(multiple of 10 sts + 3 inc'd to multiple of 10 sts + 2; 39 rnds)

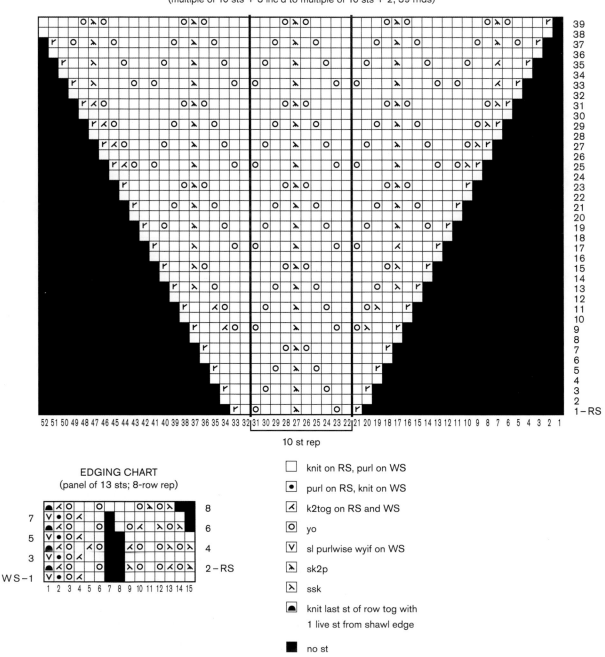

EDGING CHART
(panel of 13 sts; 8-row rep)

	knit on RS, purl on WS
•	purl on RS, knit on WS
⋌	k2tog on RS and WS
O	yo
V	sl purlwise wyif on WS
⋋	sk2p
⋌	ssk
◓	knit last st of row tog with 1 live st from shawl edge
■	no st

dpn; you now have 13 sts adjacent to your live shawl sts on the circular needle. Work Rows 2–8 of Edging Chart once. **Work Rows 1–8 of Edging Chart as Follows:** Rep 8 rows of Edging Chart, joining to outer edge of shawl as you go along (JS), until you reach the first marker. Work 4 corner sts as follows: Rows 1, 3, 4, 5, 7 and 8: As shown in Edging Chart. Rows 2 and 6: Work as shown in Edging Chart, but when you work JS, leave shawl st on needle after k2tog. You will work JS of next RS row into the same st. Essentially, you are attaching 2 RS rows to the same st in order to turn the corner. You will work 2 reps of Rows 1–8 of the Edging Chart over 4 marked corner sts. Rep Edging Chart as before around circumference of shawl, working each set of 4 corner sts in the same manner.

Note: Edging Chart will be worked over 13 sts on all rows; the last st of every RS row will be knit tog with 1 live st from the Horseshoe Lace Edging, attaching the edging as you go and eliminating need for a BO edge.

FINISHING

When you have consumed all live sts from circumference of shawl, break yarn leaving 8" tail. Use tapestry needle and Kitchener St to graft live edging sts tog with provisionally CO sts of edging with yarn tail. Weave in all ends. Block to preferred tension, pinning shawl to desired dimensions.

HORSESHOE LACE EDGING

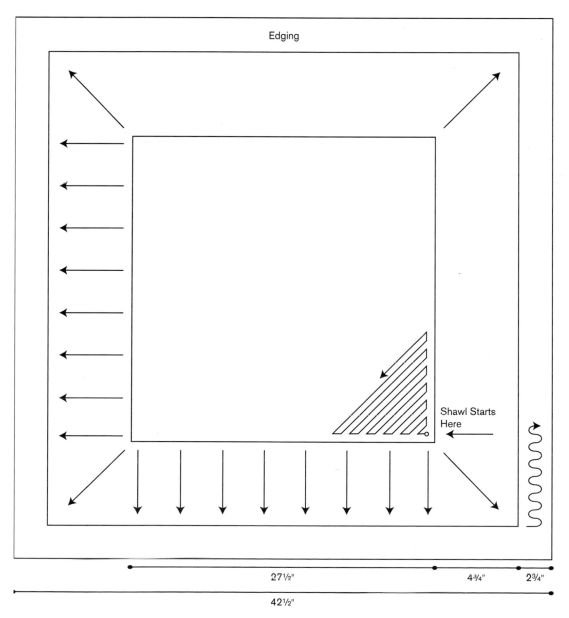

Martha Scarf

SKILL LEVEL: INTERMEDIATE

SIZE

One size

FINISHED MEASUREMENTS

12" wide and 66" long

MATERIALS

Liberty Wool by Classic Elite

(100% washable wool; 50-gram ball = approx 122 yards)

• 5 balls 7896 Sunset

Needles

• One pair size U.S. 7 (4.5 mm) **or size to obtain gauge**

• Removable stitch marker

GAUGE

19 sts and 38 rows = 4 in Garter stitch; each square measures approx 4 1/2" by 4 1/2". *Take time to save time, check your gauge.*

PATTERN STITCHES

SQUARE A (PANEL OF 41 STS, DEC'D TO 1 ST)

Rows 1, 3, 5, and 7: (WS) Knit.

Row 2 and all RS rows except Row 40: (RS) Knit to 1 st before center st marker, rem marker, sk2p, replace marker into sk2p st, knit to end—2 sts dec'd.

Rows 9 and 11: Purl.

Rows 13, 15, and 17: Knit.

Row 19: Purl.

Rows 21 and 23: Knit.

Rows 25 and 27: Purl.

Row 29: Knit.

Rows 31, 33, 35, 37, and 39: Purl.

Row 40: Sk2p—1 st rem.

Work Rows 1–40 for Square A.

SQUARE B (PANEL OF 41 STS, DEC'D TO 1 ST)

Row 1 and all WS rows: (WS) Knit.

Row 2 and all RS rows except Row 40: Knit to 1 st before center st marker, rem marker, sk2p, replace marker into sk2p st, knit to end—2 sts dec'd.

Row 40: Sk2p—1 st rem.

Work Rows 1–40 for Square B.

NOTE

Slip first st of every row purlwise wyib.

SCARF

TIER ONE

Use the Cable Method to CO 41 sts. Place removable marker into center st. (WS) Begin Square A; work 40 rows, end after RS row 40 of patt—1 st rem. Do not turn; do not break yarn. Rotate square 90° clockwise, then with RS still facing, pick-up and knit 20 sts evenly along side edge of previous square, use the Cable Method to CO 20 sts—41 sts. (WS) Beg Square B; work 40 rows, end after RS row 40 of patt—1 st rem. Fasten off.

TIER TWO, FIRST SQUARE

Use the Cable Method to CO 21 sts. With RS of previous tier facing, pick-up and knit 20 sts from the right edge of square A. (WS) Beg Square B; work 40 rows, end after RS row 40 of patt—1 st rem. Do not turn; do not break yarn. *Second Square:* Rotate work 90° clockwise, then with RS still facing, pick-up and knit 19 sts evenly along side edge of just completed square, 1 st at corner, then 20 sts along side edge of the second square from the previous tier—41 sts. (WS) Beg Square A; work 40 rows, end after RS row 40 of patt—1 st rem. Do not turn; do not break yarn. *Third Square:* Rotate work 90° clockwise, then with RS still facing, pick-up and knit 20 sts evenly along side edge of just completed square, use the Cable Method to CO 20 sts—41 sts. (WS) Beg Square B; work 40 rows, end after RS row 40 of patt—1 st rem. Fasten off.

TIERS THREE-NINE

Rep Tier Two.

TIER TEN

Rep the first and second squares as for tier two. Fasten off after second square. Do not work the third square.

FINISHING

Block pc to measurements.

Martha Diagram

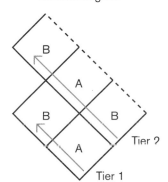

Molly

SIZE
One size

FINISHED MEASUREMENTS
5¼" wide and 72" long, unstretched

MATERIALS
Liberty Wool by Classic Elite
(100% washable wool; 50-gram ball = approx 122 yards)
• 4 balls 7897 Sunrise
Needles
• One pair size U.S. 7 (4.5 mm) **or size to obtain gauge**

GAUGE
32 sts = 5¼"; 20 rows = 4" in Ruffle pattern. *Take time to save time, check your gauge.*

NOTE

When working short rows, work each wrapped tog with its wrap.

SCARF

CO 32 sts.
Rows 1 and 2: P10, (k2, p2) 3 times, k10.

Rows 3 and 4 (short rows): K6, wrap and turn, p6, turn, k9, wrap and turn, p9, turn, k6, wrap and turn, p6, turn, P10, (k2, p2) 3 times, k10.

Rep these 4 rows until piece meas 72" or desired length end after Row 4. BO all sts. Weave in ends. Block if desired.

Sassafras

SKILL LEVEL: INTERMEDIATE

SIZES
Small (Medium, Large)

FINISHED MEASUREMENTS
17" deep and 40 (50½, 56)" circumference

MATERIALS
Magnolia by Classic Elite
(70% merino, 30% silk; 50-gram ball = approx 120 yards)
• 6 (8, 9) balls 5448 Forget-Me-Not
Needles
• One 29" circular size U.S. 6 (4 mm) **or size to obtain gauge**
• Stitch marker
• Cable needle

GAUGE
27 sts and 33 rows = 4" in Cable pattern. *Take time to save time, check your gauge.*

NOTE
Size shown is small.

PATTERN STITCHES
CIRCULAR CABLE PATTERN (MULTIPLE OF 9 STS)
Also see chart
Rnd 1: *P4, kw2, k4; rep from * around.

Rnds 2, 4, and 6: *P4, sl1p wyib dropping second wrap, k4; rep from * around.

Rnds 3 and 5: *P4, C5Fw2; rep from * around.

Rnd 7: *P4, C5F; rep from * around.

Rnd 8: *K5, p4; rep from * around

Rnd 9: *K4, kw2, p4; rep from * around.

Rnds 10, 12, and 14: *K4, sl1p wyib dropping second wrap, p4; rep from * around.

Rnds 11 and 13: *C5Bw2, p4; rep from * around.

Rnd 15: *C5B, p4; rep from * around.

Rnd 16: *P4, k5; rep from * around.

Rep Rnds 1–16 for Cable patt.

Cable Chart
(multiple of 9 sts; 16-rnd rep)

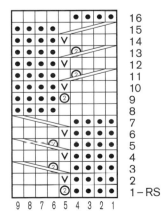

□ knit

• purl

Ⓢ kw2

Ⅴ sl1p wyib, dropping second wrap

⟋ C5Fw2

⟋ C5F

⟍ C5Bw2

⟍ C5B

COWL

CO 270 (342, 378) sts. Join, being careful not to twist sts; pm for beg of rnd. Beg St st; work 3 rnds. Change to Cable patt; work 136 rnds, end after Rnd 8 of Cable patt. Change to St st; work 3 rnds. BO all sts.

Royal Empress Shawl

SKILL LEVEL: EASY

SIZE
One size

FINISHED MEASUREMENTS
8¹⁄₂" at widest point, 55¹⁄₂" long, unstretched

MATERIALS
Magnolia by Classic Elite
(70% merino, 30% silk; 50-gram ball = approx 120 yards)
• 4 balls 5485 Persian Orange

Needles
• One pair size U.S. 8 (5 mm)
• One 32" circular size U.S. 8 (5 mm) **or size to obtain gauge**
• Removable stitch markers

GAUGE
20 sts and 30 rows = 4" in Garter stitch, after blocking. *Take time to save time, check your gauge.*

SCARF

CO 2 sts. *Beg Gtr St and Shape Scarf, Inc Row:* (RS) K1-f/b, work to end—1 st inc'd. Rep inc row every fourth row 27 more times—30 sts. (WS) Work 3 rows even, end after a WS row—112 rows/56 ridges from beg. Place a removable marker into fabric at beg of RS row. Work even for 192 rows/96 ridges from marker, end after a WS row. Pm into fabric at beg of RS row. *Dec Row:* (RS) Ssk, work to end—1 st dec'd. Rep dec row every fourth row 27 more times—2 sts rem. (WS) Work 3 rows even, end after a WS row. Next Row: k2tog and fasten off—112 rows/56 ridges from marker.

EDGING

With RS facing and circular needle, beg at CO point, pick up and knit 1 st for each ridge (st is picked up in bet ridges) as follows: working along selvedge edge of scarf, where sts were increased, pick up and knit 56 sts to marker, remove marker, pick up and knit 96 sts to next marker, remove marker, then pick up and knit 56 sts to BO point—208 sts. Cont working back and forth in rows. *Inc Row:* (WS) P1, * yo, p1; rep from * to end—415 sts. Change to St st; (RS) work 12 rows even, end after a WS row. Change to Gtr st; (RS) work 3 rows, end after a RS row. (WS) BO all sts loosely, knitwise.

FINISHING

Block pc to measurements.

Silverbell Shrug

SIZES

Extra Small (Small, Medium, Large, Extra Large)

FINISHED MEASUREMENTS

35½ (38¼, 42¼, 47¼, 50)" bust

MATERIALS

Magnolia by Classic Elite

(70% merino, 30% silk; 50-gram ball = approx 120 yards)

• 5 (6, 7, 8, 9) balls 5475 Granite

Needles

• One 32" circular size U.S. 6 (4 mm)

• One set double-pointed needles size U.S. 6 (4 mm) **or size to obtain gauge**

• Stitch holders or waste yarn

• Stitch marker (optional)

• One ⅝" button

GAUGE

22 sts and 32 rows = 4" in Reverse Stockinette stitch. *Take time to save time, check your gauge.*

NOTE

Shrug is worked from the top down. Sleeves are knit in the round. Size shown is extra small.

PATTERN STITCHES

LEAF YOKE PATTERN (MULTIPLE OF 8 STS + 5, INC'D TO MULTIPLE OF 14 STS + 5)

Also see chart

Rows 1–8: Knit.

Row 9 (WS): K5, *p3, k5; rep from *.

Row 10: P5, *k1, [yo, k1] 2 times, p5; rep from *.

Row 11: K5, *p5, k5; rep from *.

Row 12: P5, *k2, yo, k1, yo, k2, p5; rep from *.

Row 13: K5, *p7, k5; rep from *.

Row 14: P5, *k3, yo, k1, yo, k3, p5; rep from *.

Row 15, 17, 19, and 21: K5, *p9, k5; rep from *.

Row 16 and 18: P5, *k9, p5; rep from *.

Row 20: P4, *yo, ssk, k7, k2tog, yo, p3; rep from * to last st, p1.

Row 22: P5, *yo, ssk, k5, k2tog, yo, p5; rep from *.

Row 23: K5, *k1, p7, k6; rep from *.

Row 24: P5, *p1, yo, ssk, k3, k2tog, yo, p6; rep from *.

Row 25: K5, *k2, p5, k7; rep from *.

Row 26: P5, *p2, yo, ssk, k1, k2tog, yo, p7; rep from *.

Row 27: K5, *k3, p3, k8; rep from *.

Row 28: P5, *p3, yo, sk2p, yo, p8; rep from *.

Row 29: Knit.

Row 30: Purl.

Work Rows 1–30 for Leaf Yoke patt.

2 × 2 RIB (MULTIPLE OF 4 STS)

Row 1: (WS) P3, *k2, p2; rep from * to last st, p1.

Row 2: Knit the knit sts and purl the purl sts as they face you.

Rep Rows 1–2 for 2 × 2 Rib.

YOKE

With circular needle, CO 101 (109, 109, 117, 117) sts. Beg Leaf Yoke Patt; work 30 rows—173 (187, 187, 201, 201) sts. Change to Rev St st; (WS) work 8 (8, 10, 10, 12) rows, end after a RS row. **Shape Yoke, Inc Row 1:** (WS) K1 (0, 3, 2, 0), *k3 (3, 2, 2, 2), yo, k3 (3, 3, 3, 2), yo; rep from * to last 4 (1, 4, 4, 1) sts, knit to end—229 (249, 259, 279, 301) sts. (RS) Work 13 (15, 17, 19, 21) rows even, end after a RS row. **Inc Row 2:** (WS) K2 (1, 4, 3, 1), *k3 (3, 2, 2, 2), yo, k3, yo; rep from * to last 5 (2, 5, 1, 5) sts, knit to end—303 (331, 359, 389, 419) sts. Work even until pc meas 8 (8½, 9¼, 9¾, 10½)" from beg, end after a RS row. **Divide for Armholes:** (WS) Work 43 (47, 54, 61, 66) sts for left

front, sl next 62 (68, 71, 73, 80) unworked sts to st holder or waste yarn for sleeve, use the Backward Loop Method to CO 6 sts for underarm, work next 93 (101, 109, 121, 127) sts for back, sl next 62 (68, 71, 73, 80) unworked sts to st holder or waste yarn for sleeve, use Backward Loop Method to CO 6 sts for underarm, work to end for right front—191 (207, 229, 255, 271) sts for body. Cont working back and forth on body sts only.

BODY

Work even in Rev St st until pc meas 6 (6½, 7, 8, 9)" from armhole divide, end after a RS row. Change to Gtr st; (WS) work 8 rows, end after a RS row. (WS) BO all sts loosely, knitwise.

SLEEVES

Sl 62 (68, 71, 73, 80) sleeve sts from holder to dpn with sts divided as evenly as possible. Join yarn, then pick up and knit 6 sts from body underarm CO sts—68 (74, 77, 79, 86) sts. PM for beg of rnd, if desired. Join, being careful not to twist sts. Beg Circular Rev St st; work even until pc meas 1" from pick-up rnd. Change to Circular Gtr st; work 8 rnds, end after a knit rnd. BO all sts loosely, purlwise.

FINISHING

Buttonhole Band: With circular needle and RS facing, beg at lower edge of right front, pick up and knit 84 (90, 93, 98, 102) sts evenly along right front edge. (WS) Begin 2 × 2 Rib; work 2 rows, end after a RS row. **Buttonhole Row:** (WS) P3, yo, k2tog, work to end as est. (RS) Work 3 more rows even, end after a RS row. (WS) BO all sts in rib. **Button Band:** With circular needle and RS facing, beg at neck edge of left front, cont as for buttonhole band, omitting the buttonhole. Block pc to measurements. Sew button to button band opposite buttonhole.

SILVERBELL SHRUG

Leaf Yoke Chart
(multiple of 8 sts + 5 inc'd to 14 + 5; 30 rows)

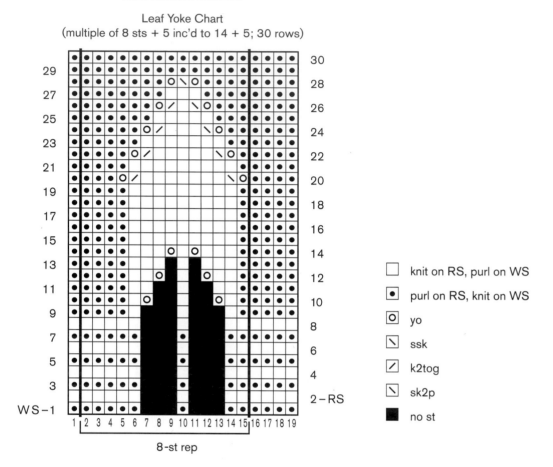

☐	knit on RS, purl on WS
•	purl on RS, knit on WS
○	yo
＼	ssk
／	k2tog
＼	sk2p
■	no st

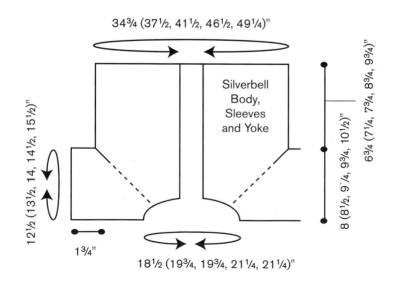

34¾ (37½, 41½, 46½, 49¼)"

12½ (13½, 14, 14½, 15½)"

1¾"

Silverbell Body, Sleeves and Yoke

6¾ (7¼, 7¾, 8¾, 9¾)"

8 (8½, 9¼, 9¾, 10½)"

18½ (19¾, 19¾, 21¼, 21¼)"

Cinder Scarf

SIZE
One size

FINISHED MEASUREMENTS
6" wide × 64" long

MATERIALS
Ariosa by Classic Elite
(90% extrafine merino, 10% cashmere; 50-gram ball = approx 87 yards)
• 6 balls 4803 Foam
Needles
• One pair size U.S. 11 (8 mm) **or size to obtain gauge**
• Cable needle

GAUGE
32 sts and 16 rows = 4" in Cable pattern. *Take time to save time, check your gauge.*

PATTERN STITCHES

CABLE PATTERN (OVER 48 STS)
Also see chart
Row 1 and all WS rows: (WS) *K2, p2; rep from * across.
Rows 2, 4, 6, 10, 12, and 14: (RS) *K2, p2; rep from * across.
Row 8: Cable, [k2, p2] 4 times, cable across.
Row 16: [K2, p2] 4 times, cable, [k2, p2] 4 times across.
Rep Rows 1–16 for Cable patt.

SCARF

CO 48 sts. (WS) Beg Cable patt; work even until a total of 15 reps of Cable patt have been worked, then work Rows 1–15 once more. BO all sts in rib.

FINISHING

Block pc to measurements being careful not to flatten ribbing.

CINDER SCARF

Cable Pattern
(multiple of 48 sts; 16-row rep)

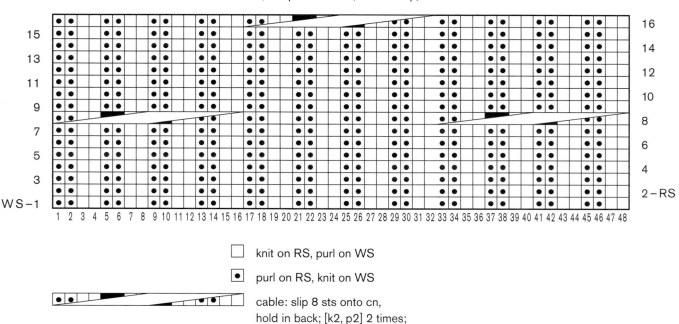

knit on RS, purl on WS

purl on RS, knit on WS

cable: slip 8 sts onto cn,
hold in back; [k2, p2] 2 times;
[k2, p2] 2 times from cn.

Encore Capelet

SIZES

Extra Small (Small, Medium, Large, Extra Large, 2X Large)

FINISHED MEASUREMENTS

$38^{1}/_2$ ($40^{1}/_2$, $42^{1}/_2$, $44^{1}/_2$, $47^{3}/_4$, $50^{3}/_4$)"; to fit bust measurements $31^{1}/_4$ ($33^{1}/_4$, $35^{1}/_4$, $37^{1}/_2$, $40^{1}/_2$, $43^{1}/_2$)"

MATERIALS

Fresco by Classic Elite

(60% wool, 30% baby alpaca, 10% angora; 50-gram hank = approx 164 yards)

• 3 (3, 3, 4, 4, 5) hanks 5315 Pea Pod

Needles

• One each 16" and 24" circular size U.S. 6 (4 mm) **or size to obtain gauge**

• Stitch markers

• Cable needle

GAUGE

27 sts and 32 rows = 4" in 6 × 1 Cable Rib. *Take time to save time, check your gauge.*

NOTES

1. A cabled capelet knit in the round from the bottom up. Size shown is extra small.

2. Row gauge is important for proper fit.

PATTERN STITCHES

CIRCULAR 6 × 1 CABLE RIB (MULTIPLE OF 7 STS)

Also see chart

Rnds 1–4: *K6, p1; rep from * around.

Rnd 5: C6F, p1; rep from * around.

Rnds 6–8: Rep Rnd 1.

Rep Rnds 1–8 for 6 × 1 Cable Rib.

CIRCULAR 5 × 1 CABLE RIB (MULTIPLE OF 6 STS)

Also see chart

Rnds 1–5: *K5, p1; rep from * around.

Rnd 6: *C5F, p1; rep from * around.

Rnd 7: Rep Rnd 1.

Rep Rnds 1–7 for 5 × 1 Cable Rib.

CIRCULAR 4 × 1 CABLE RIB (MULTIPLE OF 5 STS)

Also see chart

Rnds 1–4: *K4, p1; rep from * around.

Rnd 5: *C4F, p1; rep from * around.

Rnd 6: Rep Rnd 1.

Rep Rnds 1–6 for 4 × 1 Cable Rib.

CIRCULAR 3 × 1 CABLE RIB (MULTIPLE OF 4 STS)

Also see chart

Rnds 1–3: *K3, p1; rep from * around.

Rnd 4: *C3F, p1; rep from * around.

Rnd 5: Rep Rnd 1.

Rep Rnds 1–5 for 3 × 1 Cable Rib.

CIRCULAR 2 × 1 CABLE RIB (MULTIPLE OF 3 STS)

Also see chart

Rnds 1–2: *K2, p1; rep from * around.

Rnd 3: *C2F, p1; rep from * around.

Rnd 4: Rep Rnd 1.

Rep Rnds 1–4 for 2 × 1 Cable Rib.

6 × 1 Cable Rib Chart
(multiple of 7 sts; 8-rnd rep)

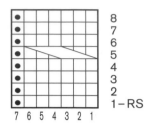

5 × 1 Cable Rib Chart
(multiple of 6 sts; 7-rnd rep)

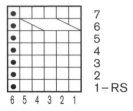

4 × 1 Cable Rib Chart
(multiple of 5 sts; 6-rnd rep)

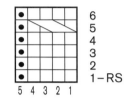

3 × 1 Cable Rib Chart
(multiple of 4 sts; 5-rnd rep)

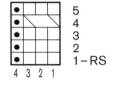

2 × 1 Cable Rib Chart
(multiple of 3 sts; 4-rnd rep)

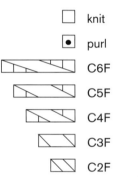

☐	knit
⊡	purl
▨	C6F
▨	C5F
▨	C4F
▨	C3F
▨	C2F

YOKE

With 24" circular, CO 259 (273, 287, 301, 322, 343) sts. Join, being careful not to twist sts; pm for beg of rnd. Begin 6 × 1 Cable Rib; work 29 (29, 29, 29, 37, 37) rnds, end after Rnd 5. **Shape Yoke, Dec Rnd 1:** *K2, k2tog, k2, p1; rep from * — 222 (234, 246, 258, 276, 294) sts rem. Change to 5 × 1 Cable Rib; work 27 (27, 27, 27, 27, 34) rnds, end after Rnd 6. **Dec Rnd 2:** *K2, k2tog, k1, p1; rep from * —185 (195, 205, 215, 230, 245) sts rem. Change to 4 × 1 Cable Rib; work 17 (17, 23, 23, 23, 17) rnds, end after Rnd 5. **Change to 16" Circular and Dec Rnd 3:** *K1, k2tog, k1, p1; rep from * —148 (156, 164, 172, 184, 196) sts rem. Change to 3 × 1 Cable Rib; work 14 (14, 14, 19, 14, 14) rnds, end after Rnd 4. **Dec Rnd 4:** *K1, k2tog, p1; rep from * around—111 (117, 123, 129, 138, 147) sts rem. Change to 2 × 1 Cable Rib; work 7 (11, 7, 7, 7, 11) rnds, end after Rnd 3. BO all sts in patt.

FINISHING

Block pc to measurements.

21¼ (22¼, 23½, 24½, 26¼, 28)"

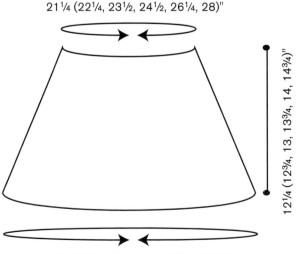

12¼ (12¾, 13, 13¾, 14, 14¾)"

38¼ (40½, 42½, 44½, 47¾, 50¾)"

Gloriole Scarf

SIZE
One size

FINISHED MEASUREMENTS
11½" wide × 73" long, excluding fringe

MATERIALS
Giselle by Classic Elite
(64% kid mohair, 25% wool, 11% nylon; 50-gram ball = approx 230 yards)
• 3 balls 4109 Moroccan Teal
Needles
• One pair size U.S. 7 (4.5 mm) **or size to obtain gauge**
• Crochet hook, size U.S. H/8 (5 mm)
• Stitch markers

GAUGE
16 sts and 22 rows = 4" in Zigzag Line patterns. *Take time to save time, check your gauge.*

PATTERN STITCHES

ZIGZAG LINE A (MULTIPLE OF 7 STS)
Also see chart
Row 1 and all WS rows: Purl.
Row 2: *K1, yo, k2tog, k4; rep from * across.
Row 4: *K2, yo k2tog, k3; rep from * across.
Row 6: *K3, yo, k2tog, k2; rep from * across.
Row 8: *K4, yo, k2tog, k1; rep from * across.
Row 10: *K5, yo, k2tog; rep from * across.
Row 12: *K4, ssk, yo, k1; rep from * across.
Row 14: *K3, ssk, yo, k2; rep from * across.
Row 16: *K2, ssk, yo, k3; rep from * across.
Row 18: *K1, ssk, yo, k4; rep from * across.
Row 20: *Ssk, yo, k5; rep from * across.
Rep rows 1–20 for Zigzag Lines A.

ZIGZAG LINE B (MULTIPLE OF 7 STS)
Also see chart
Row 1 and all WS rows: Purl.
Row 2: *K4, ssk, yo, k1; rep from * across.
Row 4: *K3, ssk, yo, k2; rep from * across.
Row 6: *K2, ssk, yo, k3; rep from * across.
Row 8: *K1, ssk, yo, k4; rep from * across.
Row 10: *Ssk, yo, k5; rep from * across.
Row 12: *K1, yo, k2tog, k4; rep from * across.
Row 14: *K2, yo k2tog, k3; rep from * across.
Row 16: *K3, yo, k2tog, k2; rep from * across.
Row 18: *K4, yo, k2tog, k1; rep from * across.
Row 20: *K5, yo, k2tog; rep from * across.
Rep Rows 1–20 for Zigzag Lines B.

SCARF

CO 46 sts. **Est Patt:** (WS) P1 (edge st, keep in St st throughout), work 21 sts in Zigzag Lines A, pm, work 2 sts in St st, pm, work 21 sts in Zigzag Lines B, p1 (edge st, keep in St st throughout). Work as est until 20 reps of Zigzag Line Patts have been completed, end after WS Row 1 of the foll rep. (RS) BO all sts knitwise.

FINISHING

Fringe: Cut 12 strands yarn, each 12" long. With WS of scarf facing, insert crochet hook from WS to RS at CO edge of the scarf, fold strands of yarn in half and pull folded end of fringe through, then pull the 2 ends of fringe through the loop and tighten. Cont attaching fringe in this manner 9 more times across CO edge, spacing evenly. Rep on BO end of scarf. Block to measurements.

Zigzag Line B Chart
(multiple of 7 sts; 20-row rep)

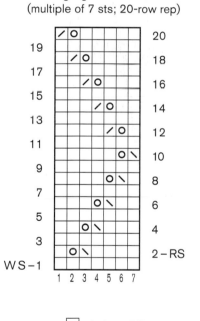

Zigzag Line A Chart
(multiple of 7 sts; 20-row rep)

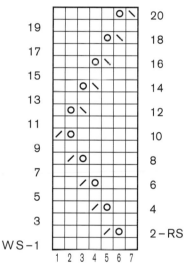

☐ knit on RS, purl on WS

☐ O yo

☐ ╱ k2tog

☐ ╲ ssk

Halo Cowl

SIZE

One size

FINISHED MEASUREMENTS

41" circumference; 18" tall

MATERIALS

Giselle by Classic Elite

(64% kid mohair, 25% wool, 11% nylon;
50-gram ball = approx 230 yards)

• 2 balls 4156 Navarra

Needles

• One 32" circular size U.S. 7 (4.5 mm)
or size to obtain gauge

GAUGE

15 sts and 24 rows = 4" in Stockinette stitch.
Take time to save time, check your gauge.

YOKE

With 2 strands of yarn held tog, CO 154 sts. Join, being careful not to twist sts; pm for beg of rnd. Beg St st; using only 1 strand of yarn, work even until pc meas 18" from beg. Join second strand of yarn and BO all sts.

FINISHING

With WS facing, block pc to measurements.

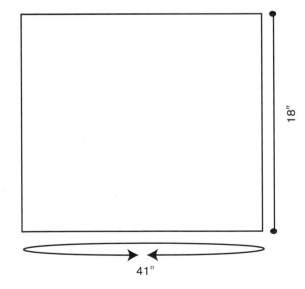

18"

41"

Corona
Pullover

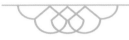

SIZES

Extra Small (Small, Medium, Large, Extra Large)

FINISHED MEASUREMENTS

31 (35, 39, 43, 47)" bust

MATERIALS

Giselle by Classic Elite

(64% kid mohair, 25% wool, 11% nylon; 50-gram ball =
approx 230 yards)

- 4 (4, 4, 5, 5) balls 4120 Darro River

Needles

- One 29 (32, 32, 32, 40)" circular size U.S. 7 (4.5 mm)
- One set double-pointed needles size U.S. 7 (4.5 mm) **or size
  to obtain gauge**
- Stitch markers
- Stitch holders or waste yarn

GAUGE

16 sts and 24 rows = 4" in Stockinette stitch. *Take time to save time,
check your gauge.*

NOTE

Size shown is small.

PATTERN STITCH

CIRCULAR 2 × 2 RIB (MULTIPLE OF 4 STS)

Rnd 1: *P2, k2; rep from * around.
Rnd 2: Knit the knit sts and purl the purl sts as they face you.
Rep Rnd 2 for 2 × 2 rib.

NOTE

For strength, CO is worked with 2 strands of yarn held
together. Work all other rows with a single strand of yarn.

YOKE

With 2 strands of yarn held tog, CO 84 (88, 84, 84, 88) sts.
Arrange needle so that yarn tail is at the needle's left point
and sts aren't twisted. Join sts as follows: Wyib, sl first st on
RH needle tip to LH needle, bring yarn to front bet needles,
sl first 2 sts from LH needle to RH needle, bring yarn to back
bet needles, sl first st on RH needle to LH needle. With single
strand, begin St st; *k28 (32, 34, 36, 38) sts, pm, k14 (12, 8, 6,
6), pm; rep from * once more. *Shape Yoke, Inc Rnd:* *K2,
yo, work to 2 sts before next marker, yo, k2, sl marker; rep
from * 3 more times—8 sts inc'd. Work 1 rnd even. Rep the
previous 2 rnds 6 (7, 11, 14, 18) more times—140 (152, 180,
204, 240) sts. *Eyelet Rnd:* *K2, yo, ssk, work to 4 sts before
next marker, k2tog, yo, k2, sl marker; rep from * 3 more times.
Work 1 rnd even. Work yoke inc rnd—8 sts inc'd. Work 1 rnd
even. Rep the previous 4 rnds 6 (6, 5, 4, 3) more times—196
(208, 228, 244, 272) sts; 56 (62, 70, 76, 84) sts each back
and front; 42 (42, 44, 46, 52) sts each sleeve. Work even, if

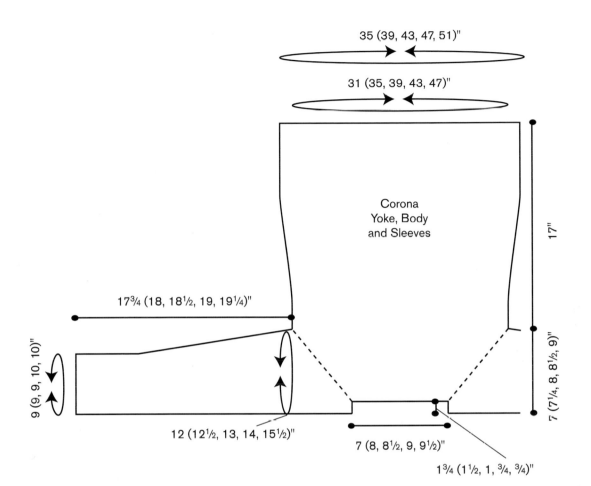

35 (39, 43, 47, 51)"

31 (35, 39, 43, 47)"

Corona
Yoke, Body
and Sleeves

17"

17¾ (18, 18½, 19, 19¼)"

9 (9, 9, 10, 10)"

7 (7¼, 8, 8½, 9)"

12 (12½, 13, 14, 15½)"

7 (8, 8½, 9, 9½)"

1¾ (1½, 1, ¾, ¾)"

necessary, until yoke meas 7 (7¼, 8, 8½, 9)" from beg. ***Divide for Sleeves and Body***: *Work 56 (62, 70, 76, 84) sts for back, remove marker, sl next 42 (42, 44, 46, 52) sts for left sleeve to st holder or waste yarn, remove marker, use Backward-Loop Method to CO 3 (4, 4, 5, 5) sts for underarm, pm for side, CO 3 (4, 4, 5, 5) more sts for underarm; rep from * once more (the second marker placed marks new beg of round)— 124 (140, 156, 172, 188) sts rem for body.

BODY

Work even until pc meas 2¼" from divide. ***Shape Sides, Inc Rnd:*** *K2, m1, work to 2 sts before next marker, m1, k2; rep from * once more—4 sts inc'd. Rep side inc rnd every 18th rnd 3 more times—140 (156, 172, 188, 204) sts. Work even until pc meas 12" from divide. Change to 2 × 2 Rib; work even until pc meas 17" from divide. Join a second strand of yarn and with 2 strands of yarn held tog, BO all sts in rib.

SLEEVE

Divide 42 (42, 44, 46, 52) held sleeve sts as evenly as possible over 3 dpns. Pick up and knit 3 (4, 4, 5, 5) sts to center of underarm of body, pm for beg of round, pick up and knit 3 (4, 4, 5, 5) more sts, then join to beg working in the rnd—48 (50, 52, 56, 62) sts. Begin St st; work 6 rnds even. ***Shape Sleeve, Dec Rnd:*** K2, ssk, work to last 4 sts, k2tog, k2—2 sts dec'd. Rep sleeve dec rnd every 6th rnd 0 (0, 0, 0, 4) times, every 8th rnd 0 (0, 2, 0, 6) times, every 10th rnd 0 (4, 5, 6, 0) times, then every 12th rnd 5 (2, 0, 1, 0) times—36 (36, 36, 40, 40) sts. Work even until pc meas 12¾ (13, 13½, 14, 14¼)" from beg. Change to 2 × 2 Rib; work even until pc meas 17¾ (18, 18½, 19, 19¼)" from underarm. Join second strand of yarn and with 2 strands of yarn held tog, BO all sts in rib.

FINISHING

Block pc lightly to measurements. Weave in ends.

Schooner Shawl

SIZE

One size

FINISHED MEASUREMENTS

Approx 60" wide × 31¾" long

MATERIALS

Inca Alpaca by Classic Elite

(100% baby alpaca; 50-gram hank = approx 109 yards)

• 5 hanks 1135 Cala Cala Moss

Needles

• 24" circular needle size U.S. 8 (5 mm) **or size to obtain gauge**

GAUGE

14 sts and 26 rows = 4" in Shawl pattern. *Take time to save time, check your gauge.*

NOTE

A shawl knit from the bottom up. The border is knit last and attached to the shawl by picking up stitches as you work. The piece is knit back and forth in rows with a circular needle to accommodate the large number of stitches.

PATTERN STITCHES

SET-UP PATTERN (PANEL OF 2 STS INC'D TO 11 STS)

Also see chart

Row 1: (RS) K1, yo, k1—3 sts.

Row 2: P1, k1, p1.

Row 3: K1, yo, p1, yo, k1—5 sts.

Row 4: P2, k1, p2.

Row 5: K1, yo, k1, p1, k1, yo, k1—7 sts.

Row 6: [P1, k1] 3 times, p1.

Row 7: K1, yo, [p1, k1] 2 times, p1, yo, k1—9 sts.

Row 8: P2, [k1, p1] 3 times, p1.

Row 9: K1, yo, [k1, p1] 3 times, k1, yo, k1—11 sts.

Row 10: [P1, k1] 5 times, p1.

Work Rows 1–10 for Set-Up patt.

SHAWL PATTERN (MULTIPLE OF 8 STS + 3)

Also see chart

Row 1: (RS) K1, yo, *p1, yo, ssk, k1, p1, k1, k2tog, yo; rep from * to last 2 sts, p1, yo, k1—multiple of 8 sts + 5.

Row 2: P2, k1, *[p3, k1] 2 times; rep from * to last 2 sts, p2.

Row 3: K1, yo, k1, *p1, k1, yo, ssk, p1, k2tog, yo, k1; rep from * to last 3 sts, p1, k1, yo, k1—multiple of 8 sts + 7.

Row 4: *P1, k1; rep from * to last st, p1.

Row 5: K1, yo, p1, k1, *p1, k1, p1, yo, sk2p, yo, p1, k1; rep from * to last 4 sts, p1, k1, p1, yo, k1—multiple of 8 sts + 1.

Row 6: P2, k1, p1, k1, *p1, k1, p3, k1, p1, k1; rep from * to last 4 sts, p1, k1, p2.

Row 7: K1, yo, k1, p1, k1, *[p1, k1] 2 times, yo, ssk, p1, k1; rep from * to last 5 sts, [p1, k1] 2 times, yo, k1—multiple of 8 sts + 3.

Row 8: Rep Row 4.

Row 9: K1, yo, p1, yo, ssk, k1, *p1, k1, k2tog, yo, p1, yo, ssk, k1; rep from * to last 6 sts, p1, k1, k2tog, yo, p1, yo, k1—multiple of 8 sts + 5.

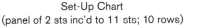

Shawl Chart
(multiple of 8 sts + 3; 16-row rep)

8-st rep

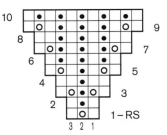

Set-Up Chart
(panel of 2 sts inc'd to 11 sts; 10 rows)

Row 10: P2, k1, *p3, k1; rep from * to last 2 sts, p2.

Row 11: K1, yo, k1, p1, k1, yo, ssk, *p1, k2tog, yo, k1, p1, k1, yo, ssk; rep from * to last 7 sts, p1, k2tog, yo, k1, p1, k1, yo, k1—multiple of 8 sts + 7.

Row 12: Rep Row 4.

Row 13: K1, yo, [p1, k1] 2 times, p1, yo, *sk2p, yo, [p1, k1] 2 times, p1, yo; rep from * to last st, k1—multiple of 8 sts + 1.

Row 14: P1, *[p1, k1] 3 times, p2; rep from * to end.

Row 15: K1, yo, [k1, p1] 3 times, k1, *yo, ssk, [p1, k1] 3 times; rep from * to last st, yo, k1—multiple of 8 sts + 3.

Row 16: Rep Row 4.

Rep Rows 1–16 for Shawl patt.

EDGE PATTERN (ANY NUMBER OF STS)

Row 1: (RS) K1, yo, knit to last st, yo, k1—2 sts inc'd.

Row 2: Knit.

Rep Rows 1 and 2 for Edge patt.

BORDER PATTERN (PANEL OF 17 STS)

Also see chart

Row 1: (RS) Knit the eyelet tog with the first st, k2, [yo, p2tog] 2 times, yo, k1-tbl, k2tog, p1, ssk, k1-tbl, yo, k3.

Row 2: K3, p3, k1, p3, k2, [yo, p2tog] 2 times, k1, wyif insert RH needle into the next eyelet hole along the selvedge edge from the RS to the WS, turn.

Rows 3–4: Rep Rows 1 and 2.

Row 5: Knit the eyelet tog with the first st, k2, [yo, p2tog] 2 times, yo, k1-tbl, yo, k2tog, p1, ssk, yo, k4—panel of 18 sts.

Row 6: K4, p2, k1, p4, k2, [yo, p2tog] 2 times, k1, wyif insert RH needle into the next eyelet hole along the selvedge edge from the RS to the WS, turn.

Row 7: Knit the eyelet tog with the first st, k2, [yo, p2tog] 2 times, yo, k1-tbl, k1, k1-tbl, yo, sk2p, yo, k5—panel of 19 sts.

Row 8: K5, p7, k2, [yo, p2tog] 2 times, k1, wyif insert RH needle into the next eyelet hole along the selvedge edge from the RS to the WS, turn.

Row 9: Knit the eyelet tog with the first st, k2, [yo, p2tog], yo, k1-tbl, k3, k1-tbl, yo, k7—panel of 21 sts.

Row 10: BO 4 sts knitwise (1 loop rem on RH needle), k2, p7, k2, [yo, p2tog] 2 times, k1, wyif insert RH needle into the next eyelet hole along the selvedge edge from the RS to the WS, turn—panel of 17 sts.

Rep Rows 1–10 for Border patt.

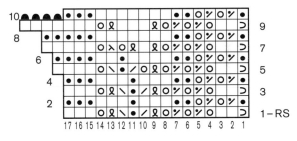

Border Chart
(panel of 17 sts; 10-row rep)

□	knit on RS, purl on WS
•	purl on RS, knit on WS
⊙	yo
＼	ssk
／	k2tog
⅄	sk2p
⅄	p2tog
⅄	k1-tbl
▲	BO

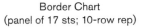

⅂ with WS facing, wyif, insert RH needle into next eyelet hole along selvedge edge from the RS to the WS, turn; knit the eyelet tog with the first st

MAIN TRIANGLE

CO 2 sts. (RS) Beg Set-Up Patt; work for 10 rows—11 sts. Change to Shawl Patt; work 160 rows (10 reps), end after WS row 16—171 sts. Change to Edge Patt; work 5 rows, end after RS row 1—177 sts. (WS) BO all sts knitwise. Do not break yarn; leave 1 loop on needle.

BORDER

Use Knitted Method to CO 1 st, then use the Cable Method to CO 15 more sts—17 sts. (WS) Purl 1 row, wyif insert RH needle into the first eyelet hole along the selvedge edge from the RS to the WS, turn. (RS) Begin Border patt; work border patt along selvedge edge until there are only 2 eyelet holes rem before the point (17 reps). **Turn Point:** Cont to work Border patt, working 2 times each into the 2 eyelet holes before the point, 3 times into the point eyelet, then 2 times each into the 2 eyelet holes after the point. Resume working once in each eyelet to end of shawl, end after WS Row 10. (RS) BO all sts knitwise.

FINISHING

Block pc to measurements, taking extra care to smooth the curve of the point.

SCHOONER SHAWL

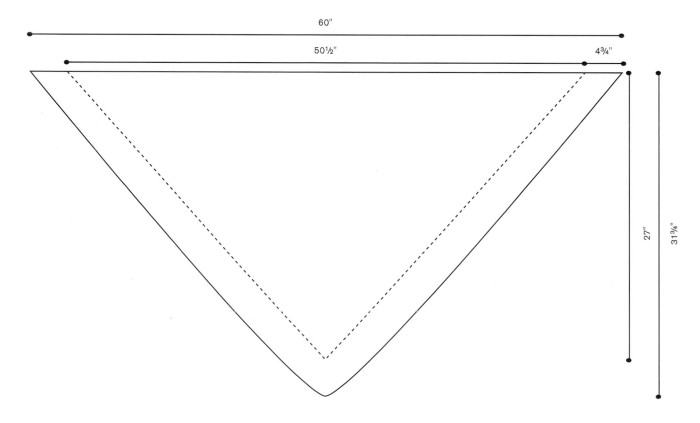

Vino Cowl

SKILL LEVEL: INTERMEDIATE

SIZE
One size

FINISHED MEASUREMENTS
35" circumference; 19³/₄" long

MATERIALS
Kumara by Classic Elite
(85% extrafine merino, 15% baby camel; 50-gram ball = approx 128 yards)
• 5 balls 5795 Thai Purple
Needles
• One 24" circular each size U.S. 8, 9, and 10 (5, 5.5 and 6 mm) **or size to obtain gauge**
• Stitch markers

GAUGE
16 sts in Ostrich Plume pattern = 3¹/₂" and 32 rows in Ostrich Plume pattern = 5³/₄" with medium needles. *Take time to save time, check your gauge.*

NOTE
The piece is shaped by short rows and by changing needle size.

PATTERN STITCHES

CIRCULAR CARTRIDGE RIB (MULTIPLE OF 5 STS)
Also see chart
Rnd 1: *K1, p1, k3; rep from * around.
Rnd 2: *P3, k2; rep from * around.
Rep Rnds 1 and 2 for Cartridge Rib.

CIRCULAR OSTRICH PLUME PATTERN (MULTIPLE OF 16 STS)
Also see chart
Rnds 1–3, 5–7, 9–11, 13–15, 17–18, 21–22, 25–26, and 29–30: Knit.
Rnds 4, 8, 12, and 16: *[K1, yo] 3 times, [ssk] 2 times, sk2p, [k2tog] 2 times, [yo, k1] 2 times, yo; rep from * around.
Rnds 19, 23, 27, and 31: *Remove marker, sl 1 st from RH needle to LH needle, replace marker, return slipped st to RH needle, knit to next marker; rep from * around.
Rnds 20, 24, 28, and 32: *Sk2p, [k2tog] 2 times, [yo, k1] 5 times, yo, [ssk] 2 times; rep from * around.
Rep Rnds 1–32 for Ostrich Plume Patt.

COWL

With largest needles, CO 160 sts. Join, being careful not to twist sts; pm for beg of rnd. Beg Cartridge Rib; work 9 rnds even. Change to Ostrich Plume patt; pm every 16 sts to easily see patt reps. Work 34 rnds even, ending after rnd 2 of patt.

Shape Cowl with Short Rows: (RS) K40, wrap and turn; (WS) slip 1 st purlwise wyif, p80, wrap and turn; (RS) slip 1 st purlwise wyib, k40. Cont with RS facing, beg with rnd 3 of Ostrich Plume Patt, work 8 rnds even, hiding wraps as they appear, ending after rnd 10 of patt. Change to medium needles; cont as est for 8 more rnds, ending after rnd 18 of patt. Rep short rows as before. Cont with RS facing, beg with rnd 19 of Ostrich Plume Patt, work 16 rnds even, ending after rnd 2 of patt. Rep from * once more changing to smallest needle after Rnd 10. Work 1 more rnd, ending after Rnd 3 of patt. Change to Cartridge Rib; work 9 rnds even. BO all sts in patt.

FINISHING

Block pc to measurements.

VINO COWL

Ostrich Plume Chart
(multiple of 16 sts; 32-rnd rep)

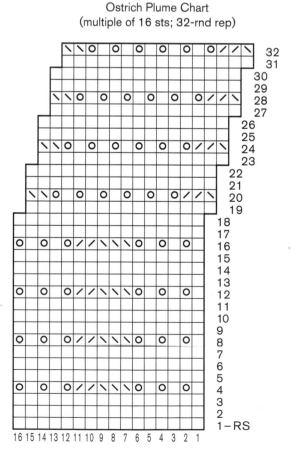

Cartridge Rib Chart
(multiple of 5 sts; 2-rnd rep)

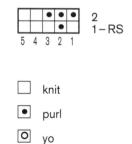

	knit
●	purl
○	yo
╲	ssk
╲	sk2p
╱	k2tog

Courtyard Scarf

SKILL LEVEL: INTERMEDIATE

SIZE
One size

FINISHED MEASUREMENTS
11" wide × 64" long

MATERIALS
Lush by Classic Elite
(50% angora, 50% wool; 50-gram hank = approx 123 yards)
• 5 hanks 4432 Peony
Needles
• One pair size U.S. 8 (5 mm) **or size to obtain gauge**
• Cable needle
• Stitch markers

GAUGE
20 sts and 24 rows= 4" in Cable Ladder pattern. *Take time to save time, check your gauge.*

PATTERN STITCHES

RIGHT EDGE (PANEL OF 7 STS)
Also see chart
Row 1: (RS) Slip 1 st purlwise wyib, k2, yo, sk2p, yo, k1.
Row 2: P5, k2.
Rep Rows 1 and 2 for Right Edge.

CABLE LADDER PATTERN (MULTIPLE OF 13 STS + 2)
Also see chart
Row 1: (RS) P2, *k1, [yo, k2tog] 2 times, p1, k5, p2; rep from * to end.
Rows 2 and 4: K2, *p4, k2, p5, k2; rep from * to end.
Row 3: P2, *k1, [yo, k2tog] 2 times, p2, k4, p2; rep from * to end.
Row 5: P2, *k1, [yo, k2tog] 2 times, p2, C4B, p2; rep from * to end.
Rows 6–9: Rep Rows 2–5.
Rows 10 and 11: Rep Rows 2 and 3.
Row 12: K2, *p5, k1, p5, k2; rep from * to end.
Row 13: P2, *k5, p1, [ssk, yo] 2 times, k1, p2; rep from * to end.
Rows 14 and 16: K2, *p5, k2, p4, k2; rep from * to end.
Row 15: P2, *k4, p2, [ssk, yo] 2 times, k1, p2; rep from * to end.
Row 17: P2, *C4F, p2, [ssk, yo] 2 times, k1, p2; rep from * to end.
Rows 18–21: Rep Rows 14–17

Rows 22 and 23: Rep Rows 14–15.
Row 24: Rep Row 12.
Rep rows 1–24 for Cable Ladder patt.

LEFT EDGE (PANEL OF 7 STS)
Also see chart
Row 1: (RS) K1, yo, sk2p, yo, k3.
Row 2: Slip 1 st purlwise wyib, k1, p5.
Rep Rows 1 and 2 for Left Edge.

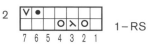

Left Edge Chart
(panel of 7 sts; 2-row rep)

Right Edge Chart
(panel of 7 sts; 2-row rep)

Cable Ladder Chart
(multiple of 13 sts + 2; 24-row rep)

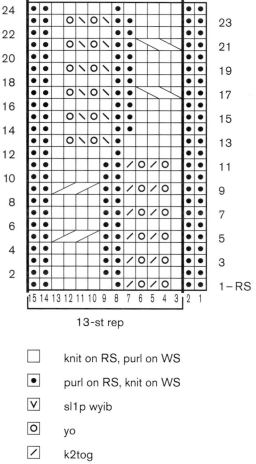

13-st rep

☐ knit on RS, purl on WS

▣ purl on RS, knit on WS

Ⅴ sl1p wyib

Ⓞ yo

╱ k2tog

╲ ssk

⅄ sk2p

▱ C4B

▱ C4F

SCARF

CO 55 sts. **Lower Edge:** (WS) Knit 1 row. (RS) Work 7 sts in
Right Edge, pm, *yo, k2tog; rep from * to last 6 sts, work last
6 sts as for Left Edge skipping the first k1. (WS) Work 7 sts in
Left Edge, pm, knit to the last 7 sts, sl marker, work to end in
Right Edge. **Est Patt:** (RS) Work 7 sts in Right Edge, sl marker,
work 41 sts in Cable Ladder patt, sl marker, work 7 sts in Left
Edge. Work even as est until pc meas approx 63½" from beg,
end after RS Row 11 or 23 of Cable Ladder Patt. **Top Edge:**
(WS) Work 7 sts in Right Edge, remove marker, knit to last
7 sts, remove marker, work 7 sts in Left Edge. (RS) Work 7 sts
in Right Edge, *yo, k2tog; rep from * to last 6 sts, work last
6 sts as for Left Edge skipping the first k1. (WS) BO all sts
purlwise.

FINISHING

Block pc to measurements.

Birch Leaf Shawl

SIZE
One size

FINISHED MEASUREMENTS
42" wide × 23" long

MATERIALS
Montera by Classic Elite
(50% llama, 50% wool; 100-gram hank = approx 127 yards)
• 5 hanks 3874 Sycamore
Needles
• One 40" circular size U.S. 10½ (6.5 mm) **or size to obtain gauge**
• Stitch markers

GAUGE
13 sts and 20 rows = 4" in Leaf Lace Pattern stretched. *Take time to save time, check your gauge.*

NOTE
A shawl worked from the top edge down to the center tip.

PATTERN STITCHES

FOUNDATION PATTERN (PANEL OF 10 STS INC'D TO 38 STS)
Also see chart

Row 1: (RS) *K2, yo, k1, yo, k2, pm; rep from * once more—14 sts.

Row 2 and all WS rows: K2, p to 2 sts before marker, k2, sl marker, k2, p to last 2 sts, k2.

Row 3: *K2, yo, k3, yo, k2; rep from * once more—18 sts.

Row 5: *K2, yo, k5, yo, k2; rep from * once more—22 sts.

Row 7: *K2, yo, k1, k2tog, yo, k1, yo, ssk, k1, yo, k2; rep from * once more—26 sts.

Row 9: *K2, yo, k1, k2tog, [k1, yo] 2 times, k1, ssk, k1, yo, k2; rep from * once more—30 sts.

Row 11: *K2, yo, k1, k2tog, k2, yo, k1, yo, k2, ssk, k1, yo, k2; rep from * once more —34 sts.

Row 13: *K2, yo, k1, k2tog, k3, yo, k1, yo, k3, ssk, k1, yo, k2; rep from * once more—38 sts.

Row 14: Rep Row 2.

Work Rows 1–14 for Foundation Patt.

LEAF LACE PATTERN (MULTIPLE OF 10 STS + 18 INC'D TO MULTIPLE OF 10 STS + 38)
Also see chart

Row 1: (RS) **[K2, yo] twice, k1, yo, *ssk, k5, k2tog, yo, k1, yo; rep from * to 4 sts before marker, k2, yo, k2, sl marker; rep from ** once more—8 sts inc'd.

Row 2 and all WS rows: K2, p to 2 sts before marker, k2, sl marker, k2, p to last 2 sts, k2.

Row 3: **K2, yo, k1, k2tog, k1, [yo, k1] twice, ssk, *k3, k2tog, [k1, yo] 2 times, k1, ssk; rep from * to 3 sts before marker, k1, yo, k2, sl marker; rep from ** once more—4 sts inc'd.

Row 5: **K2, yo, k1, k2tog, k2, yo, k1, yo, k2, ssk, *k1, k2tog, k2, yo, k1, yo, k2, ssk; rep from * to last 3 sts, k1, yo, k2; rep from ** once more—4 sts inc'd.

Row 7: **K2, yo, k1, k2tog, k3, yo, k1, yo, k3, *sk2p, k3, yo, k1, yo, k3; rep from * to 5 sts before marker, ssk, k1, yo, k2; rep from ** once more—4 sts inc'd.

Row 8: Rep Row 2.

Rep Rows 1–8 for Leaf Lace Patt.

SHAWL

CO 10 sts. (RS) Beg Gtr st; work 2 rows even. Change to Foundation patt; (RS) work 14 rows—38 sts. Change to Leaf Lace patt; (RS) work until pc meas approx 23" from beg, end after RS Row 7 of ninth rep of Leaf Lace patt— 218 sts. (WS) BO all sts knitwise.

FINISHING

Block pc to measurements.

BIRCH LEAF SHAWL

Foundation Chart
(panel of 10 sts inc'd to 38; 14 rows)

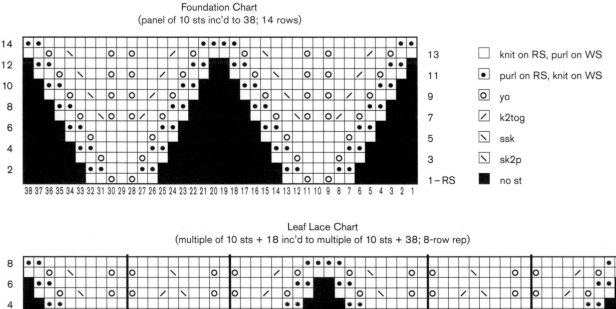

☐	knit on RS, purl on WS
•	purl on RS, knit on WS
⊙	yo
╱	k2tog
╲	ssk
╲	sk2p
■	no st

Leaf Lace Chart
(multiple of 10 sts + 18 inc'd to multiple of 10 sts + 38; 8-row rep)

10-st rep   10-st rep

186

Creek Cowl

SKILL LEVEL: EASY

SIZE

One size

FINISHED MEASUREMENTS

13" long × 93" circumference

MATERIALS

Moorland by Classic Elite

(42% fine merino wool, 23% baby alpaca, 19% mohair, 16% acrylic; 50-gram ball = approx 147 yards)

• 5 balls 2548 Blue Jay

NEEDLES

• 36" or longer circular size U.S. 7 (4.5 mm)
• One crochet hook size U.S. G/6 (4 mm)
  or size to obtain gauge
• Stitch marker

GAUGE

18 sts and 26 rows = 4" in Circular Stockinette stitch. *Take time to save time, check your gauge.*

NOTE

If you have difficulty finding the recommended yarn, you may consider using Classic Elite's Magnolia as a substitute.

COWL

CO 420 sts. Join, being careful not to twist sts; pm for beg of rnd. Beg St st; work even until pc meas 12" from beg. BO all sts loosely. Do not fasten off. Slip live loop onto crochet hook.

FINISHING

Crochet Edging: With crochet hook and RS facing, beg with live loop, and work along BO edge, *[sc, ch3, sc] in next st, sk 2 sts; rep from * around, sl st into first sc to join. Fasten off. Join yarn with a sl st to CO edge, rep edging as for BO edge. Block to measurements.

Sarsparilla Shawl

SIZE

One size

FINISHED MEASUREMENTS

Approx 59" wide × 30½" long

MATERIALS

Portland Tweed by Classic Elite

(50% virgin wool, 25% alpaca, 25% viscose; 50-gram ball = approx 120 yards)

• 5 balls 5025 Rosewater

Needles

• One 32" circular size U.S. 10½ (6.5 mm)

• Two double-pointed needles size U.S. 9 (5.5 mm) **or size to obtain gauge**

• Two stitch markers

• Cable needle

• Blocking wires (optional)

GAUGE

12 sts and 23 rows = 4" in Garter stitch very stretched and blocked.
Take time to save time, check your gauge.

PATTERN STITCH

CABLE PANEL (PANEL OF 7 STS)

Also see chart

Rows 1 and 5: (RS) P1, k6.

Row 2 and all WS rows: P6, k1.

Row 3: P1, C6F.

Row 6: Rep Row 2.

Rep Rows 1–6 for Cable Panel.

SHAWL

Using circular needle, CO 5 sts. *(RS) Beg Gtr St, and Set-Up Row:* (RS) [K1, yo] 2 times, pm, k1, pm, [yo, k1] 2 times—9 sts. (WS) Knit 1 row. *Shape Shawl, Inc Row:* (RS) K1, yo, work to marker, yo, sl marker, k1, sl marker, yo, work to last st, yo, k1—4 sts inc'd. Rep Inc Row EOR 51 more times—217 sts. (WS) Work 1 row even. Keep sts on needle, cont to work trim.

TRIM

Trim is worked back and forth over a total of 12 sts and on every RS row 1 st from the shawl and 1 st from the body are worked tog as a p2tog to join the trim to the shawl.) With RS facing, use Cable Method to CO 12 sts—229 sts. *Shape Trim, Dec Row:* (RS) Work 4 sts in St st, work 7 sts in Cable Panel, p2tog (1 st from trim and 1 st from shawl), turn. (WS) Slip 1 st purlwise wyib, work to end as est. Rep the previous 2 rows 216 more times—12 sts rem, end after WS row 2 of Cable Panel. (RS) Work 2 rows even, end after row 4 of Cable Panel.

FINISHING

Change to Dpn and Release Fringe: K4, drop these 4 sts off RH needle; *k2, k2tog-tbl, sl these 3 sts from RH needle to LH needle—1 st dec'd; rep from * 4 more times—3 sts rem. Unravel the 4 dropped sts to create the fringe. *Attached I-Cord Edging:* Holding dpn in RH, use left end of needle to pick up and knit 1 st into yo along selvedge edge of shawl—4 sts. Slip sts to RH end of needle. **K2, k2tog-tbl, pick up 1 st into yo along edge of shawl, sl sts to RH end of needle; without turning the work, rep from ** across edge of shawl picking up sts in yo's twice in each yo across. BO all sts. Thread blocking wires through fringe along fringe edges and into yo's along attached I-Cord edge, and stretch pc to its fullest extent. Pin blocking wires to hold shape and steam pc.

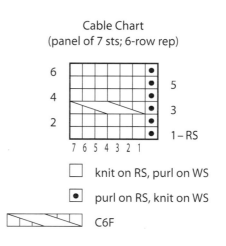

Cable Chart
(panel of 7 sts; 6-row rep)

☐ knit on RS, purl on WS

▣ purl on RS, knit on WS

▱ C6F

Sonata Cowl

SIZE
One size

FINISHED MEASUREMENTS
30" circumference at top edge; approx 22" long

MATERIALS
Waterlily by Classic Elite
(100% extrafine merino; 50-gram ball = approx 90 yards)
• 8 balls 1925 Abbey Road
Needles
• One 29" circular size U.S. 13 (9 mm) **or size to obtain gauge**
• Removable stitch markers

GAUGE
Two 8-st reps = 6" in Zig Zag Lace #2 with 2 strands of yarn held together. ***Take time to save time, check your gauge.***

NOTE
A double-stranded, lace cowl worked in the round.

PATTERN STITCHES

ZIGZAG LACE #1 (MULTIPLE OF 8 STS)
Also see chart
Rnd 1: *K2, [yo] twice, k4, k2tog; rep from *.
Rnds 2, 4, 6, and 8: Knit, dropping extra yo's off needle as they appear.
Rnd 3: *K3, [yo] twice, k3, k2tog; rep from *.
Rnd 5: *K4, [yo] twice, k2, k2tog; rep from *.
Rnd 7: *K5, [yo] twice, k1, k2tog; rep from *.
Rnd 9: *K6, [yo] twice, k2tog; rep from *.
Rnds 10, 12, 14, 16, and 18: Knit, dropping extra yo's off needle as they appear, remove marker, slip 1 st purlwise wyib, replace marker.
Rnd 11: *K4, [yo] twice, k2, ssk; rep from *.

Rnd 13: *K3, [yo] twice, k3, ssk; rep from *.
Rnd 15: *K2, [yo] twice, k4, ssk; rep from *.
Rnd 17: *K1, [yo] twice, k5, ssk; rep from *.
Rnd 19: [yo] twice, k6, ssk; rep from *.
Rnd 20: Rep Rnd 2.
Rep Rnds 1–20 for Zigzag Lace #1.

ZIGZAG LACE #2 (MULTIPLE OF 8 STS)
Also see chart
Work same as Zigzag Lace #1 but work single yo's in place of double yo's. There is no extra wrap to drop on even-numbered rnds.

Zigzag Lace #1 Chart
(multiple of 8 sts; 20 rnds)

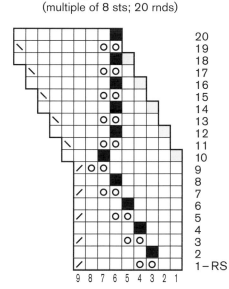

20
19
18
17
16
15
14
13
12
11
10
9
8
7
6
5
4
3
2
1 – RS

9 8 7 6 5 4 3 2 1

Zigzag Lace #2 Chart
(multiple of 8 sts; 20 rnds)

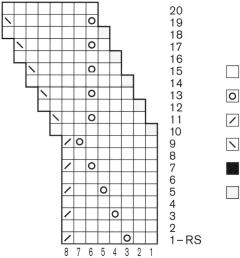

20
19
18
17
16
15
14
13
12
11
10
9
8
7
6
5
4
3
2
1 – RS

8 7 6 5 4 3 2 1

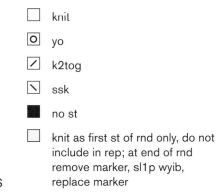

	knit
○	yo
／	k2tog
＼	ssk
■	no st

knit as first st of rnd only, do not include in rep; at end of rnd remove marker, sl1p wyib, replace marker

NOTE

Piece is worked in the rnd using a double strand of yarn throughout.

BODY

With 2 strands of yarn held tog, CO 80 sts. Join, being careful not to twist sts; pm for beg of rnd. Begin Zigzag Lace #1; work 40 rnds, end after rnd 20. Change to Zigzag Lace #2; work 40 rnds, end after Rnd 20. BO all sts loosely.

FINISHING

Block pc lightly to measurements.

Veritas Cowl

SIZE COWL
One size

FINISHED MEASUREMENTS
20³/₄" circumference × 11¹/₂" deep

MATERIALS
Wool Bam Boo by Classic Elite
(50% wool, 50% bamboo; 50-gram ball = approx 118 yards)

- 1 ball Main Color (MC)—1678 Chestnut
- 1 ball Color A—1615 Ivy
- 1 ball Color B—1672 Artichoke Green
- 1 ball Color C—1660 Treasure
- 1 ball Color D—1691 Bay Blue
- 1 ball Color E—1627 Mulled Wine
- 1 ball Color F—1634 Mulberry

Needles

- One 24" circular size U.S. 4 (3.5 mm) **or size to obtain gauge**
- Stitch markers

GAUGE
27 sts and 30 rows = 4" in Fair Isle Patt with larger needles. *Take time to save time, check your gauge.*

PATTERN STITCHES

CIRCULAR 3 × 2 RIB (MULTIPLE OF 5 STS)
All rnds: *K3, p2; rep from *.

CIRCULAR 2 × 1 RIB (MULTIPLE OF 3 STS)
Also see chart
All rnds: *K2, p1; rep from *.

NOTE

If you are interested in making the Veritas Fair Isle Mitts, see pp. 86–87.

COWL

With MC and circular needle, CO 140 sts. Join, being careful not to twist sts; pm for beg of rnd. Beg 3 × 2 Rib; work for 11 rnds. Change to St st; work 1 rnd. Change to Cowl Color patt; work 65 rnds. Change to MC and St st; work 1 rnd. Change to 3 × 2 Rib; work 11 rnds. BO all sts in rib.

FINISHING

Block pc to measurements.

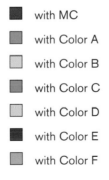

with MC

with Color A

with Color B

with Color C

with Color D

with Color E

with Color F

Cowl Chart
(multiple of 20 sts; 65 rnds)

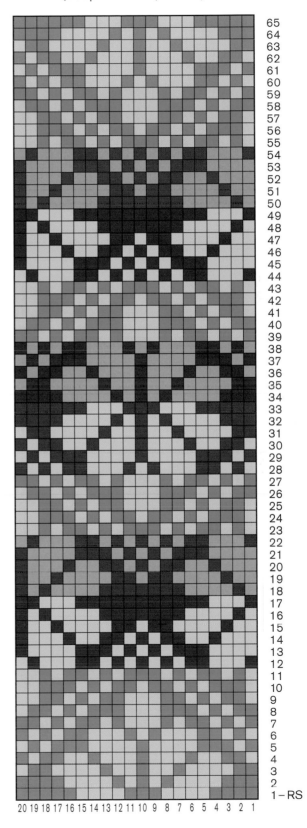

Blankets, Bags, Toys

contents

Forbidden Wrap Blanket

SIZE
One size

FINISHED MEASUREMENTS
20 (36)" wide × 54" long

MATERIALS
Forbidden by Classic Elite
(100% cashmere; 50-gram hank = approx 65 yards)
• 10 (18) hanks 10062 Putty
Needles
• One 40" circular size U.S. 15 (10 mm) **or size to obtain gauge**
• Stitch markers

GAUGE
10 sts and 14 rows = 4" in Stockinette stitch; 10 sts and 18 rows = 4" in Zigzag pattern. *Take time to save time, check your gauge.*

PATTERN STITCHES

GARTER STITCH (GTR ST)
Knit every row.

STOCKINETTE STITCH (ST ST)
Knit on RS, purl on WS.

LADDER PANEL (12 ST PANEL)
Also see chart
Row 1: (RS) K2, p3, k7 across.
Row 2: Knit the knit sts and purl the purl sts as they face you.
Row 3: K7, p3, k2 across.
Row 4: Rep Row 2.
Rep Rows 1–4 for Ladder Panel.

ZIGZAG PATTERN (MULTIPLE OF 10 STS + 2)
Also see chart
Row 1: (RS) P2, *k8, p2; rep from * across.
Row 2: P1, *k2, p6, k2; rep from * across to last st, p1.
Row 3: K2, *p2, k4, p2, k2; rep from * across.
Row 4: P1, *[p2, k2] 2 times, p2; rep from * across to last st, p1.
Row 5: K1, *k3, p4, k3; rep from * across to last st, k1.
Row 6: P1, *p4, k2, p4; rep from * across to last st, p1.

Rows 7, 8, 9, 10, and 11: Knit.
Row 12: Purl.
Rep Rows 1–12 for Zigzag patt.

NOTE
A circular needle is used to accommodate the large number of stitches.

BLANKET

CO 146 sts. (WS) Beg Gtr st; work 5 rows, end RS Row. *Est Edge Sts:* (WS) K5 (edge sts, keep in Gtr st throughout), purl to last 5 sts, k5 (edge sts, keep in Gtr st throughout). *Est Patt:* (RS) K5 (edge sts), beg Row 1 of Ladder Panel, work across 12 sts, pm, beg Row 1 of Zigzag Patt, work across 112 sts, pm, beg Row 1 of Ladder Panel, work across 12 sts, k5 (edge sts). Work as est until piece meas approx 18½ (34½)" from beg, end WS Row 6 of Zigzag Patt. Est St st: (RS) Maintaining edge sts, work 2 rows even. *Change to Gtr St:* (RS) Work 6 rows, end WS row. (RS) BO all sts.

FINISHING

Block pc lightly to measurements being careful not to flatten texture.

Zigzag Chart
(multiple of 10 sts + 2; 12-row rep)

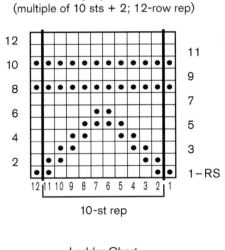

10-st rep

Ladder Chart
(multiple of 12 sts; 4-row rep)

☐ knit on RS, purl on WS

⊡ purl on RS, knit on WS

Cabled Baby Blanket

SKILL LEVEL: INTERMEDIATE

SIZE

One size

FINISHED MEASUREMENT

35" wide × 35" long

MATERIALS

Princess by Classic Elite

(40% merino, 28% viscose, 10% cashmere, 7% angora, 15% nylon; 50-gram ball = approx 150 yards)

• 10 balls 3416 Natural

Needles

• One pair each size U.S. 5 and 7 (3.75 and 4.5 mm) **or size to obtain gauge**

• Cable needle

GAUGE

26 sts and 30 rows = 4" in Patt A; 25 sts and 26 rows = 4" in Patt B; 20 sts of Patt C = approx 2½". *Take time to save time, check your gauge.*

PATTERN STITCHES

SEED STITCH (MULTIPLE OF 2 STS)

Row 1: (RS) *K1, p1; rep from * across.

Row 2: Knit the purl sts and purl the knit sts as they face you.

Rep Row 2 for Seed st.

PATTERN A (MULTIPLE OF 12 STS + 2)

Also see chart

Row 1 and all WS rows: (WS) Purl.

Rows 2 and 6: (RS) Knit.

Row 4: K1, *C4B, k4, C4F; rep from * to last st, k1.

Row 8: K1, *k2, C4F, C4B, k2; rep from * to last st, k1.

Rep Rows 1–8 for Patt A.

PATTERN B (MULTIPLE OF 24 STS + 13)

Also see chart

Foundation Row: (RS) Knit.

Row 1 and all WS rows: (WS) Purl.

Row 2: (RS) K1, C4F, k4, C4B, *k2, C4B, C4F, k2, C4F, k4, C4B; rep from * across.

Row 4: K3, C4F, C4B, k2, *k2, C4B, C4F, k4, C4F, C4B, k2; rep from * across.

Row 6: K3, C4F, C4B, k2, *C4B, k4, C4F, k2, C4F, C4B, k2; rep from * across.

Row 8: Knit.

Row 10: K3, C4B, C4F, k2, *C4F, k4, C4B, k2, C4B, C4F, k2; rep from * across.

Row 12: K3, C4B, C4F, k2, *k2, C4F, C4B, k4, C4B, C4F, k2; rep from * across.

Row 14: K1, C4B, k4, C4F, *k2, C4F, C4B, k2, C4B, k4, C4F; rep from * across.

Row 16: Knit.

Rep Rows 1–16 for Patt B.

PATTERN C (20-ST PANEL)

Also see chart

Foundation Row: (RS) K1, p5, k8, p6.

Row 1 and all WS rows: (WS) Knit the knit sts and purl the purl sts as they face you.

Row 2: K1, p5, C4B, C4F, p6.

Row 4: K1, p3, C4BP, k4, C4FP, p4.

Row 6: K1, p1, [C4BP] twice, [C4FP] twice, p2.

Row 8: Knit the knit sts and purl the purl sts as they face you.

Row 10: K1, p1, [C4FP] twice, [C4BP] twice, p2.

Row 12: K1, p3, C4FP, k4, C4BP, p4.

Rep Rows 1–12 for Patt C.

PATTERN D (16-ST PANEL)

Also see chart

Rows 1, 3, 5, and 7: (RS) P2, k4, [p1, k1] twice, p1, k3, p2.

Rows 2, 4, 6, and 8: (WS) K2, p4, [k1, p1] twice, k1, p3, k2.

Row 9: P2, sl 3 sts to cn, hold in back; [k1, p1, k1]; k3 from cn, sl 3 sts to cn, hold in front; k3; [p1, k1, p1] from cn, p2

Rows 10, 12, 14, 16, and 18: K2, p1, k1, p7, k1, p1, k3.

Rows 11, 13, 15, and 17: P2, k1, p1, k7, p1, k1, p3.

Row 19: P2, sl 3 sts to cn, hold in back; k3; [k1, p1, k1] from cn, sl 3 sts to cn, hold in front; [p1, k1, p1]; k3 from cn, p2.

Row 20: K2, p4, [k1, p1] twice, k1, p3, k2.

Rep Rows 1–20 for Patt D

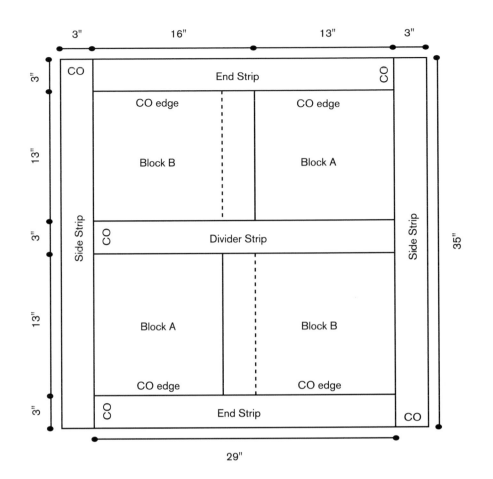

NOTE

Blanket is worked as a set of blocks and strips, which are assembled upon completion. See schematic for layout.

BLOCK A (MAKE 2)

Using larger needles, CO 86 sts. (WS) Beg Patt A; work even until piece meas 13" from beg, end WS row. BO all sts.

BLOCK B (MAKE 2)

Using larger needles, CO 105 sts. **Est Patt:** (RS) Beg with Foundation Rows, work 85 sts Patt B, pm work 20 sts from Patt C. Work as est until piece meas 13" from beg, end WS row. (RS) BO all sts knitwise.

DIVIDER STRIP (MAKE 1)

Using larger needles, CO 16 sts. (RS) Beg Patt D; work even until piece meas 29" from beg, end WS Row 6 of patt. BO all sts knitwise.

END STRIP (MAKE 2)

Using larger needles, CO 20 sts. **Est Patt:** (RS) Work 4 sts in Seed st, pm, 16 sts in Patt D. Work as est until piece meas 29" from beg, end WS row 6 of patt. (RS) BO all sts knitwise.

SIDE STRIP (MAKE 2)

Using smaller needles, CO 20 sts. (RS) Beg Seed St; work 4 rows even. **Change to Larger Needles** and est patt as for end strip; work even until piece meas 34½" from beg, end WS row. **Change to Smaller Needles and Seed St:** (RS) Work 4 rows even, end WS row. (RS) BO all sts knitwise.

FINISHING

Block all pieces to measurements, being careful not to flatten texture. Sew pieces tog as shown in schematic with CO edges and Seed st edges toward outer edge.

CABLED BABY BLANKET

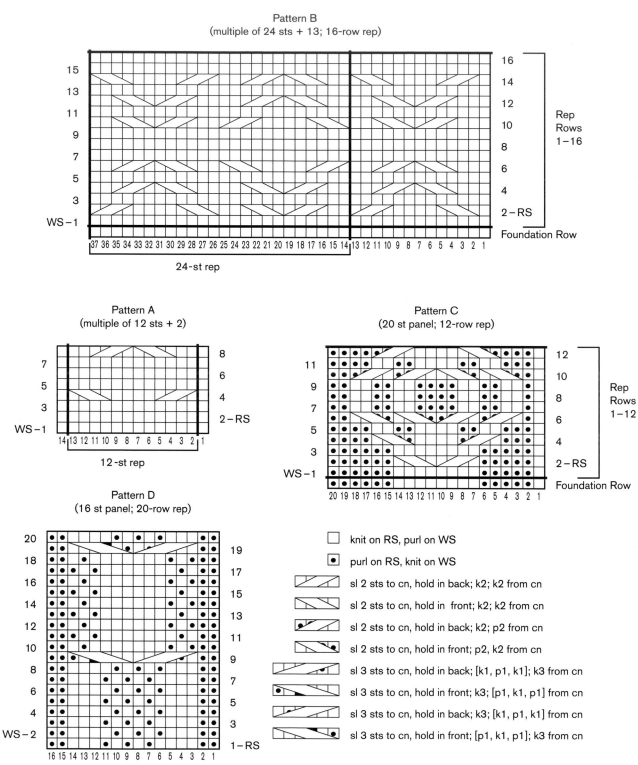

Pattern B
(multiple of 24 sts + 13; 16-row rep)

Rep Rows 1–16

24-st rep

Pattern A
(multiple of 12 sts + 2)

12-st rep

Pattern C
(20 st panel; 12-row rep)

Rep Rows 1–12

Pattern D
(16 st panel; 20-row rep)

☐ knit on RS, purl on WS

▪ purl on RS, knit on WS

sl 2 sts to cn, hold in back; k2; k2 from cn

sl 2 sts to cn, hold in front; k2; k2 from cn

sl 2 sts to cn, hold in back; k2; p2 from cn

sl 2 sts to cn, hold in front; p2, k2 from cn

sl 3 sts to cn, hold in back; [k1, p1, k1]; k3 from cn

sl 3 sts to cn, hold in front; k3; [p1, k1, p1] from cn

sl 3 sts to cn, hold in back; k3; [k1, p1, k1] from cn

sl 3 sts to cn, hold in front; [p1, k1, p1]; k3 from cn

Cozy Blanket

SIZE
One size

FINISHED MEASUREMENTS
48" wide × 60" long

MATERIALS
Montera by Classic Elite

(50% llama, 50% wool; 100-gram hank = 127 yards)

• 17 hanks 3816 La Paz Natural

Needles

• Osne pair size U.S. 10 (6mm) **or size to obtain gauge**

• Cable needle

GAUGE
16 sts and 28 rows = 4" in Garter stitch.
Take time to save time, check your gauge.

NOTE
Patchwork throw made of 20 squares worked separately then sewn together.

PATTERN STITCHES

SQUARE 1: GARTER RIDGE (GTR RIDGE)
Row 1: (RS) Knit.

Rows 2 and 3: Purl.

Row 4: Knit.

Rep Rows 1–4 for Gtr Ridge.

SQUARE 2: SEED STITCH (EVEN NUMBER OF STS)
Row 1: (RS) *K1, p1; rep from * to end.

Row 2: (WS) *P1, k1; rep from * to end.

Rep Rows 1–2 for Seed st.

SQUARE 3: DOUBLE MOSS STITCH (MULTIPLE OF 4 STS)
Row 1: (RS) *K2, p2; rep from * to end.

Row 2: rep Row 1.

Rows 3 – 4: *P2, k2; rep from * to end.

Rep Rows 1–4 for Double Moss st.

SQUARE 4: BASKETWEAVE (MULTIPLE OF 8 STS + 4)
Rows 1, 3, 6, 8, 9, and 11: K4, *p4, k4; rep from * to end.

Rows 2, 4, 5, 7, 10, and 12: P4, *k4, p4; rep from * to end.

Rep Rows 1–12 for Basketweave.

SQUARE 5: REVERSIBLE CABLE (MULTIPLE OF 8 STS)
Row 1: (RS) *K2, p2; rep from * to end.

Rows 2–6: Rep Row 1.

Row 7: * Sl 4 sts to cn, hold in back; k2, p2; k2, p2 from cn; rep from * to end.

Row 8: Rep Row 1.

Rep Rows 1–8 for Reversible Cable.

Cozy Chart

1	3	5	2
4	1	3	5
2	4	1	3
5	2	4	1
3	5	2	4

BLANKET (MAKE 4 OF EACH SQUARE; 20 SQUARES TOTAL

Square 1 (Square 2, Square 3, Square 4): CO 48 sts. Beg Gtr st; work 4 rows, end after a WS row. *Est Patt:* (RS) work 2 sts in Gtr st, work 44 sts in Gtr Ridge (Seed st, Double Moss st, Basketweave), work 2 sts in Gtr st. Cont as est until 15 (30, 15, 5) reps (60 rows) of Gtr Ridge (Seed st, Double Moss st, Basketweave) have been completed. Change to Gtr st; (RS) work 4 rows even, end after a WS row. BO all sts.

Square 5 CO 48 sts. Beg Gtr st; work 3 rows, end after a RS row. *Inc Row:* (WS) K3, *[k1, m1] 6 times, k1; rep from * to last 3 sts, K3—84 sts. *Est Patt:* (RS) work 2 sts in Gtr st, work 80 sts in Reversible Cable, work 2 sts in Gtr st. Cont as est until 7 reps of Reversible Cable are complete (56 rows), then work Rows 1–4 of Reversible Cable 1 more time (60 rows). *Change to Gtr St, Dec Row:* (RS) K3, *[k2tog] 6 times, k1; rep from * to last 3 sts, k3—48 sts rem. Work 3 rows even, end after a WS row. BO all sts.

FINISHING

Block squares to 12" by 12". Sew squares together as indicated on chart (4 squares wide by 5 squares long).

Irresistible Blanket

SKILL LEVEL: INTERMEDIATE

SIZE
One size

FINISHED MEASUREMENTS
33" wide × 35x½" long

MATERIALS
Posh by Classic Elite
(30% cashmere, 70% silk; 50-gram hank = approx 125 yards)
• 11 hanks 93048 Pale Pink
Needles
• One 36" circular needle size U.S. 7 (4.5 mm) **or size to obtain gauge**
• Cable needle

GAUGE
24 sts and 26 rows = 4" in Staggered Cable pattern; 18 sts and 29 rows = 4" in Seed stitch. *Take time to save time, check your gauge.*

PATTERN STITCHES

SEED STITCH (MULTIPLE OF 2 STS + 1)
Row 1: (RS) K1, *p1, k1; rep from * across.

Row 2: Knit the purl sts and purl the knit sts as they face you.

Rep Row 2 for Seed st.

STAGGERED CABLE PATTERN (MULTIPLE OF 12 STS + 2)
Also see chart

Row 1: (WS) *K2, p10; rep from * across to last 2 sts k2.

Rows 2, 6, and 10: (RS) P2, *C4B, k6, p2; rep from * across.

Row 3 and all WS rows: Knit the knit sts and purl the purl sts as they face you.

Rows 4, 8, 12, 16, 18, 22, and 24: P2, *k10, p2; rep from * across.

Rows 14, 20, and 26: P2, *k4, C6F, p2; rep from * across.

Row 28: P2, *k10, p2; rep from * across.

Rep Rows 1–28 for Staggered Cable patt.

BLANKET

CO 151 sts. (RS) Beg Seed st; work even until piece meas
1 1/2" from beg, end WS row. **Increase Row:** (RS) Work 7 sts in
Seed st as est, inc 45 sts evenly across center 137 sts as shown
on chart or as foll: p2, *k1, [k1-f/b, k1] 3 times, p2; rep from
* across to last 7 sts, work 7 sts in Seed st as est—196 sts. **Est
Patt:** (WS) Work 7 sts in Seed st as est, 182 sts in Staggered
Cable patt, 7 sts in Seed st as est. Work even until piece meas
32 1/2" from beg, end RS Row 12 of Staggered Cable patt.

Dec Row: (WS) Work 7 sts in Seed st as est, dec 45 sts evenly
across center 182 sts as shown on chart or as foll: *k2, [p2,
p2tog] 3 times, p1; rep from * across to last 9 sts, k2, work 7 sts
in Seed st as est—151 sts rem. Change to Seed St; work even
until piece meas 1 1/2" from Dec Row.

FINISHING

Block lightly to measurements, if necessary, being careful not
to flatten texture.

IRRESISTIBLE BLANKET

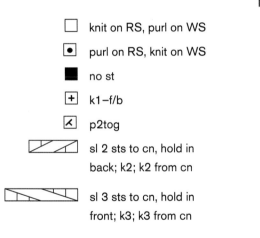

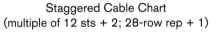

Staggered Cable Chart
(multiple of 12 sts + 2; 28-row rep + 1)

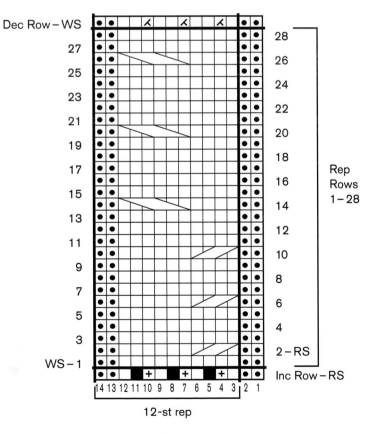

Basketweave Blanket

SIZE
One size

FINISHED MEASUREMENTS
37" wide × 29" long

MATERIALS
Sundance by Classic Elite
(50% cotton, 50% microfiber;
50-gram ball = approx 83 yards)
• 12 balls 6267 Arizona Blue
Needles
• One 29" circular size U.S. 6
(4 mm) **or size to obtain gauge**

GAUGE
20 sts and 29 rows = 4" in Basketweave pattern. *Take time to save
time, check your gauge.*

PATTERN STITCHES

GARTER STITCH (GTR ST)
Knit every row.

BASKETWEAVE PATTERN (MULTIPLE OF 8 STS)
Also see chart
Rows 1, 2, 3, and 4: * P4, k4, rep from * across.
Rows 5, 6, 7, and 8: *K4, p4, rep from *across.
Rep Rows 1–8 for Basketweave patt.

NOTES

1. A circular needle is used to accommodate the large number of stitches.

2. Join all new balls of yarn immediately after the Garter stitch edge.

3. If you have difficulty finding the recommended yarn, you may consider using Classic Elite's Solstice as a substitute.

BLANKET

CO 174 sts. Beg Gtr st; work 6 rows even, end WS row.
Est Basketweave Patt: (RS) K3 (edge sts; keep in Gtr st
throughout), work 168 sts, in Basketweave patt, k3 (edge
sts; keep in Gtr st throughout). Work even until piece meas
28¼"from beg, end WS Row 4 or 8 of Basketweave patt.
Change to Gtr st; work 6 rows even. BO all sts loosely.

Basketweave Pattern
(multiple of 8 sts; 8 row rep)

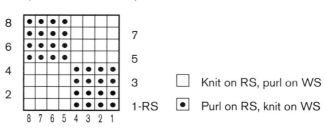

☐ Knit on RS, purl on WS

▣ Purl on RS, knit on WS

Sunshine Bag

SKILL LEVEL: INTERMEDIATE

SIZE

One size

FINISHED MEASUREMENTS

13³/₄" wide × 18³/₄" tall

MATERIALS

Chesapeake by Classic Elite, Verde Collection

(50% merino, 50% organic cotton; 50-gram ball = approx 103 yards)

• 3 balls Main Color (MC)—5985 Mandarin Orange
• 2 balls Color A—5955 Shanghai Red
• 1 ball Color B—5912 Meyer Lemon
• 1 ball Color C—5904 Scuba Blue
• 1 ball Color D—5981 Tendril Green

Needles

• One 24" circular size U.S. 4 (3.5 mm)
• One set double-pointed needles size U.S. 4 (3.5 mm)
  or size to obtain gauge

GAUGE

26 sts and 31 rows = 4" in Fair Isle Stockinette stitch working Motif, Arrow, and Diamond Patterns. *Take time to save time, check your gauge.*

PATTERN STITCHES

See charts

I-CORD

Using 2 dpn, CO specified number of sts onto 1 needle. *Knit 1 row; without turning the work, slide the sts to RH end of needle, pull yarn tightly from the end of the row, (behind the sts); rep from * until cord meas desired length.

BAG

With MC and circular needle, CO 180 sts. Join, being careful not to twist sts. Begin Circular St st; work 4 rnds.

Change to Motif patt; work 29 rnds.

Change to Arrow patt; work 17 rnds.

Change to Motif patt; work 29 rnds.

Change to Diamond patt; work 13 rnds.

Change to Motif Patt; work 29 rnds. Change to Arrow patt; work 17 rnds. Change to Motif patt; work Rnds 1–4. Change to MC; work 4 rnds even.

Turning Rnd: Purl 1 rnd.

CASING

Knit 1 rnd, turn. Beg working back and forth in rows. Change to St st; work even until pc meas 1" from turning rnd. BO all sts.

FINISHING

Weave in ends and block pc. Hold bag so beg of round is centered on 1 side edge. Seam CO edge of bag to close bottom of bag. Fold casing to inside and sew BO edge to WS of bag.

I-Cord: Using dpns and MC, CO 3 sts. Beg I-Cord; work until pc meas 66" from beg. BO sts. Thread cord through casing so that ends come through casing opening on WS of bag. Sew ends of cord to bottom corners of bag.

Motif Chart
(multiple of 20 sts; 29 rnds)

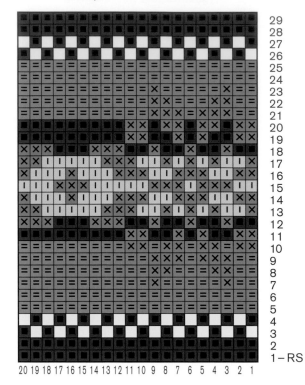

29
28
27
26
25
24
23
22
21
20
19
18
17
16
15
14
13
12
11
10
9
8
7
6
5
4
3
2
1–RS

20 19 18 17 16 15 14 13 12 11 10 9 8 7 6 5 4 3 2 1

Arrow Chart
(multiple of 6 sts; 17 rnds)

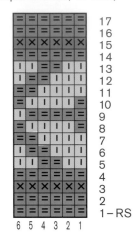

17
16
15
14
13
12
11
10
9
8
7
6
5
4
3
2
1–RS

6 5 4 3 2 1

Diamond Chart
(multiple of 12 sts; 13 rnds)

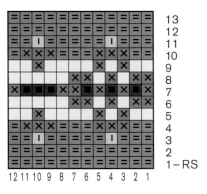

13
12
11
10
9
8
7
6
5
4
3
2
1–RS

12 11 10 9 8 7 6 5 4 3 2 1

= MC

■ Color A

□ Color B

✕ Color C

Ɪ Color D

Alternate Colorway

= MC — 5920 Oxford — knit

■ Color A — 5981 Tendril Green — knit

■ Color B — 5948 Bronte Blue — knit

✕ Color C — 5955 Shanghai Red — knit

Ɪ Color D — 5904 Scuba Blue — knit

Renaissance Doll

SKILL LEVEL: INTERMEDIATE

SIZE
One size

FINISHED MEASUREMENT
11" tall

MATERIALS
Renaissance by Classic Elite

(100% wool; 50-gram hank = approx 110 yards)
- 1 hank Color A—7111 Lime Infusion
- 1 hank Color B—7157 Botticelli Blue
- 1 hank Color C—7195 Aster
- 1 hank Color D—7188 Kumquat
- 1 hank Color E—7136 Cork

Needles
- One set double-pointed needles size U.S. 7 (4.5 mm) **or size to obtain gauge**
- Tapestry needle
- Crochet hook size U.S. F/5 (3.75 mm)
- Stitch holder
- Polyfill for stuffing

GAUGE
20 sts and 28 rows = 4" in Stockinette stitch. *Take time to save time, check your gauge.*

NOTE
If you have difficulty finding the recommended yarn, you may consider using Classic Elite's Liberty Wool as a substitute.

PATTERN STITCHES

STOCKINETTE STITCH (ST ST)
Knit on RS, purl on WS.

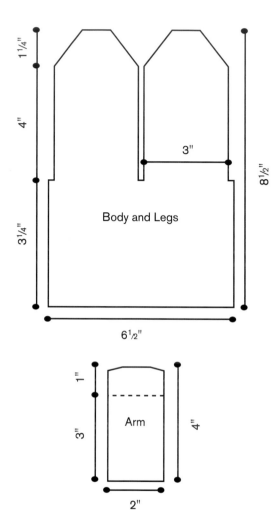

RENAISSANCE DOLL

1¼"

4"

3¼"

8½"

3"

Body and Legs

6½"

1"

3"

Arm

4"

2"

BODY

Using Color A and Longtail Cast-On Method, CO 33 sts. (WS) Knit 1 row. (RS) Begin St st; work even for 2 rows, end WS row. *Est Patt:* (RS) Work 10 sts in St st, work 13 sts from Star Chart in Intarsia St st, work 10 sts in St st. Work as est until Chart is completed. Using Color A, work 3 rows even in St st, end RS row. (WS) Knit 1 row. *Leggings:* Change to Color C; (RS) work even in St st for 6 rows, end WS row.

LEGS

(RS) BO 1 st, work 15 sts, place on holder for second Leg; BO 1 st, work 16 sts for first leg. (WS) BO 1 st, knit across first leg—15 sts rem. Working on first leg only, *Change to Color D; work 2 rows even in St st. Cont for 24 more rows, alternating Color C and Color D every 2 rows, end WS row, Color D. Change to Color C; (RS) knit 2 rows. *Foot:* (RS) Dec 1 st each side this row, then EOR 4 times—5 sts rem, end RS row (last dec row). (WS) BO rem sts. *Second Leg:* With WS facing, sl 15 sts on holder back to needle and attach Color C. (WS) Work 1 row in St st; rep from * as for first Leg. Beg at feet, sew up each leg and up rear of doll. Stuff body to desired thickness, leaving top open.

ARMS (MAKE 2)

Using Color A and Longtail Cast-On Method, CO 10 sts. (WS) Begin St st; work 1 row. *Note:* Work on dpn, beg each row at side where the next color begins. Change to Color B; work 1 row even, *Change to Color A; work 1 row even, Change to Color B; work 1 row even; rep from * 9 times, end WS row. Change to Color A; (RS) knit 2 rows, end WS row. Change to Color E; (RS) work 6 rows even in St st, end WS row. *Hand:* (RS) K2tog 5 times—5 sts rem. Break yarn and pull tail through the 5 sts on needle. Remove needle, pull tight. Beg at hand, sew up arm, stuffing as you go. Sew onto body as shown in photo on p. 209.

HEAD

Sew shoulders tog leaving 1" in center for neck. Using Color E, with RS facing, beg at left shoulder seam, pick up 18 sts around neck hole, pm for beg of rnd. Rnd 1: Knit. Rnd 2: *M1, k3; rep from * around—24 sts. Rnd 3: Knit. Rnd 4: *M1, k12; rep from * once—26 sts. Rnd 5: *M1, k13; rep from * once—28 sts. Rnd 6: *M1, k14; rep from * around—30 sts. Rnds 7–10: Knit. Rnd 11: K15, ssk, k11, k2tog—28 sts rem. Rnd 12: Knit. Rnd 13: K15, ssk, k9, k2tog—26 sts rem. Rnd 14: Knit 13, pm, knit 13. Rnd 15: BO 2 sts, knit to marker (head front), BO 2 sts, knit to end of rnd (head back). **Head Back:** Change to working back and forth, (WS) working on back sts only. **Shape Head:** BO 2 sts at beg of next row, then BO 3 sts at beg of next 3 rows. Fasten off. Attach yarn with WS facing to head front. BO 2 sts at beg of row, then BO 3 sts at beg of next 3 rows. Fasten off. Stuff head, sew top of head closed.

FINISHING

Hair: Cut several pieces 3½" long of Color D and with a crochet hook, attach one piece into each stitch on back of head, along seam and around edge of front of head as follows: pull center of yarn through st, pull two tail ends of yarn all the way through the loop on the hook, pull tight. **Face:** Using Color D and Backstitch technique embroider a smile onto the face. Using Bolor B and French Knot technique, embroider 2 eyes onto the face.

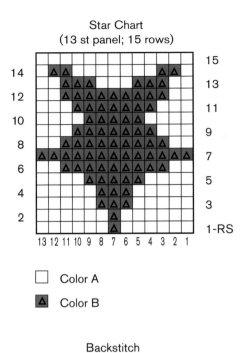

Star Chart
(13 st panel; 15 rows)

☐ Color A
△ Color B

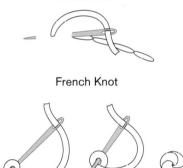

Backstitch

French Knot

Paintbox Frog

SKILL LEVEL: INTERMEDIATE

SIZE
One size

FINISHED MEASUREMENT
20" tall

MATERIALS
Paintbox by Classic Elite
(100% merino wool; 100-gram ball = approx 110 yards)
• 3 balls 6897 Watercolor Green
Needles
• One pair U.S. size 10½ (6.5 mm) **or size to obtain gauge**
• Tapestry needle
• Black embroidery thread
• Polyfill for stuffing

GAUGE
14 sts and 24 rows = 4" in Seed stitch. *Take time to save time, check your gauge.*

PATTERN STITCH

SEED STITCH (MULTIPLE OF 2 STS + 1)
Row 1: K1, *p1, k1; rep from * across.
Row 2: Knit the purl sts and purl the knit sts as they face you.
Rep Row 2 for Seed st.

NOTES

1. Seed St looks the same on both sides. Indications for RS and WS are for clarification of instructions only. Place marker at beginning of Row 1 to indicate beginning of RS rows.

2. If you have difficulty finding the recommended yarn, you may consider using Classic Elite's Sprout as a substitute.

BODY (MAKE 2)
CO 11 sts. **Beg Seed St and Inc:** (WS) CO 2 sts at end of this and next 3 rows, then inc 1 st at end of next 8 rows—27 sts. Work even for 12 rows, end WS row. **Dec:** (RS) Dec 1 st each side this row, then every 4 rows 4 times, then EOR 2 times—13 sts rem. BO rem sts.

LEGS (MAKE 2)
CO 15 sts. (RS) Beg Seed St; work even until piece meas 5½" from beg, end WS row. (RS) BO all sts.

FEET (MAKE 4)
CO 4 sts. **Beg Seed St and Inc:** (RS) CO 3 sts at end of this and the next row, then CO 2 sts at end of next 2 rows—14 sts. Work even for 6 rows, end WS row. **Dec:** (RS) BO 2 sts at beg of next 2 rows, then BO 3 sts at beg of next 2 rows—4 sts rem. BO rem sts.

ARMS (MAKE 2)

CO 11 sts. (RS) Beg Seed st; work even until piece meas 4½" from beg, end WS row. (RS) BO all sts.

HANDS (MAKE 4)

CO 4 sts. **Beg Seed St and Inc:** (RS) CO 1 st at end of this and next 7 rows—12 sts. Work 1 row even, end RS row. **Dec:** (WS) Dec 1 st at beg of next 8 rows—4 sts rem. BO rem sts.

HEAD (MAKE 2)

CO 7 sts. **Beg Seed St and Inc:** (RS) CO 3 sts at end of this and next row, 2 sts at end of next 8 rows, then 1 st at end of next 4 rows—33 sts. Work 5 rows even, end RS row. **Dec:** (WS) Dec 1 st at beg of next 4 rows, BO 2 sts at beg of next 8 rows, then 3 sts at the beg of next 2 rows—7 sts rem. BO rem sts.

EYES (MAKE 4)

CO 14 sts. (RS) Beg Seed st; work 1 row even. **Dec:** (WS) Dec 1 st at beg of next 6 rows—8 sts. BO 2 sts at beg of next 2 rows—4 sts rem. BO rem sts.

ASSEMBLY

Legs and Feet: Sew tog long edges of one leg piece to form a cylinder. Sew tog two foot pieces leaving open the area shown on schematic as a dashed line; stuff foot with polyfill. Sew foot onto CO edge of leg cylinder; stuff leg. Sew end of leg closed. Rep for second leg. **Arms and Hands:** Sew tog long edges of one arm piece to form a cylinder. Sew tog two hand pieces leaving CO edges open for stuffing; stuff hand. Sew hand onto CO edge of arm cylinder; stuff arm; sew end of arm closed. Rep for second arm. **Body:** Sew tog the CO edges of both body pieces. Sew legs to body on either side of sewn seam. Sew body sides tog, leaving open about 1" down from BO edges on both sides. Sew arms onto body; stuff body. **Head:** Sew together head pieces, leaving CO edges open; stuff head. Sew head onto body. **Eyes:** Sew together two eye pieces leaving CO edges open. Sew to top of head as shown in photo, stuff as you sew. **Embroidery:** With 2 strands of black embroidery thread, using Backstitch as shown in the diagram, embroider the mouth onto the head, and eye balls onto the eyes as shown in photo.

Paintbox Frog

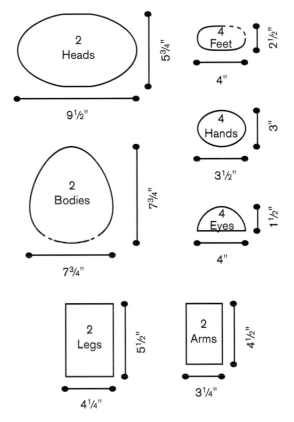

Designers

Index